Leo Lyons,
the Rochester Jeffersons
and the Birth of the NFL

ALSO OF INTEREST AND FROM MCFARLAND

Pop Warner: A Life on the Gridiron
(Jeffrey J. Miller, 2015)

Leo Lyons, the Rochester Jeffersons and the Birth of the NFL

JEFFREY J. MILLER *and*
JOHN D. STEFFENHAGEN

McFarland & Company, Inc., Publishers
Jefferson, North Carolina

All photographs and images are from
the Leo V. Lyons Collection except where noted.

ISBN (print) 978-1-4766-9221-0
ISBN (ebook) 978-1-4766-5603-8

LIBRARY OF CONGRESS CATALOGING DATA ARE AVAILABLE

Library of Congress Control Number 2025018506

© 2025 Jeffrey J. Miller and John D. Steffenhagen. All rights reserved

No part of this book may be reproduced or transmitted in any form or by any means, electronic or mechanical, including photocopying or recording, or by any information storage and retrieval system, without permission in writing from the publisher.

Front cover: (top, left to right) Leo Lyons in uniform, 1915, and in 1970 holding the 1916 New York State Championship trophy; (bottom) the Rochester Jeffersons in action versus Lancaster, 1919 (photographs from the Leo V. Lyons Collection)

Printed in the United States of America

*McFarland & Company, Inc., Publishers
Box 611, Jefferson, North Carolina 28640
www.mcfarlandpub.com*

To Leo Lyons

Table of Contents

Acknowledgments	ix
Preface	1
1. "I'd like to try out with the Jeffersons" (1908–1913)	5
2. "Champions of New York State" (1914–1916)	25
3. "I thought we were pretty good" (1917–1919)	45
4. "Hay had the good cigars" (1920)	57
5. "The finest Jeffs team to ever scar up a gridiron" (1921)	68
6. "I nearly went broke a half-dozen times" (1922–1923)	85
7. "We never played a game expecting to lose" (1924–1925)	103
8. "I already knew my part was caput" (1926–1927)	127
9. "I miss my team badly"	132
10. "His loyalty to the NFL never wavered"	152
Appendix 1—Items from the Leo V. Lyons Collection	155
Appendix 2—Season-by-Season Results	161
Appendix 3—Player Register	169
Chapter Notes	189
Bibliography	195
Index	199

Acknowledgments

John D. Steffenhagen

The journey to piece together my great-grandfather's life in football led me to meet so many incredible individuals with whom I would not have otherwise been acquainted. Their help and guidance helped us immeasurably while writing this book. My sincerest gratitude begins with my good friend Jeff Miller, an accomplished football historian and author. Jeff has authored several outstanding books, including *Buffalo's Forgotten Champions: The Story of Buffalo's First Professional Football Team*, *Rockin' the Rockpile*, *Game Changers: The Greatest Plays in Buffalo Bills Football History* (with Marv Levy), *100 Things Bills Fans Should Know and Do Before They Die*, and *Pop Warner: A Life on the Gridiron*. Jeff provided the proverbial push to do this book when it seemed too big a project to me, and my family and I are forever grateful. Jeff was the perfect blend of friend/historian/author. He was a stickler for detail, which I learned was a most important asset.

Thank you, Robert Wheeler, for sharing so many stories about Leo and providing the rare recordings of Leo speaking about the early years of the National Football League (NFL). Robert wrote the acclaimed *Jim Thorpe: Pathway to Glory*, widely considered the definitive book on the great Olympian. He was also the cofounder, with his wife Dr. Florence Ridlon, of the Jim Thorpe Foundation and served as its first president. *Sports Illustrated* credited them with the primary responsibility in the restoration of Jim Thorpe's Olympic gold medals in 1982. Wheeler managed public relations for ABC Sports, FOX Sports, and the White House Conference for Children and Youth. In 2022, both were team members of the American Indian nonprofit organization Bright Path Strong, which convinced the International Olympic Committee to fully reinstate Jim Thorpe as the sole champion of the pentathlon and decathlon in the 1912 Olympics. My great-grandfather knew both Jim Thorpe and Bob Wheeler and held them in high regard.

I am indebted to Ken Crippen, accomplished football historian, author, and founder of the Football Learning Academy. He was one of the first NFL historians I reached out to for help with my Rochester Jeffersons research back in 2001, providing me with invaluable information and direction. He helped me develop a website for the Jeffersons and offered his assistance whenever I asked.

To Leo "Vin" Bosner, Pat, Kevin, and Mary Catherine Bosner, and John and Mary Pat Bosner—without your help and support the whole story on Leo Lyons would have been full of holes. Over the years, you have all been so very generous providing so many important pieces from Leo's life to my Leo Lyons collection. Unknown to us, those scraps of paper and old boxes, which looked unimpressive, contained so many important details. Of course, that is not counting the one shiny piece my uncle Leo Bosner gave to me years back, the 1916 Jeffersons state championship trophy. It is now my most cherished possession and it will never leave our family—I promise! The stories that you have shared with me have provided great detail for this book.

Thank you to the family members of former Rochester Jeffersons players, Hugh Irwin (son of Dutch Irwin), Gary Maybee (relative of Art Webb), Andrew Loughlin (great-grandson of John Loughlin), Tom McShea (grandson Joe McShea), and Jane Flaherty and John Caufield (relatives of Bill Caufield and Jack Slattery). Thank you to the always friendly and helpful staff at the Rundel Memorial Library in Rochester, New York, where I had my share of troubles using the new microfilm machines. Thank you to the *Rochester Democrat & Chronicle* for the excellent coverage on the Jeffersons for more than a century. They have recently published several articles relating to the Jeffs including some front-page articles on Leo Lyons. Bob Matthews, Sal Maiorana, James Johnson, and my dear friend Scott Pitoniak, I am most appreciative of your support. Thank you to many other Rochester media people like Virginia Butler, Jim Aroune, Joe Versage, Zac Bell, Mike Hedeen, Kimberly and Beck, Brother Weese and Jane Flashe. Thank you to the staff, former and present, at the Pro Football Hall of Fame, Joe Horrigan, Jon Kendle, Jason Aikens, Saleem Choudhry, and Jim Campbell. Thank you, Chris Willis (head of NFL Films research library and acclaimed author), Joe Ziemba (pro football author and historian), Denny Lynch (former executive with several NFL teams), Christopher Bensch (curator at the Strong Museum of Play), and Joe Bock (former Buffalo Bills and Houston Gamblers player who shared a great story about Leo when he was a boy).

Thank you also to Gary Mitchem and Mark Durr. Partnering with a distinguished publisher like McFarland means the world to me. My personal library is full of books published by your company, and they are all of high standard and quality. I would also like to thank Mark Fenner and Kevin O'Donnel, my "brothers" in Dayton, Ohio, with ties to the Dayton Triangles and former Triangle players Lee Fenner and Norb Sacksteder. Thank you to the famous Vince Lombardi memorabilia collector Jack Giambrone, Lancaster town historian Mary Jo Monnin, and immensely talented photographer Steve Desmond for his wonderful work shooting the Rochester Jeffersons memorabilia pictures used in this book. Thank you to all my PFRA "family" who have supported me over the years through podcasts, news articles, and friendships. A special note of gratitude and love for my beautiful wife Julie and our children Victoria, Sara, Jessica, and David V. who all had the patience with and confidence in me to complete this book.

My last thank you is for Sabina Steffenhagen, Leo Lyons' granddaughter and known to me as "Mom." There would be no story to write without her and I probably would never have known the extent of my great-grandfather's involvement in the city of Rochester, the NFL, and the Pro Football Hall of Fame. Nor would the rest of my family or others with an interest in Rochester sports, for that matter. My mother was in fair health when I told her this book was going to be written and this news almost sent her to the grave. She was so excited and so happy! As the book was being written, she always asked how it was going and said she had jotted down more recollections from the past to help us. She told everyone she knew, including nurses and doctors who said, "What? Rochester was in the NFL and played teams like the Packers, Giants, Bears, and Cardinals?" I knew she was proud of me, and that means the world to me. I wanted this page to have a storybook ending. The Lord, however, had other plans as Mom was called to His side before my book was completed. But it gives me peace knowing she is with Leo keeping tabs on our progress. Thank you, Mom, for everything!

Jeffrey J. Miller

There are so many people deserving of acknowledgment that I am bound to omit someone from my list. If I failed to include someone I should have, I am deeply sorry and will do my best to let it be known in other ways.

The list of people I wish to acknowledge begins with my friend and coauthor John Steffenhagen. I am honored—and humbled—that John invited me to partner with him in telling Leo's story. This is an important and long-overdue undertaking. I hope you are pleased with the result, John, and that we have made your family proud.

My deepest gratitude goes to my dear friends Jeff Mason and John Maxymuk, who diligently and skillfully proofread this manuscript. Jeff is a retired educator, noted historian, and fellow Lime Laker. This is the eighth book on which we have collaborated (and won't be the last!). John is a reference librarian at Rutgers University and author of more than a dozen books focusing on football history. He has assisted me with my past several books as well. As always, I stubbornly reserved the right to occasionally ignore their advisements, so any errors in typography, omission, or historical accuracy are fully my responsibility.

Steve Desmond is an outstanding photographer who shared his talents in shooting the artifacts featured in this book. Photographing in black and white can be challenging, and Steve was equal to the task. Great work, my friend!

A thank-you is owed to Joe Gibbon and the fine folks at Finger Lakes Coffee Roasters in Canandaigua for giving us a place to meet (and a great cup of "Joe").

I had the pleasure—and good fortune—of interviewing three gentlemen who were acquainted with Leo during his lifetime: former professional football player Joe Bock, pro football historian and former librarian at the Pro Football Hall of Fame Jim Campbell, and renowned author Bob Wheeler, writer of the definitive biography of Jim Thorpe. Thank you all for taking part in this project and adding color and depth to Leo's story.

Thanks to Chris Willis, noted football historian and head research librarian at NFL Films, for sharing sound and video recordings of Leo Lyons interviews from Films' fabled archives. Your historiography proved invaluable as we stitched together the narrative of this book.

Thank you also to Mark Durr and Gary Mitchem at McFarland, with whom I had the pleasure of collaborating on my book *Pop Warner: A Life on the Gridiron*. They believed in this project from the very beginning and have been supportive throughout.

And, of course, my beautiful wife Cathaline and our amazing son Benjamin. Thank you for being there!

Preface

John D. Steffenhagen

If someone had asked me a driver's name and car number in auto racing—NASCAR or Formula 1—back in 1985, I could easily have supplied the answers. A young Dale Earnhardt drove the bright blue-and-yellow Wrangler Jeans Chevrolet #3, and veteran driver Niki Lauda had the red-and-white McLaren sponsored by Marlboro. My father Eddie was a NASCAR modified driver for many years, so my life was all about racing and very little about the National Football League (NFL), let alone the league's history. When my loving mother Sabina gifted me several boxes full of old papers, pictures, and "junk" (what I called it at the time), I was honored but not overly interested. She told me they contained some of "Leo's football things" from way back, given to her by her grandfather Leo V. Lyons. I knew at that time Leo was acquainted with football legends such as Jim Thorpe, George Halas, and Art Rooney, Sr., and had an NFL team called the Jeffersons, but without a computer or Google to research further, the boxes simply gathered dust in my bedroom closet for several years. My sister Joann and I spent many weekends at my great-grandparents' house in Pittsford, New York, a suburb of Rochester. We lived in Fairport—the next town over—and were there quite often over the years, from my infant days until I reached the ripe old age of ten in 1976, when Leo passed away. My great-grandmother Catharine (or "Gaga," as we called her) died a year later.

Since I was so young at the time, I only remember bits and pieces of our visits, but one memory remains vivid to this day. I recall playing with my Hot Wheel cars on the enclosed porch out back and being told by my mother to "keep it down" because Leo had friends over. At that time, I was six or seven (1973 or 1974) and what I remember is Leo and two old guys with hats and cigars laughing. Many years later, my mother told me that those two old guys were Chicago Bears owner George Halas and Pittsburgh Steelers owner Art Rooney, Sr. I was also oblivious that the downstairs of the home, full of file cabinets, desks, stacks of files with papers, and 8 × 10 photographs wall to wall was a veritable mini–Pro Football Hall of Fame. Joe Horrigan, longtime Hall of Fame president and highly regarded historian who visited the house shortly after Leo's death, referred to his office as "the first man cave." Nope, all my sister and I were interested in was the bright-colored pool table that stood off to the side. My mother said Leo told me stories about old-time football games and the legends of pro football, knowing all along I was too young to care or remember.

By the summer of 2001, I had already become a huge football fan, thanks in part to #13 (Dan Marino) and the exciting "Marks Brothers," having to hear "squish the fish" from family and friends who were fans of the local team, the Buffalo Bills. Now being

1

into football and with the availability of computers and search engines at my fingertips, I took a more serious look into those boxes that Leo gave my mother back in the early 1970s. It is only by divine intervention that these boxes and their contents survived so long with me. The more I delved in and researched, the more surprised I became.

I soon learned that a group of 14 men gathered in Canton, Ohio, in 1920 to form the first organized professional league of football. One of those visionaries was my great-grandfather Leo Lyons, representing his hometown of Rochester, New York, and its football team, called the Jeffersons. Along with Leo were Jim Thorpe of the Canton Bulldogs and George Halas of the Decatur Staleys, which later became the Chicago Bears. I came across Halas' induction speech on the Pro Football Hall of Fame's website and found that Papa Bear mentioned only a few names in his speech, one being Leo Lyons. It soon began to overwhelm me, so much history, so much information.

Overwhelmed, I reached out to the Professional Football Researchers Association (PFRA) and their president Ken Crippen. He soon developed a website called "Reconstructing the Rochester Jeffersons, an NFL Franchise." I talked with fellow football researchers and historians like Jeff Miller, who helped me unearth a century-old player and his team. I was still unsure of what the relics in the boxes actually were, an old leather football torn and restuffed, a pair of canvas football pants, and a dog-eared helmet. An ornate wood-and-glass box with a nameplate, crude football shoes with nails poking out of the cleats, a large Johnson & Johnson first aid kit that looked very old, two old orange-and-blue New York State license plates stamped "NFL-1," an old whistle with a keystone logo, and lots more. Many documents, letters, photographs, notes, and a journal were thrown in. The collection grew as more items were given to me by aunts and uncles years later, such as the Jeffersons' NFL franchise certificate from 1923, the 1916 Rochester Jeffersons New York State championship trophy, and many of Leo's handwritten notes from the early days of pro football. I always thought they were just Leo's things like his helmet, pants, and football.

In 2020, I was moving into a new house with my wife Julie, and among the boxes of belongings were ones containing Leo's "junk." While I was transferring the items out of the old boxes into new ones, something dropped out of an old Hall of Fame program. There were two sheets of paper that shed new light on the relics I possessed. One was a letter from NFL commissioner Pete Rozelle to Leo in 1961, asking for an inventory list of the historical league mementos he had collected going back to the league's founding. The second sheet was an actual inventory (though not complete) dated the same month. On the list were many items I had sitting in those boxes. With the help of Wilson Athletics, the Smithsonian, football historians, old newspaper articles, NFL team historians, and museum curators, I was able to verify that what I had were indeed many of the same items on Leo's list. Of course, it made me feel nauseous when I saw so many historical items on the list that I did not have, their whereabouts probably ended at the Hall of Fame in Canton.

Which brings me to the present time and my desire to write Leo's story. However, I am not an author, let alone one who could do justice to Leo's life. Jeff Miller, an accomplished author and historian whom I had met in the early 2000s through the PFRA, had been closely following my journey and the "Leo Lyons Collection." These items are only part of the story, however, as I truly wanted to gather all of the history on Leo that I had in my possession combined with documented sources already available and piece together with Jeff Miller the sixty-plus years Leo was involved in pro football and the NFL.

I strongly believe that people like my great-grandfather should not be forgotten and their lives should be known to generations of his family that follow. I have four grandchildren, and I have peace of mind knowing that if they want to know about their distant relative, they can. I would like people in Rochester to know about Leo and his team and the historical events in which he was involved. I would like football fans to know that there was a kid more than a century ago who dreamed of having a pro football team long before the NFL existed—and did it! From starting in the sandlots of Rochester along Jefferson Avenue to playing the Chicago Bears at Wrigley Field (Cubs Park), to the Polo Grounds to take on the New York football Giants and Green Bay to battle Curly Lambeau and his Packers. All the interesting events in his career—trying to create football trading cards, an "NFL" exclusive logo, having league divisions and playoffs, having a football museum like Cooperstown, and having unique football uniforms with a logo on the front. All before any of those were invented or used.

I should have known he was not your typical football fanatic. My mother would tell me years later that his football Sundays found him sitting in his chair with the television on mute showing one football game while listening to another game on the radio. And boy, if you ever entered "the zone" in his living room on Sunday afternoon during football season, especially if you were a loud and energetic eight-year-old, you would be promptly scolded with the phrase "go light someplace" (a phrase I never did understand … I am guessing it is a reference from long ago, equivalent to "scram," "beat it," or "get out of here!").

I still have a picture of my sister and me in that living room and I always think of his endearing phrase and chuckle.

1

"I'd like to try out with the Jeffersons"

(1908–1913)

To commemorate its 100th anniversary in 2019, the National Football League (NFL) held a yearlong series of events saluting the game, its history, and its millions of fans. As part of the celebration, the league acknowledged its charter members by holding special draft-day events in several cities that were either represented at the league's founding meeting held September 17, 1920, in Canton, Ohio, or played during its inaugural season. Draft-day festivities were held April 27, 2019, in eight cities, all of which once—but no longer—proudly hosted NFL teams, including Akron, Canton, Columbus and Dayton in Ohio, Hammond and Muncie in Indiana, Rock Island in Illinois, and Rochester in New York.

The celebration in Rochester featured Mayor Lovely Warren announcing the Buffalo Bills' sixth-round selection in that year's college draft (safety Jaquan Johnson of the University of Miami). Joining her for the event was Buffalo Bills legend Darryl Talley, along with a large group of students from Rochester city schools clad in T-shirts replicating the red-and-white jerseys once worn by the city's first NFL team, the Rochester Jeffersons.[1]

There was another face among the crowd of revelers that day, one who was not a public figure, a former pro football player, or a public school student. Standing inconspicuously at the back of the crowd was a 52-year-old man whose interest in the Jeffersons went far beyond the publicity or photo op this event offered the city or the league. In fact, his interest was arguably greater than anyone else's present that day. That man, John D. Steffenhagen, was there to represent Rochester's only NFL team and Leo V. Lyons, his great-grandfather and the man responsible for bringing the Jeffersons into the league.

Steffenhagen is the proud vessel carrying Lyons' legacy, along with the man's expansive collection of artifacts relating to pro football's earliest days. Among those artifacts are Lyons' personal notes documenting the events leading up to and including the league's organizational meeting held a century earlier. Lyons was there, an important member of the group of visionaries recognized today as the league's founders. He worked alongside the likes of George Halas, Joe Carr, Ralph Hay, and Jim Thorpe to midwife the league from a ragtag collection of geographically limited sandlot and semi-pro clubs into a national professional league that would one day overtake major league baseball as America's pastime. Yet Mr. Lyons is often overlooked despite his role in the

NFL draft day celebration in Rochester, April 27, 2019. John Steffenhagen is seen in the back row, fifth from left (photograph by Kim Joris).

birth of the NFL, though he can claim as much responsibility for its origin as those better-publicized figures.

So how did Lyons wind up a forgotten founder? How could someone so integral to the creation of the most successful sports enterprise on earth be rendered a mere footnote in its history? The primary answer can be found in the very city in which his team played. Sports enthusiasts in Rochester simply did not share his passion for the pro game the way fans did in Chicago, Philadelphia, or New York. Football-loving fans in Rochester were not interested in the game as it was played by highly-paid mercenaries with no inherent attachment to their city. If the game did not feature familiar, homegrown talent played by men compensated by the passing of a hat, they were not interested.

Lyons, however, believed the game of pro football was going to be big. He put everything he had—literally—into his team and the new league. For six seasons he kept the Jeffersons alive as members of the NFL until he could no longer withstand the losses, not just on the field but also in his bank account. He was relegated to the sidelines as his place at the owners table—and history—was assumed by the now-familiar names of Mara, Bell, Rooney, Marshall, and Lambeau.

But Lyons was a fighter. That predominant trait was developed early in life, being raised by a stern, domineering patriarch with whom he was at constant odds. When 14-year-old Leo developed a love for the relatively young sport of football, his father, Edward Lyons, forbade him to play. Edward believed the sport was not only dangerous but a complete waste of time. Leo continued to participate despite fears that his father would find out. As Leo's passion for the game grew, his father's dictate was a bone of contention that eventually became the wedge that caused a lifelong estrangement. Football blossomed into an obsession, one that placed nearly everything else in his life in the back seat, including family. From early adulthood, Leo had little contact with his father, who viewed his son's football dreams with disdain. When Leo returned from Canton shortly after attending that first league meeting in September 1920, he had occasion to speak to his father about it. His father's reply was, according to family lore, a simple, "Who cares?"

The two never spoke again.

1. "I'd like to try out with the Jeffersons"

* * *

Edward A. Lyons was born in Ireland in 1866. He left the Emerald Isle at age 19 after hearing of great opportunity available in the United States. He settled in the Rochester area, a busy hub of activity and work, with the Genesee River and Erie Canal running through. It was a time of great innovation in the United States with the advent of the steam turbine, the transformer, and the telephone. These modern marvels were destined to change the world forever, and the city of Rochester played a significant role in the country's growth. The city was expanding at a rapid pace, with a population in excess of 160,000 by the turn of the century.[2] Bausch & Lomb, a highly successful optical business, rose to prominence with high-quality microscopes and soon-to-be-patented spectacles. George Eastman founded the Eastman Dry Plate and Film Company, responsible for the first cameras for everyday use and the popularization of roll film. Good paying jobs were available at Western Union Telegraph, the R.T. French Mustard Company, the New York Central Railroad, and more.

With so many opportunities available, it was not long before Edward found work as a bridge foreman. Within a year, however, he moved to nearby Fairport upon learning of the availability of a milk delivery route. In 1890, he entered into partnership with a gentleman named Menzo Bort in a cigar and grocery store located in the Snow & Parce Building on Main Street in Fairport. He continued to operate the milk delivery service but hired an employee to run his routes.

At some point in late 1890 or early 1891, Edward met the woman who was destined to be his bride, Miss Ellen T. Tehan, whose family hailed from the Batavia suburb of South Byron. Nellie—as her loved ones called her—was born in 1869, one of ten children born to Timothy and Bridget Tehan. Her father and all seven brothers worked for the New York Central Railroad at some point. Timothy was killed in 1886 when he was thrown against a mailbag post while exiting a moving car at the train station in South Byron. Her brother James was also killed in the line of duty in 1895 when he was struck by a moving passenger train at the same station, not far from the spot where his father had been killed.

Nellie had moved to Fairport in 1890 to find work. Exactly how or when she and Edward became acquainted is not known, but what is certain is that the two eventually met and fell in love. They were married in Batavia on May 6, 1891, and settled in Fairport to begin raising a family. Ten months after entering into holy matrimony, the couple were blessed with their first child, a son, Leo Vincent, born March 11, 1892.

It was around this time that Edward's name began popping up in local papers for a series of minor offenses or other run-ins that had him appearing before local magistrates on a fairly regular basis. On October 1, 1892, he was scheduled to appear in court to answer to a charge of petit larceny.[3] In July 1893, Edward and two accomplices were sentenced to six months' imprisonment for the crime of being "knights of the road."[4] He was taken to court in September 1897 by a Clark W. Bly, who was seeking recompense in the amount of $23.43 which he claimed Edward owed him.[5]

Meanwhile, the Lyons family continued to grow as Nellie gave birth to a second son, Edward, in January 1894 and a third, William, in April 1895 before finally blessing the hearth with daughters Irene (April 1897) and Mary (August 1899).

Whether trying to stay ahead of creditors, the law, or a deteriorating reputation, Edward relocated his family frequently during this period. He moved them out of Fairport in 1897 and settled briefly at 188 Champlain Street in Rochester, where Edward partnered in a milk delivery service under the name of O'Brien & Lyons. In 1898, he moved the family to 10 Champlain Street and a year later to 72 Campbell Street. He uprooted the brood again in 1900, moving them this time to 55 Cady Street in Rochester's 19th Ward, where Edward found employment working for an electrical lighting company.

Edward then moved the family to 154 Adams Street. He took a position as a fabricator at the Merchants Despatch Transportation (MDT) Company in the village of Despatch (later the site of East Rochester). MDT served as the main plant within the New York Central Railroad system specializing in construction of refrigerator cars. Nellie gave birth to three more sons, Donald in June 1904, Frank in September 1906, and John in August 1909.[6]

The Lyons children were enrolled at Immaculate Conception Catholic School on Edinburgh Street in the 19th Ward, about a half-mile's walk from their home on Adams Street. The family were weekly communicants and the children raised in strict Catholic tradition. Leo was athletically gifted and highly competitive. He participated in all of the sports the school offered young men. In the winter months he played basketball and, in the spring, played multiple positions on the baseball team.

His best friend was a classmate named Walter Mellody, whom everyone called "Dutch." The Mellody family lived on Doran Street, a short walk from Leo's house.

It was while Leo was at Immaculate Conception that he became acquainted with Miss Catharine Long, the young lady with whom he was destined to spend the rest of his life. "In grade school, I met the love of my life, Catharine," Lyons recalled, "a shy but confident doll in the eighth grade."[7]

Immaculate Conception only went as far as the ninth grade, after which students had to choose whether to continue with their education into high school or enter the working world. Leo chose the latter. It was a decision he regretted the rest of his life.

"I'd give my right arm to have had high school or college," Lyons recalled years later. "All I could say was that my education ended when I got out of the ninth grade at Immaculate Conception School in Rochester, New York."[8]

Leo took part in Immaculate Conception's graduation ceremony in June 1908, along with girlfriend Catharine and

Immaculate Conception School on Edinburgh Street, Rochester.

best friend Dutch. He later recalled wondering whether he was going to finish at all and believed he would not have had it not been for his two closest companions.[9]

With his son's education now as complete as it was going to be, Edward Lyons made it his mission to help the young man find steady employment. Leo began spending his Saturdays hanging around the train yard in Despatch where his father worked. Edward had befriended a blacksmith at MDT named William Hagen, who often brought along his son Walter as well. William was hoping his son might pick up some mechanical skills in case his dream profession did not work out. Walter, however, was less likely to be found watching the welders and fabricators than he was behind the plant driving golf balls. It was not long before Leo and Walter became acquainted and began to spend most of their time finding ways to avoid work. They were known to "borrow" drills from one of the shops so they could dig holes for an improvised golf course. Although Leo had only a fleeting interest in the game of golf, the two shared a love for baseball. They both played throughout the summer, though on different teams, and eventually competed against each other as pitchers for opposing teams.

While Leo had learned his love of competitive sports at Immaculate Conception, there was one athletic pursuit the school did not offer—football. Leo left no record of how or when he became aware of the grid sport, but he recalled his first efforts at taking part.

"In nineteen-hundred and six," he remembered, "I was fourteen years of age and I saw some football pictures. I didn't have enough money to buy a pair of shoes, so I went down to a shoemaker to have him cut up some hard leather and put cleats on my old shoes. He didn't know what I was talking about. He was deaf, and I tried to show him by motions. I went home and got a football picture out of a magazine and imitated kicking a football and throwing a football and showing him the pictures and he got the idea. He put the cleats on my shoes and I went over to Reynolds Field and played sandlot football and the cleats did not stand over five minutes and I played the balance of our choose-up game in my stocking feet."[10]

Like so many other young boys in the Flower City at that time, Leo became an ardent follower of the growing local football scene. "Rochester virtually brimmed with football activity," wrote noted football historian Bob Carroll. "Although the university eleven was usually of indifferent quality, fans supported a whole gaggle of sandlot teams. By far, the biggest game each season was played by the town's two high schools. Huge crowds turned out, betting was rampant, and play was for blood."[11]

Due to the city's rapid growth, its public high school—Rochester Free Academy—was bursting at the seams. A second school—Rochester East High—was opened in 1903 and a third—Rochester West—in 1905. Rochester Free Academy dropped football from its program, leaving the fall sport to the two newly created schools. This resulted in deep rivalries among the respective student bodies, as former teammates became opponents on the fields of athletics. East High's football team, nicknamed the Orientals, faced the West High's Occidentals before crowds that sometimes approached 6,000.

The city was agog with football fever and eventually nearly every section was represented on the local sandlots. Among the teams active during this period were the Columbias (representing the Columbia Athletic Club and Social Center), the Belmonts (from the Belmont Street area of the city's 14th Ward), the Oxfords (from the area in the city's northeast section known as the Butterhole), the X-Rays (formed in 1896 and representing the Exchange Street area in downtown Rochester), the Genesees (from the Genesee Street area in the city's south side), and the Scalpers (representing the 15th Ward in the west-central part of the city).[12] Then there was the Jeffersons, who represented the 19th Ward in the city's southwest section and the neighborhood in which the Lyons family lived.

The Jeffersons traced their history back to 1898, when a group of football players from the University of Rochester were expelled by newly installed president Joseph T. Alling for gambling and other "unseemly conduct." Alling insisted on a strict adherence to Christian ethics and found the players' conduct in stark contrast with the standards to which he wished the college to be held. The expelled athletes wanted to continue playing football but were in need of a sponsor. Most of the boys came from the Jefferson Avenue area in the 19th Ward, which was also home to the prominent Jefferson Avenue Clubhouse. The organization, most commonly referred to simply as the Jefferson Club, at the time served as a headquarters for the city's Democratic Party. Legend has it that the players asked the club to sponsor the team, but no evidence has been found to prove any financial support was provided. Regardless, the Jeffersons slowly grew in prominence, eventually becoming one of the top sandlot teams in the city and idols to many young men residing in the 19th Ward, including Leo and his friend Dutch.

Most of the sandlot teams played other squads within their own weight class to minimize injury to smaller players. The Jeffs at this time were playing in the 110-pound class. Teams ran ads in the local papers seeking opponents for open weekends. Leo's

The first known photograph of the Rochester Jeffersons football team, 1906. Back row: (fourth from left) Jim Weldon, (sixth from left) Bill Caufield, (ninth from left) Bill O'Brien. Front row: (far left) Shorty Caske, (third from left) Jack Slattery, (fourth from left) Jack Forsyth, (sixth from left) Ray Spiegel.

parents forbade him from playing, but by 1908, after learning that Dutch had joined the Jeffersons, Leo was beseeching his friend to get him on the team.

"I said, 'Dutch, I'd like to try out with the Jeffersons.'" But since 16-year-old Leo's parents refused their consent, he would have to do so on the sly. To keep his folks from finding out, Leo told them he was going to be spending the day at Dutch's house. Dutch's parents, however, were just as much against their son playing football as the Lyonses.

"Leo was not the only kid around sneaking off to play football," recalled Lyons' granddaughter Sabina Steffenhagen. "He had a friend who also did the same thing. That kid already had a brother or sister die at a young age and that was why the parents were overprotective."[13]

But Dutch was not to be denied. He had devised a means of getting to the playing field undetected.

"He took me up to a hotel," Lyons recalled. "We went upstairs, climbed a ladder into a blind attic without lights, put on our clothes and walked over to the field where we were going to play. From then on, I really got the idea to pursue it."[14]

It turned out that Leo's audition was in actuality a baptism by fire, as the Jeffersons were playing their crosstown rivals the Scalpers that afternoon, and he was going to be taking part. Managing the team that season was William Glavin, who was well known for managing local baseball teams in the city. He reportedly knew very little about the game of football, serving more as a father figure for the young men on the team.[15]

Since coverage of local grid activity was sparse at that time, there is no newspaper account of this game to verify the actual date (most likely October 4), the final score, the venue, or size of the crowd. Lyons recalled there being an admission fee of ten cents, though most of the attendees—approximately 100—sneaked in through a wooded area near the field.

Whenever there was a mention of the Jeffersons in the local *Rochester Democrat & Chronicle*, that bit of intelligence was provided by Eddie Benz, the team's right guard. Dutch had an agreement with Benz that his real name would not be used when listing the Jeff players in the box scores. Since Leo was still wary of being caught, he too asked that his name be kept out of the box scores, so both were listed under aliases. He borrowed the last name of teammate William Doane and employed several different first initials to keep his parents off the scent.

"My family saw the game of football pointless and barbaric," said Lyons. "They forced me to use fake names and I had to make sure my name was not listed in the newspaper. My brothers and sisters knew, and often covered for me when needed."[16]

It appears other members of the team had the same fears and also used Doane's surname while employing a variety of first initials (A, F, G, H, and J). Since William had one brother (Cam)—and possibly one other—who also played on the team, this made it nearly impossible to determine which was Leo, which were disguised teammates, and which might actually have been members of the Doane family.

The Jeffs were victorious in their next two outings, defeating the Belmonts 15–0 at Sheehan's Field (located near the corner of Monroe Avenue and Winton Road in Brighton, just outside the southeast section of city), then dispatching the Columbias 5–0 at Reid's Field (on Lyell Avenue near Burrows Street in the city's northwest section). As the Jeffs prepared to face the X-Rays on Sunday, November 8, Lyons approached Benz with the offer to take over the duties of reporting the team's scores to the newspaper. This was to be the first instance of a Jeffersons box score—with full lineup and scoring summary—appearing in the *Democrat & Chronicle*.[17]

"Promising teams from the sandlots were breaking into print with marked regularity along toward the close of the 1908 campaign," wrote former Jeff player Elbert Angevine in his book *Parade of the Grid Ghosts: The Story of Football in Rochester*. "Among them were the Jeffersons of the 19th Ward who, within a few years, were to provide the city's major football attractions."[18]

The game, as reported, ended in a 6–0 victory for the Jeffersons. They were scheduled to face the Genesees the following Sunday, the same day the X-Rays were slated to meet the Columbias in a game they claimed was for the city championship. William Glavin, as manager of the Jeffersons, protested the claim, pointing out the fact that the Jeffs had defeated both of these teams during the season.[19] Glavin's protest was for naught, however, as the Jeffs were defeated, 11–6, thus allowing the Genesees to claim the city title at their weight class.[20]

The Jeffs closed out the season with a meaningless 5–0 win over a team from nearby Churchville. In all, the Jeffersons played five verifiable games in 1908. Not counting Lyons' undocumented initial game against the Scalpers or any games before that, the team posted a respectable record of four wins and a single loss.

* * *

By this time, the relationship between Leo and his father was becoming contentious. They did not see eye to eye on many things, especially Leo's growing love of football. As tensions grew, Leo was at Catharine's more than he was at his own home. "My father was not pleasant to be around," Lyons recalled. "I found myself at Catharine's more often than not. Her family was very nice to me. They took me and my pals to see Harry Houdini [the world-famous escape artist and stunt performer] jump off a bridge downtown in 1907."[21]

Leo's granddaughter Sabina Steffenhagen provided some insight into the tension that existed in the relationship between Leo and his father:

> None of us knew much about his parents; he never talked about them or had pictures of them. I did know a lot of her [Catharine's] family, her mom and dad, brothers, sisters. They were nice, down-to-earth people. I only know what I have heard from other family members about Leo's parents. They said he was a strict Irishman who liked beer. Guess he was a baseball fan but hated football. I think he liked the Giants but not sure about that. Both parents were against any of their sons playing football. Leo didn't like when his father would constantly show him newspaper articles about nasty injuries or deaths from playing football. They would remind him a lot about the president of the United States [Theodore Roosevelt] having to do something about football violence. Knowing Leo, it didn't matter. If he wanted to play football, he would play football in any way he could conjure up. He lied to them and secretly played for years. He was always surprised that he got away with it for so long. He used his brothers and sisters, friends, kids from the teams, anyone who could keep the ruse or lie or whatever you want to call it, going.[22]

He had very little spare time to spend at home anyway. By 1909, Leo was working three jobs—as a stock keeper at Rochester Electrical Contractors, in a similar capacity at Rochester Gas Light Company, and as a laborer with Rochester Telephone. This was in addition to the athletic pursuits he refused to yield. Graduates of Immaculate Conception were allowed to continue playing on the school's so-called Seconds teams up until the age of 19. Leo and Dutch took advantage of this rule by competing on the Immaculate Seconds' basketball team in the winter and baseball team in the spring and summer, with Leo acting as manager for both teams. He was also pitching for the Willows amateur baseball team. Just how he found time to pursue his love of sports, work three jobs, and maintain his romantic relationship with Catharine is a mystery, but somehow Leo managed.

Leo also recalled having his first experience on an actual golf course that summer. His friend Walter Hagen had been hired as a caddie and golf instructor at the Country Club of Rochester and invited Leo to spend a day with him on the links, though Leo was nervous he was going to be asked to leave since he was not a member. They grabbed some clubs and headed out to the course. Leo remembered it not being very busy that day due to gusty winds, but the golfers who were there would say, "Hello, Walter" as they passed by. There was a moment of uncertainty when a club pro came over to the pair and asked who Leo was. Walter interjected, "He is with me." The pro responded, "Any friend of Walter's is a friend of mine." Leo recalled Walter regaling him with stories of caddying for George Eastman, the Rochester native and founder of the Eastman Kodak film and camera company.[23]

* * *

The Jeffs had a new man, Frank Dunning, in charge for the 1909 season. Dunning's tenure as manager, however, proved short and uneventful, as he succeeded in arranging just three games during the entire season, all played at Rochester's West End Park.

The Rochester Jeffersons, 1909. Back row (from left): Bill Caufield, unknown, unknown, Bill O'Brien, Pop Morrison, unknown, Ade Groot, Bill Kretchmer. Middle row: Dutch Mellody, Eddie Benz, Jack Forsyth, Bill McCarty, Charles Morrison. Front row: Mike Pfaudler, Ray Spiegel, Shorty Caske, unknown, Leo Lyons (courtesy Jane Flaherty).

The campaign opened on October 31 with a 0–0 tie against Columbia. A week later, the Jeffs defeated the Geneva Hogarths, 14–0, before finishing with a 16–0 skunking of the Oxfords.

Unhappy with the job Dunning had done and eager to take control of the team's destiny, Lyons declared himself manager and owner of the team in anticipation of the 1910 football season.

"He was only 18 years old," wrote grandson Kevin C. Bosner for an oral history in 1969, "but he saw this as an excellent opportunity to have a football team of his own, and to work to making them the best in the country. From the start, Leo knew he had to set himself apart from the rest of the sandlot teams."

Lyons purchased a used typewriter on which he typed letters to his players, advising them of the change in management and philosophy. He advised them there were going to be formalized scheduled practices, new plays to learn, and most important, a commitment to being the top team in the city.[24]

"From the start, Lyons poured his heart and soul into the Jeffersons," wrote football historian Bob Carroll. "He was much more than just a player-manager. One job description had him as the team's 'travel-agent, ad man, ticket hustler, doctor, road secretary, mentor, marriage counselor, recruiter, and financier.'"[25]

In April 1910, the public high schools in Rochester announced that football was being discontinued as an athletic activity. School officials cited several reasons for the ruling, including player injuries, excessive gambling, and ill-mannered behavior of fans. It was also pointed out that the teams' coaches were earning a greater weekly salary than teachers. Even though the decree was intended to be a temporary measure "to allow time for a thorough canvass of the entire school football situation," it ultimately deprived local fans of high school ball for the next three decades.[26]

The ban, however, turned out to be a boon for the sandlot teams in the city. "Deprived of high school football," Carroll observed, "Rochester grid fans increased their interest in the sandlotters. Nineteen ten saw a bonanza for the semi-pros. In addition to bigger crowds, the sandlot teams gained player windfalls as many potentially fine high school players joined them."[27]

Lyons, diving headlong into his role as the Jeffs' chief recruiter, sent letters to many of the displaced high school football players in hopes he could attract some to join the team. A good number of these fellows eventually found their way into the Jeffersons lineup.[28]

Managing the team also meant preparing the field at West End Park for the games on Sundays. Most of the players were content to let Lyons worry about such trivialities, but good old Dutch was usually on hand to pitch in. Kevin C. Bosner provided a detailed description of his grandfather's game-day routine:

> The day before the game, Leo and Dutch were the official grounds crew, nailing two-by-fours together for goalposts and putting them into the ground, drawing marks on the field with white paint or lime for every yard and marking up the sidelines and end zones. It took them all day to set up at Reid's Field near the railroad tracks on Emerson Street. That night Leo packed a first aid kit, a bucket for water along with a ladle, a notebook with plays, pencils, a hammer, tiny nails and a small box of cleats, towels, two footballs, and a bucket of other little extras. Walter Hagen had his father's Model T pickup truck because he became the official transporter of the Rochester Jeffersons. Leo and Walter loaded the truck, covered everything with a canvas tarp and hauled the new franchise to its playing field. After everything was

unloaded and set up, the team had a warm-up and pep talk. Leo wanted to manage the game from the sideline more than he wanted to play, and he would play only sparingly. It is believed to have been one of the largest sandlot crowds in Rochester at that time. Leo had snuck a cooler in with the other equipment. Ice-cold bottles of Coca-Cola and Cracker Jack for the team afterwards, a small gesture but one that was not forgotten.[29]

The list of responsibilities was daunting, to be sure, especially for one who had never managed a football team before. Leo had some experience overseeing the Immaculate Seconds' baseball and basketball teams, but now he was going to be managing a team that did not have the built-in mechanisms for practice and equipment, the scheduling of games with other schools, or a dedicated venue in which to play. He was also going to be in charge of a team comprised primarily of adult men, some of whom were hardboiled veterans of the city's sandlot circuit.

To help keep order, Lyons recruited an old friend named Bill Caufield to serve as his comanager. Caufield had been a teammate of Lyons on the Seconds' baseball team and also assisted him as comanager of the basketball team. He later recalled the litany of duties he and Lyons performed throughout the 1910 football season:

> Those days were rough. From placing challenges to other teams in the paper to a Sunday contest to reserving the field to finding a printer for tickets to getting players to show up for practice especially when horrible weather to making sure they were ready on game day to promising they would at least make a dollar for playing to double-checking that the lines on the field were good to making sure the goalposts were the same making sure there was a place for people to relieve themselves, filling the water bucket with fresh drinking water for teams, and trying to keep onlookers from entering the playing field. ALL BEFORE GAME.[30]

The Jeffs' lineup at this time included quarterback Shorty Caske, halfback Cam Doane, halfback Adrian Groot, tackle Al Horth, center John Loughlin, fullback Stewart "Pop" Morrison and his brother Charlie at end, end Punk O'Brien, halfback Henry Olin, tackle Howard Pfaudler, tackle Ray Rice, and guard Richard Sweeney. Lyons played sparingly, concentrating primarily on his role as the team's manager. Whereas his friend Dutch was no longer using an alias, Lyons continued to do so to keep peace at home.

The season opened on October 23 with a matchup against the Scalpers, the pride of Lyell Avenue in the city's 15th Ward. The Jeffs prevailed by a score of 11–0, with Adrian Groot and Pop Morrison going over for touchdowns. Two weeks later, the Jeffs downed the West High Independents, 5–0. Punk O'Brien scored the game's only touchdown, returning a fumble 30 yards to paydirt.

A rematch with the Scalpers ended in a 0–0 tie, followed by scoreless ties against the Oxfords and a team called Rox. The Jeffs finished their first campaign under Lyons' management at a very respectable 2–0–3.

The effectiveness of his leadership was apparent, but all the time spent concentrating on football matters detracted from spending time with Catharine. Leo's sister Irene joked that she had forgotten what her brother looked like. Leo began setting time aside during the week to spend with his love. He did not yet own an automobile, so the sweethearts usually walked to the nearby Lyceum Theater to catch a play or silent movie starring Mary Pickford, Arthur V. Johnson, or perhaps the rising cowboy sensation named Tom Mix.[31]

Leo turned 19 years of age in March 1911. By this time, he had graduated from school, was holding down at least two jobs (sometimes three) while managing baseball and basketball teams during the spring and summer months and the Jeffersons every other waking moment. He was now a responsible young man who no longer felt the need to hide his football activities from his father.

"Leo had grown older and finally stood up to his dad," granddaughter Sabina Steffenhagen explained. "[It was] a big moment in his life. He told him something to the effect that he was and had been playing football for years and he was not going to stop. Obviously, I don't know what was said exactly, but it was hostile. It was the first time he had challenged his dad, and the two had a very strained relationship after it. He spent almost all his time at Catharine's parents' house nearby after that until he was married."[32]

* * *

Nineteen eleven kicked off on October 15 against the Oxfords at the Butterhole boys' home field of Premier Park. The Oxfords took the game's first lead when a speedy halfback named Henry McDonald sprinted 90 yards for a touchdown. The Jeffs tied the score at five apiece (five points being the value of a touchdown at the time) when Bill McCarty recovered a muffed punt in the Oxfords' end zone. The tie stuck as the final score.

Lyons had his hands full holding down the center position in the Jeff line, but he certainly had occasion to witness the fleet-footed McDonald zooming past him for several long gains. He also observed that whenever the Jeffs managed to bring him down, none of McDonald's teammates were there to offer a hand to help him up like they would for the other men on the squad. When he made a great play or even when he scored that breathtaking touchdown, no one was there to congratulate him or pat him on the back. They celebrated among themselves while McDonald made his way back for the next play. Lyons did not understand why this was.

Lyons was familiar with McDonald. The Haitian-born halfback was very well known around the city after a standout athletic career at Canandaigua Academy before transferring to Rochester's East High, where he starred on both the baseball and football teams. Despite enduring inevitable hardships along the way, McDonald became the first person of color to graduate from that school when he was handed his sheepskin in the spring of 1911.[33] That fall, he joined the Oxfords who, along with the Scalpers and Jeffersons, were considered one of the top three sandlot teams in the city. Lyons always kept a vigilant eye open for top talent in his quest for municipal supremacy. The sight of McDonald streaking almost the entire length of the field to paydirt left an indelible impression on his memory.

A week later the Jeffs faced off against a new team called the Dreadnaughts at Keifer's Field. The game was forgettable except for the eight combined fumbles and the several times play was delayed when kids or dogs ran onto the field. The 0–0 final score said it all.

Next up for the Jeffs was a 60-mile jaunt to Lockport, New York, for a matchup with the North Ends, a team they had never played before. Leo purchased 15 tickets for the Buffalo, Lockport and Rochester Railroad to take the team on its longest road trip yet.

"It was not cheap," wrote Kevin Bosner, "but Leo liked these away games to gauge the competition in other cities around them. The team was surprised to see a sizable number of rooters going along to see the game. Leo had asked Catharine if she wanted to go but she told him she would rather watch paint dry than sit in the rain and cold watching boys try to score a touchdown."[34]

Catharine's analogy was not far off the mark as the game was completely devoid of offense. The game ended in a scoreless draw, the team's third tie in three games.

The Jeffs' season came to an early close on November 5 with a second meeting against the Oxfords. It was yet another scoreless outing for the Jeffs as they failed to muster any offensive punch in going down to a 5–0 defeat. Although he was not in the starting lineup that day, McDonald was spectacular when he entered the game, breaking away for several long runs, just as he had when the teams met three weeks earlier.

Lyons recalled how well McDonald had played in that first game, but it was the pattern of behavior he observed in McDonald's teammates that stood out in this one. He had noticed in the first meeting with the Oxfords that his teammates did not seem to treat McDonald as one of their own. Here again, they were not congratulating him for outstanding plays or helping him off the ground after being tackled. Lyons had seen enough. After the game, he made a beeline for McDonald, sitting by himself on the Oxford bench, stuck out his hand, and congratulated him for another fine performance. McDonald was taken by surprise as this sort of gesture was quite unfamiliar to him. Lyons sat down next to him and asked McDonald why he was not leaving with his teammates to attend the party at the team manager's house. He looked at Lyons incredulously and said, "Seriously?" Lyons asked McDonald to join the Jeffersons, promising he would always be treated just like everybody. Color would never be an issue! McDonald accepted the offer and joined the team the following season. The two men became lifelong friends.[35]

With their season over, Lyons and Jeffs teammates Dutch Mellody and Bill McCarty were invited to play a game with the Scalpers, who were scheduled to meet up with the Oxfords the following Sunday. Despite the influx of talent, the Scalpers took it on the chin by a 20–0 score.

The Jeffs' loss to the Oxfords had brought the final record to 0–1–3. Lyons tried to arrange more games for the team, but scheduling conflicts and cancellations ultimately resulted in the short, four-game campaign. It was a disappointing finish, to be sure, but Lyons was becoming aware of the limitations of the intracity sandlot circuit, which included playing the same old teams on the same old fields week after week for porkchop money. The trip to Lockport on October 29 had revealed that there were numerous teams outside the city that might draw bigger crowds if he could bring them in. It had served as an acid test of his team's capability and affirmed his belief that the Jeffs could compete with the better clubs from beyond the confines of Monroe County.

Once football season had ended, Lyons turned his competitive interests elsewhere. He was still working two jobs (Rochester Electrical Contractors, Inc. and Rochester Telephone), yet somehow found time in the winter to play for and manage two basketball teams. He was an active member of the Immaculate Seconds until March 1912 when he turned 20, the mandatory "retirement" age for the team. Lyons also organized a basketball team made up of players from the Jeffersons, including Dutch Mellody, Ade Groot, and Bill McCarty. When summer came, he busied himself playing baseball with the Willows and Regals.

Leo still managed to find time for Catharine, though. On a rare free evening, the two would ride in Leo's new Model T to the Lyceum Theater to take in a movie.

* * *

Lyons was determined to instill an air of professionalism in the Jeffersons, not just in the way they were managed but also how they looked and played on the field. By 1912, he felt it was time to bring style and uniformity to the Jeffs' appearance. If major league baseball and college football teams wore sharp, matching uniforms, why not sandlot football teams?

One day that summer, he and new friend Henry McDonald took a drive down to Marietta Street in Leo's Model T to watch his friend Walter Hagen pitch for the Ramlys in a game against the Court Plymouths. After witnessing Hagen's masterful performance in winning 20–5, the three sat for a chat. Walter revealed that he was leaving Rochester shortly for Canada to play in the Canadian Open, his first major tournament as a professional. The conversation eventually turned to football, and Leo asked Walter—well known as a flamboyant dresser—his opinion on a design for the team's uniforms. Walter told Leo to go with red, "the color of blood in that sport you love so much." Walter pointed to the bright red beret he was wearing at the moment and said, "Go with that color. It will most definitely stand out, and you don't want to be like everyone else."[36]

"I needed to stand out from the rest, so he proposed bright red togs," Lyons recalled. "I went to Scrantoms, a local sporting goods store, and purchased 18 red tops for around $25."[37]

The initial uniform design was a red jersey with white stripes on the sleeves and a plain letter "J" on the front, mimicking the style used by many university teams at that time. This combination stood as the team's standard look through the 1914 season.

The year 1912 also saw the Jeffs move to Sheehan's Field as a regular home field. With the loss of scholastic ball in Rochester, the sandlot variety had been enjoying an upsurge in interest from displaced fans. The small fields on which teams such as the Jeffs, Oxfords, and Scalpers played were ill-equipped to handle the increased numbers turning out for their games. With no fencing to hold back the crowds, bedlam often ensued.

"Recalling these fiery battles," noted Angevine, "oldtimers have many a chuckle. If the score was close near the finish of the game, the excited fans almost invariably swept out onto the gridiron for a better view. Then the boys of both teams would have to lock arms and drive them back to the sidelines—but the crowd would be out there again a play or two later. Many a forward pass, hurled into a row of spectators in the gathering dusk of a late Sunday afternoon, went for a long gain. More than once, the ball-carriers got the day's best 'blocking' from persons in the crowd."[38]

Although located in the suburb of Brighton just outside the city limits, Sheehan's was more spacious than West End or Genesee Valley parks and was easily accessed by the city's trolley service. Moving the Jeffs' home games there also provided Lyons the opportunity to put up a barrier to keep the crowds from pouring onto the playing field. The *Democrat & Chronicle* lauded Lyons' efforts at cultivating a higher standard for the local football scene: "Most of the local Sunday games for several years have been met with considerable wrangling, a condition of affairs that naturally has not tended to please the spectators. Manager Lyons proposes to see that such features will be eliminated. Crowding onto the field, which has marred most of the games, will also be prevented as a low wire fence has been erected to keep the spectators from the gridiron. Competent officials will handle the contests and every attempt made to raise the game to the standard set by college football."[39]

Lyons later recalled that the construction of the fence required a great deal of elbow grease, a good amount of teamwork, and a fair share of resourcefulness:

1. "I'd like to try out with the Jeffersons"

We moved to Sheehan's Field at the corner of Monroe Avenue and Elmwood and played there and charged twenty-five cents. The crowd in those days stood right on the sidelines. I decided to put a fence around the field. I was the night wire chief with the telephone company at the time. Cables were being put underground and the overhead wires and crossarms being thrown away. I got the president's chauffer, who had an open Packard, to put the old wire and crossarms into the car and take them out to Sheehan's Field around midnight. One of our players, Joe Still, who had the Empire Fence Company, had all the equipment for building fences. I bought a post-hole digger from Joe. I worked [for the telephone company] from midnight until eight o'clock in the morning. When I got through, I took a streetcar with the post-hole digger to Monroe Avenue and Harlem, the end of the line, and walked from there about two miles to the field. I worked all day digging holes for the new fence, went home about four o'clock, took a nap, and then went to work at midnight. Went out the next day digging holes for the fence. Saturday morning I had the holes dug and two of my players came out and helped me. We put the crossarms in the hole, filled in with the dirt, packed it down, put the wire on, tied one end of it to the bumper of Don Gray's old Buick to stretch it, and I went around the field stapling the wire on. We also marked the field Sunday morning. Sunday afternoon we played. I played the whole game. In the first quarter, the crowd tore down the fence.[40]

The *Democrat & Chronicle* continued, "It is only fitting that the Jeffersons, through Manager Lyons, should be the ones to attempt to put local semi-pro football in the position that it belongs, as that team is undoubtedly the best in its class in these parts. His record of having lost only two games in four years is striking proof of that fact. Local teams seem to be wary when it comes to meeting the Jeffersons and it is probable that Manager Lyons will schedule most of his games with out-of-town elevens."[41]

The Rochester Jeffersons, 1912. Back row (from left): Ade Groot, Ray Rice, Harry Driscoll, Bill McCarty, Tom Burke, Pop Morrison, Charles MacLellan, Henry McDonald, Charles McFadden, Dutch Mellody, Charles Morrison. Front row: Mike Pfaudler, Leo Lyons, Jack Slattery, Ben Ziegler, Chuck Ashton, Oliver Angevine.

Of the seven games the Jeffs played in 1912, however, only two were against teams from outside of Rochester. The Jeffs opened the campaign with a 3–0 win against the Fairport Athletic Club, a team from the namesake suburb on the city's east side. Quarterback Bill McCarty was the hero, kicking a field goal to give the Jeffs the margin of victory.

Henry McDonald made his debut a week later (November 3) against a new aggregation calling itself All-Rochester, made up primarily of members of the dissolved Oxfords. He was spectacular in leading the Jeffs to a 6–0 win, scoring the game's only touchdown on an 11-yard scamper.

"After the game," Lyons recalled several years later, "the players shouted 'Henry! Henry!' and crowded around him to congratulate him on a great day's work. [I] was happy that Henry was fitting in nicely with the squad and was becoming a spectacular addition to the team."[42]

The Redshirts faced their first real test of the campaign the following Sunday when they hosted Lancaster, a formidable team that had scored 196 points in six games played thus far, while allowing their opponents no points. The Jeffs were flush with confidence after their 2–0 start but were totally outclassed in this outing. Their fans were initially optimistic, as the Jeffs managed to register the first points against Lancaster this year on a McCarty dropkick and trailed by a slim 9–3 score at halftime. But the Lancasters used their weight advantage to batter the Jeff line in the second half, scoring two more touchdowns en route to a 23–3 win.

The Jeffs shook off the disappointing loss and played another new team, the Atlantics, representing the city's Sixth Ward. Bill McCarty, Dutch Mellody, and Charles McLellan all scored touchdowns in leading the Jeffs to a 19–0 win.

Next up was a Thanksgiving Day visit from All-Syracuse, a team that had not lost in three years or yielded a single point in three games this year. The Jeffs proved up to the challenge, dispatching the visitors 18–0 on a snow-covered gridiron at Sheehan's Field. Dutch Mellody, Chuck Ashton, and Pop Morrison each contributed a score for the Jeffs.

Three days later, the Jeffersons met up with the Scalpers at Sheehan's Field, ostensibly for the city championship. The bitter rivals slugged it out for 58 scoreless minutes, at which point the Scalpers took possession and drove all the way to the Jeffs' five-yard line. But just as they were about to execute their next play, the whistle blew. The game ended in the scoreless deadlock.

Unsatisfied, the mortal enemies agreed to a rematch. With Sheehan's Field unavailable, however, the managers were forced to move the game to Reid's Field. The Jeffs had not played at Reid's in a few years, but it was all that was available for this mid–December contest.

Another Jeff-Scalper game, another dustup. When a dispute arose over an officiating decision, one of the teams—though which is not clear—walked off the field with time remaining on the game clock. Since both teams were accusing the other of leaving the field of play, the game was ruled a cancellation.

An account of the incident appeared in the next day's *Democrat & Chronicle*:

WHY NOT BE SPORTS, BOYS?
No Need of an Official If You Don't Abide by His Decision.

The football game at Reid's Field yesterday afternoon between the Scalper and Jeffersons wound up in a row. Both teams submitted contradictory reports of the contest, in which each claimed the other left the field. The Scalpers claimed to be within two yards of a touchdown when a dispute arose over the referee's decision. On the other hand, the Jeffersons contend the ball was rightfully in their possession further down the field when the trouble arose.

No matter what did occur the two teams should have abided by the official's decision. What's the use of having one if a team is going to walk off the field because a decision is not to its liking. And right here it may be said that the best team is bound to win. So, ye Scalpers and Jeffersons, be sports.[43]

The nondecision left the Jeffs with a final mark of four wins, two losses, and two ties. It was a major improvement over the previous season's record of 0–1–3 but not quite good enough. The Scalpers claimed municipal honors with an overall record of 8–1–1, having outscored their opponents 187–12 in the process.

* * *

The sharp new uniforms and upgraded playing fields introduced in 1912 gave the Jeffersons a more professional aura than their city rivals, but for many players it still came down to dollars and cents. To build a roster of highly talented players, teams had to recruit and pay them. Sometimes this resulted in bidding wars as teams sought to sign the best players in an effort to build a winning combination that could draw large crowds and ultimately generate money that could be reinvested to continue the cycle year after year. For Lyons, who had visions of football grandeur from the first time he stepped onto a gridiron, it was a constant struggle to generate the revenue he needed to elevate the Jeffs—and the game of paid football—from sandlots to stadiums.

"My biggest concern now was being able to keep the best players on the team despite the lack of funds," Lyons remembered. "Other teams and rivals made enticing offers throughout the season to top players, even for a just a game or two. Players contracts were not popular in Rochester, not enough money to hold on to a player. Nope, in Rochester, semipro teams were on their own, none financed by the wealthy. I knew that would have to change somehow, someday down the road. To reach the pro level, a team would have to be able to field a team of highly paid players to compete, like in professional baseball."

Somehow, Lyons managed to finagle a meeting with Rochester entrepreneur George Eastman, the founder of the Eastman Kodak Company, to ask for his sponsorship. Eastman was well known for his philanthropic work through which he provided funding to the Eastman School of Music, Rochester Philharmonic Orchestra, the University of Rochester, the Rochester Athenaeum and Mechanics Institute (today known as the Rochester Institute of Technology), and several other projects. If Lyons could only secure the support of a wealthy benefactor such as Eastman, he would be all set.

"I dressed up in my best suit and tie and met Mr. Eastman downtown at his factory office," he recalled. "It was not what I was anticipating, an unimpressed and uninterested response from the giant, 'professional football, are you serious?' Not that Eastman was being unfair to me, football was considered, at that time, a foolish and pointless sport with no future. Even small businesses felt professional football had no future, though I did try to drum up support for it. One meeting after another would end the same, not one business establishment would offer any financial support to the team, and it frustrated me to no end. I saw how successful teams out west were and knew it could be the same here in this city, but it all fell on deaf ears. But it would not deter me from my dream of professional football, if there is major league baseball there can be major league football."[44]

It was the first of many setbacks Lyons was destined to face along the way, but he was undeterred. He was as bold as he was indefatigable and came up with many ideas to promote his team and the sport over the next several years. In the meantime, he would have to rely on gate receipts to sustain his enterprise.

The 1913 edition of the Rochester Jeffersons featured several former members of the crosstown rival Oxfords, which had ceased operations after the 1911 season. Boys from the Butterhole joining the Jeffs included tackle Pete Heinlein, quarterback Hermie Klehr, and fullback Harry "Dutch" Irwin. Irwin, a former star at East High in Rochester before moving on to play at Mercer College, was brought in by Lyons to double as an assistant coach overseeing the backfield men. Heinlein had suited up for the Jeffs for the final game of the 1912 season and was now becoming a permanent member of the squad. Both he and Irwin would enjoy long careers with the Jeffersons.

Lyons was pleased to have some experienced veterans returning from the previous year as well, including center Chuck Ashton, tackle Denny Cahill, halfback Don Gray, quarterback Adrian Groot, tackle Al Horth, quarterback Bill McCarty, guard Charles McClellan, end Dutch Mellody, fullback Pop Morrison, guard Howard Pfaudler, and end Harold Spiegel. One player who was not going to be with the team to start the season was Henry McDonald, who had accepted an offer to play for the Lancaster team. In addition to an offer of more money than Lyons could pay, McDonald was dating a young

The Rochester Jeffersons, 1913. Back row (from left): Pete Johnson, Don Gray, Eddie Benz, Ray Spiegel, Denny Cahill, Charles MacLellan. Middle row (from left): Chuck Ashton, Babe Clark, Dutch Mellody, Jimmy O'Toole, Pete Hardy. Front row (from left): Leo Lyons, William Lyons.

lady from that town named Laura Scott and the couple planned to be married soon. The man McDonald replaced in the Lancaster backfield, Joe McRae, left that team and subsequently joined the Jeffersons.

The Jeffs assembled at the New York Central train station at eight the morning of Sunday, October 5, to board the train taking them to their season opener against Lancaster. Lancaster had a very strong team, having gone undefeated in 1912 (which included a 23–3 triumph over the Jeffs) and winning the *Buffalo Evening News* Cup as Western New York semipro champions.

The one thing they would not have going for them in this contest was newly acquired Henry McDonald, who was inexplicably absent when the teams trotted onto the field at Lancaster's American Malleable Park. It did not matter, though, as the host team ran roughshod over the red-clad invaders from Rochester. Playing in a sweltering heat before 1,000 partisans, the Lancaster boys rolled up four first-half touchdowns to take a 26–0 lead into intermission. The game then devolved into a defensive battle as the players grew sluggish from the unseasonable warmth. The halftime score stuck as the final.

The Jeffs suffered an even greater loss a week later, dropping a 30–0 decision to the Buffalo-based Cazenovias. Now standing at 0–2, the team rebounded to win their next three contests, 12–0 against the Pullmans at Genesee Valley Park, 7–0 over a team from Tonawanda, New York, called the Irontons, and 46–0 drubbing of All-Brockport in which six different Jeffs crossed the goal line.

The turnaround left the Jeffs with a respectable record of 3–2, good enough to qualify to once again meet the Scalpers (4–1) for the city championship. Barring an episode similar to the 1912 tilt when the teams failed to finish the game over a disputed call, this contest figured to be the first in which the title was decided on the field of play. The Jeffs held a slight weight advantage over their antagonists from the 15th Ward, but the teams were otherwise evenly matched.

As expected, a large crowd turned out to witness the grudge match. The teams traded blows for the better part of three and a half quarters before Scalper quarterback Billy Bauer scored the game's only touchdown on a one-yard plunge. The extra point gave the Scalpers a 7–0 lead that held until the final whistle.

The *Democrat & Chronicle* reported:

> ### Much Lighter Scalper Team Beats Jeffersons For Title
> #### Losers Three Times Advance Ball to Within Few Yards of Goal Line but Don't Possess Punch to Push It Over for Touchdown
>
> Outweighed fifteen pounds to the man, the plucky Scalper eleven outplayed the Jeffersons yesterday afternoon at Reid's Field and made history by settling for the first time the question of supremacy between the semi-pro football teams of this city. The final score was 7 to 0 in favor of the Northsiders. The visitors uncovered an attack that was far superior to anything that the Jeffersons pulled off. In fact, the latter, on account of their great superiority in weight, relied on the old game of football for the most part, and even in this they were surpassed by their lighter opponents who managed to find openings somewhere in the big Jefferson line.
>
> The appearance of the field resembled somewhat the old days of high school football in this city except that there were no bleachers and there was no waving of pennants, but there was cheering and there was a good-sized crowd out to see the game, estimated to be in the neighborhood of 4,000 persons. Old high school days were further recalled by the fact that each team was coached by onetime high school stars, Harry Irwin, a former East High halfback,

having had charge of the Jeffersons this season while Frank Niven, a former West High fullback, was responsible for the plays pulled off by the Scalpers. Then, too, each team had a number of players who learned the game under such instructors as Sullivan, the old East High and University of Rochester crack; Acton Langslow and Hogan Yancey, former coaches at West High School.

The influence of these coaches upon the players was quite apparent in the manner in which the game was played. It was the cleanest semi-pro contest ever seen in this city. There were times when the players were a little rough but not enough to mar the contest, despite the intense rivalry that exists between the teams and the title that was at stake.[45]

The Jeffs assembled one last time to take on the East Ends, winning 32–0. The otherwise meaningless game was notable for being the first known appearance of Leo's brother William in the lineup as a guard. The Redshirts' final record of 4–3 was a slight comedown from the 4–2–2 season posted in 1912, but competing for the city championship in back-to-back seasons cemented their place as one of the top two teams in the area. Those big losses suffered against Lancaster and Cazenovia informed Lyons that his team still had some ground to cover if it was going to compete with the best elevens from other parts of the state.

2

"Champions of New York State"

(1914–1916)

After seven years of courtship, Leo and Catharine decided the time had come to get married. Leo's family situation caused some problems, so they chose to have a small ceremony with just a few close friends attending. The events leading up to and the nuptials were retold by Leo and Catharine's daughter, Sabina, as the story was passed down to her:

> Leo and Catharine had set a wedding date, April 18, 1914, and they planned on a short "honeymoon" in Niagara Falls right after. They both were working steady at their jobs at the telephone company and city office. Rochester Jefferson basketball was still rolling along, comprised of several of the Jeffs players including Henry, who joined the basketball team for the first time. Leo was enjoying his managerial position on the basketball team and in February, was honored at the Immaculate Conception Reunion Dinner for his managing of a baseball, basketball, and football team at age 22. Catharine attended the dinner with Leo and were congratulated by their former classmates who were happy to see the two together, not at all surprised the two would "tie the knot." Whenever the upcoming wedding was being planned at either house, both families disliked the other, making it all very difficult. Leo's father Edward refused to attend their wedding, which led to even more drama. This family rift had started long before this; Leo had moved out of his parents' house at an early age and lived with Catharine's parents. As the wedding approached, Leo and Catharine talked about it, and in frustration, they went the day before the wedding on Tuesday and got their marriage certificate and were planning to get married the next day minus both families. Leo talked to his friend Dutch Mellody, who he asked to be his best man months earlier and asked if he could be at the church the next day, and of course said "yes." Catharine called her best friend Mayme Weber and explained the situation and if she could be at the church on Wednesday, and of course she said "yes." And so, on Wednesday morning, April 15, 1914, at the Immaculate Conception Church in Rochester, Leo and Catharine were wed by the Reverend Augustine O'Neil, with Dutch and Mayme alongside. Marrying a couple like this during the week without family was not something the Reverend O'Neil was supposed to do, not something the Catholic Church had in mind. He told them he was only doing it because he liked Leo and Catharine and was familiar with the family trouble, and it would be his first and last marriage performed like this. There was a large group of boys sitting in the back of the church, who did not walk up to the front pews until the ceremony began. Leo and Catharine were shocked to see the entire Rochester Jefferson football team along with Walter Hagen. Dutch had hurriedly gathered the players together the night before to tell them about the early Wednesday wedding, and Walter Hagen got wind of it somehow and showed up.[1]

Leo and his bride then spent a few days honeymooning at Niagara Falls before moving into a small dwelling at 124 Hobart Street on the city's west side. Yet, as he settled into a life of domestic bliss, Leo's thoughts never strayed far from the football field. Whether it was devising new offensive plays, personnel moves, or uniform designs, the Rochester Jeffersons had become an obsession. Unfortunately, the team was not successful enough to become a full-time vocation. There were bills to pay, so Leo went right back to working his two jobs as an electrician with Rochester Electrical Contractors and as a general laborer with Rochester Telephone.

* * *

The focus was still on family as the 1914 football season was getting underway. Leo was thrilled to have his younger brother William—who had joined the Jeffs as a substitute a year earlier—joining the Jeffersons on a full-time basis. His parents were no happier about Willie playing football than they had been with Leo. Willie's decision to play caused strain in his relationship with the parents as well, but he was 19 by this time and there was little they could do or say to stop him.

Newlyweds Leo and Catharine Lyons, circa 1914.

Leo, on the other hand, had different forces with which to contend. Although not explicitly expressed in their wedding vows, Catharine had asked him to give up his role as an active player and concentrate strictly on his managerial duties. But just as he had when his parents forbade him to participate in the scary grid sport, Leo simply asked the reporters covering the game to refrain from using his real name in the next-day summaries. After playing in the season opener under the name "Lines," Leo was assigned the name "Jackson" for the balance of the year. Whether Catharine ever caught on is not known, but it seems unlikely she didn't at least suspect he was taking part, especially if he came home after a game bruised and muddied.

Aside from Leo and his brother, players returning from the 1913 squad were guard Denny Cahill, fullback Harold "Babe" Clark, end Dutch Dow, halfback Don Gray, tackle Pete Heinlein, quarterback Joe Klehr, center Nelson Lengeman, halfback and team captain Dutch Mellody, tackle Pop Morrison, end Ray Spiegel, and quarterback Dutch Irwin. Irwin was returning in his dual roles of quarterback and coach, though it was announced on August 16 that Lyons had secured the services of Dr. Ray Brown, assistant football coach at Georgetown University, to work alongside Irwin until it was time for him to return for the Stonewalls' training camp.[2]

New players joining the team this year included tackle Walter Frickey, end Mike Hall, and center Art Webb. Webb would enjoy a long tenure with the Jeffs and become one of Lyons' most reliable players.

Another nonplayer brought into the fold was Dave Cansdale, whom Lyons had secured to serve as the team's athletic trainer. Cansdale had held the same position at West High in Rochester from 1906 to 1909 and then the Rochester Hustlers International League baseball team. "Dave is something more than a trainer on the football field," wrote the *Democrat & Chronicle*. "He insists that every man out for the team report for each practice as well as respecting strict training rules during the season. With him looking after the squad, the Jeffersons should be fit as a fiddle as they enter the big games."[3] He too was destined to become one of Lyons' most trusted team members.

The season opened on October 4 with a trip to Lockport, where the Jeffersons escaped with a 0–0 tie. The home portion began a week later against the Atlantics, a squad made up of players from several area teams including the Scalpers, Westcotts, Senecas, and others. As another example of Lyons' efforts toward legitimizing the Jeffs, the game was scheduled to be played at Rochester Baseball Park, located at Bay and Greeley Streets in the city's east side. This was significant since only college and high school teams had been allowed to use the Baseball Park up to that point. The park was a major improvement over Reid's and Sheehan's Fields as it offered a large, covered grandstand and could hold as many as 10,000 spectators. It featured fencing around the entire field, which reduced the possibility of people sneaking in without paying.

"The contest will be handled by experienced officials," the *Democrat & Chronicle* reported, "and there will be police to maintain order, so that there should be no

Rochester Jeffersons in action in game believed to be October 17, 1914, versus the Atlantics at Rochester Baseball Park.

wrangling or vexatious delays. The independent football players hail this as an excellent opportunity to demonstrate the strength of the game in Rochester."

The Jeffersons proved worthy of the upgraded accommodations, getting two touchdowns from Joe Klehr and one each from Dutch Mellody and Babe Clark in rolling to a 26–6 win. The triumph was a costly one, however, as Jeffs end Harold McCrary was badly injured while being tackled. McCrary, still a student at West High in Rochester, suffered a couple of cracked ribs and required the removal of his appendix as a result.[4]

As a result of cancellations, scheduling conflicts, and an inability to find teams willing to face them, the Jeffs did not have another game scheduled for several weeks. They continued to practice regularly while Lyons worked the phones to find a team to play. He also had time to negotiate with local sports figure Acton Langslow to join the Jeffs as an advisory coach. Langslow was a bit of a legend on the athletic fields of the Flower City, having starred on the gridiron at West High and later the University of Rochester. The *Democrat & Chronicle* announced Langslow's signing in its November 6 edition. Although he was nearly 30 years old, there was speculation that he might actually suit up and play at some point.

The Jeffs would not play again until Sunday the 22nd when they were scheduled to face the Scalpers at Reid's Field. Since these teams were considered to be the best two in the city, the game was designated to be for the city championship, making it the third straight year these teams were going to meet for the honors.

"After prolonged dickering, challenges, calumny and oratorical Roman candles," chirped the *Democrat & Chronicle*, "the managements of the Jefferson and Scalper football teams, leading pigskinners of this city, had a peaceable talk last night and agreed to a game the coming Sunday. It has been hoped for a long time that the Jeffersons and their perennial rivals would find time to stage a series, but the lateness of the season dissuaded them yesterday from arranging anything but a single game."[5]

It was a battle of evenly matched teams, the Jeffersons reportedly outweighing their opponent by just a mere pound per man. They used those 11 pounds to their advantage by taking the game's first possession and marching from their own 15-yard line down to the Scalpers' 10 in just six plays. Moments later, fullback Babe Clark smashed through the Scalper line for the touchdown. But the conversion attempt failed, leaving the Jeffs ahead by six. The Scalpers finally put together a sustained drive of their own late in the fourth, marching all the way to within a foot of the Jefferson goal line. From there, halfback George Nier bulled over to tie the score. Quarterback Billy Bauer added the extra point, and the Scalpers had a tenuous 7–6 lead. The Jeffs received the ensuing kickoff and began a drive from their own 35. They marched down to the Scalpers' 10-yard line with one minute left on the clock. The decision was made to go for the field goal to win it. Pop Morrison dropped back to attempt the dropkick, but a bad snap threw off his rhythm. He recovered in time to get the kick away, but just as it left his foot, the pigskin bounced off Dutch Mellody's back and fluttered to the ground, along with the Jeffs' last hope. The Scalpers held on to win 7–6 and were again awarded the city championship.

The disappointed Jeffs pulled themselves together to play four days later against the Pullmans on Thanksgiving Day. Fullback Lyman Avery gave the Jeffs a 6–0 lead in the opening frame with a short touchdown run, and a safety shortly before halftime made it 8–0. Dutch Mellody set up a touchdown for himself by racing 75 yards with the pigskin to the Pullmans' 5. He went over two plays later, and the Jeffs now led 15–0. Lyons (playing under the alias of Jackson) capped the scoring in the fourth with a thrilling

13-yard dash on an end-around, making the final Jeffs 22, Pullmans 0. Acton Langslow was given a chance to relive some old glories when he trotted onto the field to rousing applause in the third quarter. However, after being away from the playing field for so long, the man was unable to be of much help.

The season came to a close with a 39–6 destruction of All-Rochester in which the Jeffs found the end zone six times, getting touchdowns from Bob Argus and Dutch Mellody and two each from Babe Clark and Jackson (Lyons).

The victory left the Big Red with a final season mark of 3-1-1. Despite losing the city title to their archnemesis Scalpers, it was a successful season that saw the Jeffersons moving away from the smaller fields in town for the more professional accommodations of the Baseball Park. Lyons was determined to continue to advance his team's reputation in the city and throughout the state.

* * *

The city of Rochester could not seem to get enough of the grid sport. Its citizenry loved athletic endeavors in the winter months, especially basketball, but that was hardly a replacement for what seemed to be the consensus first love. But what if there was a way fans could enjoy football year-round? Maybe the football-crazed city could enjoy the sport in those months normally dominated by basketball and ice hockey.

Leo Lyons believed it could be so.

INDOOR FOOTBALL APPEARS TO BE A VERY FAST GAME
Not So Dangerous as Outdoor Rugby Play.

The local townspeople will soon have a chance to affix their official stamp of approval or disapproval, whichever the case may be, on a form of indoor athletics new to these parts but patterned after that great old game, so dear to the hearts of every rah rah boy in the country, whether that youth obtained his football knowledge in a high school or college. An indoor football game is to be played at the New York State Armory on Friday night, February 19th, and the promoters are looking for a capacity crowd to witness the struggle which is to be between the Jeffersons and Scalpers athletic clubs.

Now you must not picture the players appearing on the floor carefully packed in excelsior or anything of that sort. The fact is the paraphernalia used in the indoor game is practically the same as that used on the frozen ground with the exception of footgear. Instead of wearing the cleated leather shoes as in the outdoor game, the players will be equipped with rubber sneaks so as to insure a firm footing on the slippery floor.

With the shoulders, hips and knees well-padded there is less danger of injury in the indoor game than in the outdoor game and it is said by people that have witnessed the former that it is much faster, the ball traveling through the air via forward passes a far greater portion of the time. The element of chance plays a more prominent part also, thus making it abound in exciting moments.[6]

Where Lyons got the idea of playing games in an indoor venue is not known, but it is likely that he was aware of similar games being played in other large cities throughout the Northeast. The concept itself was certainly not new. The first known indoor games were played at New York's Madison Square Garden in the winter of 1902–1903. The World Series of Football, as it was called, was a series of football games played among five teams, all of which were composed of men being paid for their services. The teams participating represented the Knickerbocker Athletic Club (New York), the Warlow (Long Island) Athletic Club, the Orange (New Jersey) Athletic Club, a squad comprising eight members of the major league baseball Philadelphia Phillies and four Philadelphia Athletics playing as the nominal "New York" team, as well as a team representing the Syracuse Athletic Club featuring legendary football coach Glenn "Pop" Warner and his brother Bill. The timing of the event was to take advantage of the downtime over the Christmas–New Year holiday season (December 29–January 1). Even though that first attempt at indoor football was considered a failure, it inspired other cities with large venues to hold indoor games of their own. The nearby city of Buffalo had a fairly successful circuit going. That no one in Rochester had thought to try it before 1915 is somewhat surprising.

There were differences between the Armory and Madison Square Garden, of course. The Garden's playing surface was only 70 yards long, while the Armory's was 110. The Garden's wooden floor had been removed and replaced with dirt. At the Armory, the combatants were going to be playing on the building's hardwood floor wearing basketball shoes. Since there were no goalposts, attempts at points after touchdown and field goals were not permitted. Quarters were limited to eight minutes due to excessive warmth and poor ventilation in the building.

The game was scheduled for the evening of Friday, February 19. Some 700 football-starved fans turned out, finding refuge from the brisk winter weather within the Armory's fortified walls. The Jeffs emerged on the upside of a chippy 18–0 final, getting two touchdowns from Babe Clark and one from Dutch Mellody.

Despite the sparse crowd, the *Democrat & Chronicle* declared the game a success. "From a spectator's point of view the game far surpasses the outdoor game, as was predicted, but the heat was too intense to allow the teams to do battle more than eight minutes at a time. The injuries that were looked for by many failed to make their appearance and time was taken out only three times during the whole game, in each instance for the Scalpers. All the players were in fine condition after the indoor battle and the spectators went away pleased with the exhibition."[7]

Several of the participants interviewed after the game also expressed a preference for the indoor variety. Clement Lanni, who served as referee for the game, declared, "It's a great game from the spectator's point of view but it must be hard on the players on account of the heat."

"It's better than the outdoor game," remarked Dutch Mellody. "I like it."[8]

The event was successful enough to inspire Lyons to plan more games at the Armory. They were going to have to wait, however, as a more pressing matter was taking precedence. Leo and Catharine had been expecting their firstborn child at any moment, and fortunately for them the baby was willing to wait until the week after the Armory clash to make her grand entrance. Catherine Zelda Lyons was born Thursday, February 25, 1915, at Rochester Homeopathic Hospital at 224 Alexander Street. Although named after her mother, with a slightly different spelling, she was destined to be called Zelda by family and friends her whole life.

Leo and Catharine's granddaughter Sabina Steffenhagen related the story as it was told to her by her mother (the couple's second daughter, also named Sabina):

> Leo and Catharine were "over the moon"—Leo's words—with the arrival of their first child. It was a stressful time before the birth, money and his football team were making it very hard to get by, and was going to be harder with a new addition and Catharine out of work. But the sight of his first child made him the "happiest man on earth." Seemed like every time Leo and Catharine were at their wit's end with the way their lives were going, something would bring their love for one another closer. This was one of those times.[9]

The proud papa was not away from his team for long, though. Just three weeks after Zelda's arrival (March 13), Lyons had arranged for the Jeffs to return to action at the Armory for a game against Lancaster, a team they had faced twice on grass but had never beaten. Lancaster was the reigning champion football team in New York State, having defeated a team from Syracuse the previous fall to claim the title. Remarkably, they had lost just 12 games over the previous 17 seasons. They also had one of the finest halfbacks in all of sandlot football playing for them in Henry McDonald, the former Jeff.

Lyons had not played in the game against the Scalpers, bowing to his wife's wishes that he stick to managing the club. He could no longer resist the urge, however, and decided to pull on the moleskins for this one. It was a decision he would soon regret.

The Jeffs put up a noble fight but were no match in this one, coming up on the short end of a 12–6 final.

To hide the fact that he was playing, Lyons had again asked his contact at the *Democrat & Chronicle* to not to publish his name in the next day's box score. The reporter agreed, telling Lyons he would use an "Indian"-sounding name this time. He was a man of his word. The game account appearing in Sunday's *Democrat & Chronicle* showed an unfamiliar player at left end named "Manafraid" (short for "Man Afraid of His Wife"). It did not really matter, though. The cat was out of the bag just a few hours after the contest, when Leo walked through the door with his face bruised and bloodied. "I needed 11 stitches in my head after one long slide along the floor," he recalled. "Not all of us wore headgear in those days."[10]

Nearly 50 years later, Henry McDonald still had vivid memories of the event. "It was a good football game," he told a *Democrat & Chronicle* reporter in 1963, "with plenty of room to move and throw. We wore sneakers, but when we were tackled we'd still slide. Outside of a few burns on our hands, playing conditions were ideal."[11]

A third indoor game had been scheduled for later in the spring, but after a disappointing crowd described as a "few hundred" had shown for the Lancaster tilt, it was called off.

* * *

Lyons was unrelenting in his quest to develop a culture of professionalism with the Jeffs. From the very beginning, he managed his team differently from the other sandlot squads in the area. He started by recruiting the best players from other teams in the city and scheduling games with the top teams from cities outside of Rochester including Lockport, Lancaster, and Syracuse. In 1914, he moved the Jeffs from the smaller venues such as Reid's and Sheehan's Fields into the larger Bay Street Baseball Park, which featured a covered grandstand and could accommodate bigger crowds. In 1912, with an assist from his friend Walter Hagen, Lyons standardized the team's look with the adoption of the now-familiar red-and-white jerseys. Now three years later, he was looking to take the team's appearance a step further. What Lyons had in mind was something more distinctive than the simple letter "J" the team had sewn on its jerseys. He sketched out several ideas, but nothing seemed right until he drew the shortened variation of his team's name in cursive lettering. Eureka! The Jeffs' script logo, with which the team became most commonly associated, was born. Thus, the Jeffersons became one of the first, if not *the* first, pay-for-play football teams to have its own emblem.[12]

"I then had the player's mother sew on the Jeffs name," Lyons recalled. "The first year, the uniforms were anything but uniform. Some were too low, too high, or offsides.

So I hired my wife and a few other ladies to be the official seamstresses of the Rochester Jeffersons."[13]

Not only did designing the players' uniforms fall under Lyons' list of responsibilities as owner and manager of the team, he was also the groundskeeper and equipment manager. He rose at 6:00 a.m. on game day to load his Model T with tools and various necessities before driving over to pick up Dutch Mellody and then head over to the field. The two would spend much of the morning measuring the lines and marking them off with paint, erecting goalposts out of two-by-fours and setting up benches for both teams. They then drove back to Leo's place and packed towels, water buckets, first aid kit, footballs, a megaphone, blankets, bottles of Coca-Cola, notebooks, pencils, and a roll of paper tickets. By the time they returned to the field and unloaded these items, it was time to start signal drills. Water was obtained from a hose at a neighboring house, and when nature called, the woods near the field proved acceptable accommodations.[14]

Leo and Dutch had the gridiron at Sheehan's Field in good shape for the opening of the 1915 season. The Jeffs were scheduled to launch the campaign on Sunday, October 17, against the Syracuse Westcotts, a team the Jeffs had never faced before. The teams battled on even terms for over three quarters, carrying a 0–0 score late into the final frame. The Jeffs had a chance to win it with the ball at the Syracuse 8-yard line and about three minutes remaining. On fourth down, Pop Morrison dropped back to the 15 to attempt a

The Rochester Jeffersons, 1915, showing off their new jerseys with the now-iconic script logo. Back row (from left): Eddie Benz, Cliff Brothers, William Lyons, Pete Heinlein, Charles MacLellan, Art Webb, Nels Lengeman, Pop Morrison, Denny Cahill, Pete Nicholson, Dave Cansdale (trainer). Middle row (from left): Walter Frickey, Joe O'Brien, Henry McDonald, Don Gray, Dutch Mellody, Ham Connors, Bob Argus, Babe Clark, Leo Lyons. Front row (from left): Dutch Irwin, Oliver Angevine, Ray Spiegel, Billy Warren, Shorty Caske.

Jeffs back Stewart "Pop" Morrison, circa 1915 (courtesy Hugh E. Irwin).

dropkick. But the kick was no good, and the game ended with the score still knotted at zero.

The *Democrat & Chronicle*, no longer restricted from using the Jeffs' manager's surname in print, singled out Lyons for his outstanding performance. "The Jeffs showed a good knowledge in all departments, several of their forward passes being good for long gains. One, Irwin to Frickey to Lyons, being good for thirty yards. The Jefferson manager also skirted the Westcott ends on several occasions on a trick play for from ten to twenty-five yards. It was the best game that he ever played."[15]

Jeffs lineman Art Webb, circa 1915 (courtesy Gary S. Maybee).

A week later, the Jeffs played host to All-Buffalo, another team they were facing for the first time. The All-Buffalos were touted for having a well-developed passing game and featuring several former college men in their lineup. They were fresh off a 32–0 drubbing of defending New York State champion All-Lancaster, and local papers were already speculating a state title for the Bison City boys.[16] The Jeffs, for their part, were looking for an infusion of offensive might with the return of Henry McDonald and Dutch Irwin, who had not played the previous game against Syracuse.

What was anticipated to be a shootout, however, was anything but. Both teams relied heavily on a ground attack, with each able to threaten the other's goal only once throughout the contest. In the first quarter, All-Buffalo drove down to the Rochester ten, but the Jeffs held on downs. The Jeffs had their lone opportunity in the fourth quarter after Lyons recovered a fumble at his own 30. They drove into All-Buffalo territory and attempted one of the few passes in the game, but the pass to the end zone fell incomplete and the ball reverted to All-Buffalo. The game ended shortly after in a 0–0 deadlock.

"If a person was looking for lots of thrills, long runs and successful forward passes," wrote the *Democrat & Chronicle*, "he was sadly out of place at Sheehan's Field, for of these plays were none, but for the steady grind of line plunging for a gain of a few yards and real football between two teams that were practically evenly matched, the game could hardly be equaled."[17]

The Jeffs then hosted the celebrated Lancaster 11 at Sheehan's Field. The defending state champs were accompanied to the game by a large contingent of hometown rooters, one of whom led the team onto the field with the exhortation, "Come on now boys, let's give 'em the Beefsteak yell," to which came the collective refrain, "Beefsteak and pork, beefsteak and pork. Lancaster, champions of Western New York!"[18]

It was another hard-fought game with neither team able to get closer than their enemy's ten-yard line. It was the third straight week the Jeffs failed to score while at the same time keeping their opponent off the scoreboard and second straight against a recognized power. If Lyons was looking for a sign that the Jeffersons had moved into the upper echelon of teams in the state, the back-to-back scoreless ties against All-Buffalo and Lancaster could not have made it any clearer. The Big Red offense finally broke the dam a week later with a four-touchdown performance against the Geneva Glenwoods at Sheehan's Field. Fullback Babe Clark reached the payoff patch in the opening frame, while Dutch Mellody found it in the second, giving the Jeffs a 14–0 lead at the half. After a scoreless third period, the Jeffs put the game out of reach with Mellody scoring a second time and Henry McDonald also going over, making the final Jeffs 27, Glenwoods 0.

Next up was a rematch with All-Buffalo, this time to be played in the Bison City. Two thousand fans turned out at Ryan's Park to witness what was expected to be a close contest. The All-Buffalos had different ideas, however. With five different players finding the end zone, including an 80-yard return of a fumble by Ray Provensha, the Buffalos rolled to an easy 34–0 win.

With their hopes of a shot at the state title vanquished, the Jeffs turned their focus instead to winning municipal honors. For three years running, the Jeffs and Scalpers rode herd over the rest of the city and met each year for the right to call themselves champion. After playing to scoreless tie in 1912, the Scalpers emerged victorious to be crowned undisputed champion in 1913 and '14. For the fourth straight year, the two would meet to determine city supremacy.

The crowd at the Bay Street Ball Park was treated to a classic. The teams slugged it out on even terms for the first two quarters, and it looked as if it was going to be a repeat of the 1912 title bout when the score at halftime read 0–0. But the Scalpers took a 3–0 lead early in the third quarter when quarterback Billy Bauer—who had missed on three previous tries—booted a 35-yard field goal. The Jeffs responded early in the fourth period with a scoring drive of their own. Babe Clark crossed the goal line after a short run to put his team on top, 6–3. The ensuing kickoff was fumbled, and the Jeffs recovered at the Scalpers' 30-yard line. After several short runs, Dutch Mellody bulled into the end zone to give the Jeffs their second touchdown. He then converted the extra-point attempt, and the score stood at 13–3. The Scalpers made a valiant effort to come back and appeared to be on the verge of closing the gap when a Jeff fumble was picked up and returned for a substantial gain, only to be called back as an incomplete pass. The Redshirts held the Scalpers at bay the rest of the way and the city championship was finally theirs.

The *Democrat & Chronicle* reported,

JEFFS SHAKE JINX OF THREE YEARS' STANDING AND WIN
INDIANS' LINE LACERATED IN END

The Jeffersons got satisfaction yesterday for the cuffs they have taken the last three successive years from the Scalpers in a game that rioted with action. Some of the action trickled over the brim, climaxing when Kline, of the Scalpers, was dismissed from the field for leaping cleats first on McDonald, of the Jeffersons, after the latter had been thrown by a tackle. The score was 13–3.

Memory Harks Back to Old Days

Baseball Park was suggestive of the age of interscholastic football. The red and white pennons of the Jeffs were unfurled in one section, and the blue and white [the Scalpers' colors were purple and white] of the Scalpers waved in other blocks—a bank of color etched by the rainbow shades of feminine dress, with the yellow splashes of chrysanthemums.

Individual honors will go to Argus, Babe Clark and Lyons of the Jeffersons, and Gordiner, Brown and Bauer of the Scalpers.[19]

Despite having been declared city champs, the Jeffs had a game scheduled just three days after their battle with the Scalpers. Lyons had agreed to have his team face the Glenwoods at Geneva the following Sunday as the second part of a home-and-home series. The Jeffs had soundly defeated the Glenwoods 27–0 in the previous encounter and were not expecting any different in the rematch. The Glenwoods played their home games at Standard Optical Field, which was notable for very little other than the fact that it lacked goalposts, meaning there could be no field goals or extra points by kick.

The Glenwoods were able to keep this one a little closer than the first game but not by much. After a scoreless first quarter, the Big Red took a 6–0 lead on a one-yard plunge by Bob Argus. Dutches Irwin and Mellody scored six-pointers in the final frame, and the Jeffs claimed an 18–0 win.

Lyons had one more game scheduled for his team the following Sunday, but what was supposed to be the season finale pitting the Jeffs against a collection of city all-stars was called off at the last minute—and with good reason! Leo's wife Catharine was pregnant with their second child and went into labor that week. On Friday, December 3, Catharine gave birth to a daughter, Sabina Ellen, at Rochester Homeopathic Hospital.

Catharine and Leo with their daughters Catherine (called Zelda, held here by her mother) and Sabina, circa 1916.

"A stressful time again," said Leo and Catharine's granddaughter and namesake Sabina Steffenhagen. "Leo was heavily involved with the football team but dropped everything when the second child was born. He was again 'over the moon'!"[20]

The 1915 season was certainly a benchmark for Leo Lyons. On the home front, he and Catharine were giddy over the arrivals of their two baby girls. On the playing field, his Jeffersons had established themselves as one of the top teams in the entire state by holding both All-Buffalo and Lancaster to scoreless ties and claiming their first city championship by beating the hated Scalpers.

However, could the upward progression continue?

* * *

The indoor football series Lyons promoted in 1915 had been a less-than-resounding success, but he still believed the concept was a good one, so much so that he decided to give it another go in the dark winter months of 1916.

"This will be the second attempt of Manager Lyons to stage indoor football games," wrote the *Democrat & Chronicle*, "and if his idea meets with the approval of the Rochester sporting public it will be a weekly or semi-monthly affair at the State Armory."[21]

Lyons' hopes of fomenting sustained interest in the enclosed variety of the game were dashed almost as soon as they were hatched. After announcing that he had arranged for All-Buffalo to visit the Armory for the year's initial game, he learned the Bison City 11 were not going to be able to keep their commitment. To fill the void, Lyons arranged for several players from the area's other clubs—Scalpers, Gibsons, Crimsons, Pullmans, Syracuse Westcotts—to create a quasi–all-star team hastily dubbed All-Rochester. Things got worse the night of the game, however, when the All-Rochester team failed to field 11 players, forcing Lyons to lend them some of his men just so a game could be played for the 100 folks who came out to witness the debacle.

"The game was so completely irregular," reported the *Democrat & Chronicle*, "that they didn't even keep the score."[22]

And just like that, Rochester's dalliance with indoor football was over.

* * *

It was late 1915 or early 1916 when Leo Lyons found himself looking over a bunch of baseball cards pulled from boxes of Cracker Jack candy. As he was poring over the colorful cardboard-backed images of the day's baseball greats, Lyons had an epiphany—why couldn't the same concept used to promote major league baseball be applied to football? He had already arrived at the belief that football could someday rival baseball in popularity, and perhaps a smidgen of promotion was all the grid game needed to rise above the diamond game in the power rankings of American sport. Baseball cards had been a popular collectible for several decades by this time, used to promote sales of tobacco, candy, and other goods having little or no connection to baseball. Lyons' confidence in the growth potential of football had him believing American kids would eventually be as passionate about collecting Jim Thorpe or Charlie Brickley cards as they were for those of Ty Cobb or Honus Wagner.

He put that belief into action by writing up a plan in which he listed business contacts, the scope of the product he wished to promote, the target market for the product, and his reasoning for believing the idea was viable:

2. "Champions of New York State" 39

PROPOSAL No. 1   July 13, 1916

                                  American Chicle Company
                                  North Goodman Street, Rochester
                                  Thomas B. Dunn, retired

                                  Pulver Gum Co.
                                  F. Pulver, 295 State Street, Rochester

                                  George Eastman
                                  Eastman Kodak Co.
                                  343 State St., Rochester

Options: Individual or team trade cards

                                  Size of said card   2⅛ × 4

                                                                                                                    2 × 3¾

                                                                                                                    1¾ × 3¾

Target: children gum (chewing) or candy

                                  Tobacco not option

                                  Background of picture solid color or field backdrop

                                  Sports themed College football all stars

                                  Professional football Ohio, Penn., West Coast

In Theory: Pictures of football players taken by Kodak or team photographers, printed on postcard stock with or without coupon or advertising, cut out to size of product, packed and shipped by (American Chicle or Pulver Co.). Would need legal assistance with individuals, teams, and league officers to proceed.

    Currently chewing gum is a huge hit with all ages and sexes. Product, Chicle, from Yucatan, inexpensive and shipping here is not a problem.

    Would propose speaking with Zeenut and Wrigley companies soon.

    Target price is 5 cents sold everywhere. Advertising urgent. We have an advisor in retired businessman Thomas B. Dunn in Rochester, who is a genius in advertising this type of product.

    Wrigley using profit sharing coupons with gum.

    Various companies using a collect coupon for cards, not popular.

    Cracker Jack popular with kids, football cards in these boxes?[23]

Lyons' notes indicate that he sent letters of proposal to at least three companies mentioned in his plan—the American Chicle Company, Eastman Kodak, and Rueckheim Bros. & Eckstein (manufacturer of Cracker Jack). Although no contemporaneous responses from these companies survive, Lyons wrote several years later, "The 1917 deal with American Chicle and Eastman Kodak fell through. Eastman decided not on board with football trade cards." This claim is substantiated in a letter received from George Eastman in 1921.

As for Rueckheim Bros. & Eckstein, Lyons wrote, "The deal in 1917 to produce football trade cards modeled after their previous baseball sets (1914 & 1915) did not pan out as planned. War in Europe, rationing and specific tax increase put plan on shelf."[24]

It was a bold plan, though ill-timed. It was one Lyons believed in, however, and would return to a few years later.

* * *

The 1916 edition of the Big Red was nearly identical to the one that had delivered a successful campaign in 1915, with Angevine, Argus, Bachmaier, Cahill, Clark, Connell, Connors, Frickey, Gray, Heinlein, Irwin, Lengeman, McDonald, MacLellan, Mellody, Morrison, and Webb all set to return. The only newcomer was Walter Schiebel, former end and captain of the University of Rochester 11. It was a well-seasoned squad that Lyons trusted. His faith was ultimately rewarded with one of the best years the Jeffs would ever have.

The season was set to kick off on Sunday, October 8, at Sheehan's Field with a contest against a team representing the city of Niagara Falls. However, when seven players from the Falls' team were stranded after their automobile became disabled, Lyons had no choice but to refund the admission fee to those who had already purchased tickets. The Jeffersons instead used the opportunity to hold an intrasquad scrimmage, free of charge to those who stuck around to watch.

The campaign finally got underway a week later when the Lancaster squad visited Sheehan's Field and played the Jeffs to a scoreless draw. The Jeffs then hosted East Syracuse and gave the crowd at Sheehan's Field one of the most exciting finishes they had seen in recent memory. East Syracuse took a 3–0 lead with a dropkick field goal in the first quarter. The teams then battled for two scoreless quarters, and it appeared

The Rochester Jeffersons, 1916. Back row (from left): Acton Langslow, George McIntosh, Charles MacLellan, Walter Scheibel, Eddie Benz, William Connell, Oliver Angevine, Art Webb, Harry Wilson. Middle row (from left): Nels Lengeman, Bob Argus, Leo Lyons, Dave Cansdale (trainer), Dutch Irwin, Pete Heinlein. Front row (from left): Denny Cahill, Joe Bachmaier, Shorty Caske, Walter Frickey, Don Gray.

a Syracuse victory was certain until late in the fourth. The Jeffs drove all the way to the Syracuse two-yard line with less than a minute remaining. On third down and needing a touchdown to win it, Henry McDonald pushed over to give the Jeffs a 7–3 come-from-behind victory.

Lyons himself was the star of the Jeffs' next game, scoring two touchdowns in leading the Big Red to a 48–0 trouncing of the Onondaga Indians at Sheehan's Field. The head Jeff scored on a run in the second quarter and on a pass from Dutch Irwin in the third. It was the greatest margin of victory in the team's history, besting the previous mark set in 1913 in a 46–0 win over Brockport.

The Big Red remained undefeated with a scoreless tie against the North Tonawanda Frontiers but then suffered a crushing 32–0 loss at the hands of the Syracuse University freshman team. They redeemed themselves a week later with a 26–6 defeat of a local squad called the Crimsons, with Lyons scoring on a 30-yard run to daylight in the first quarter. The game was a rough one, with the crowd becoming unruly at one point, necessitating a stoppage in play so referee Rip Benzoni could clear the spectators who had spilled onto the field. One "fan" was left with a bloody nose after hurling a racial epithet toward Henry McDonald.[25]

A 13–0 triumph over the Rogan & Johnson team from Geneva was followed by a 6–6 tie against the Westcotts, giving the Jeffs a 4–1–3 record and the opportunity to face the Scalpers on Thanksgiving Day for the city championship. The game marked the fourth straight year these teams competed for city honors, with the Jeffs winning 13–3 the previous year and the Scalpers grabbing the two previous years.

Several Jeffs were nursing injuries during the week, and some players were considered doubtful for the big game. With the prospect of playing shorthanded looming, the Jeffs were struck by a bit of good fortune when a scruffy-looking stranger walked into their dressing room at the South Avenue Bath House and asked for a tryout. The man identified himself as John McCrohan and claimed he had once played for Princeton. Since none of the other players had ever heard of him and he appeared too slovenly to have once attended an Ivy League college, no one believed his story. But needing players, McCrohan was given an audition.[26] He did well enough to make the team and would be in the lineup as a reserve tackle for Thursday's game. It was later discovered that his story was true, and he played with the Jeffersons on and off for another three years.

The bitter rivals battled through a scoreless first quarter, but the Redshirts seized a 7–0 advantage in the second when Lyons intercepted an errant throw and raced 30 yards for a touchdown. Later in the same quarter, Dutch Irwin hauled in a scoring pass from reserve halfback Earl Jones to put the Jeffs up by 14. The Jones-to-Irwin combination worked its magic again in the third, giving the good guys a 21–0 lead. The defense did the rest, holding the Scalpers scoreless the rest of the way to give the Jeffs the win and their second straight pennant.

The Jeffs' fine season merited the honor of facing All-Buffalo for the state title. The Bison City 11 had earned their appointment with a less-than-stellar 5–3–1 record. The game was scheduled for Sunday, December 3, at Buffalo.

The Jeff players reported to the New York Central train station at eleven Sunday morning for the trip to Buffalo. The teams arrived at Ryan's Park that afternoon to find the gridiron a sea of mud from the early December precipitation. Despite the conditions, the game got off to a fast start with All-Buffalo claiming a disputed touchdown midway through the first quarter. The Jeffs had stopped an All-Buffalo drive and forced a punt by halfback Doug Jeffrey. As the kick sailed toward the Rochester end zone, All-Buffalo quarterback Gene Dooley raced downfield and caught the pigskin before it hit the ground or could be fielded by a Rochester player. He then carried the ball into the end zone for what the Buffalo side thought was a touchdown. Referee Rip Benzoni, however, ruled the play was off-side and disallowed the score, resulting in vehement protests from the All-Buffalo players. After conferring with the team captains, Benzoni awarded the ball to All-Buffalo at the Rochester 20-yard line but no points. Play resumed, but the Jeffersons held and the first quarter ended in a scoreless tie. The Jeffs found the end zone in the second period when Dutch Irwin returned another All-Buffalo punt 80 yards for a touchdown, putting his team in front 6–0, or so they thought. During the halftime intermission, Benzoni and his crew met and ruled to restore the six points All-Buffalo insisted they had scored on Dooley's disputed play in the first quarter.

The second half devolved into a defensive battle with neither team able to muster a viable offense in the muck. The game ended in either a 6–0 triumph for Rochester or a 6–6 tie, depending on whose side of the field one stood. After time had expired, however, All-Buffalo—feeling they were owed the opportunity to try for the extra point they were deprived as a result of Benzoni's original ruling—took the field and executed a successful conversion and thus claimed a 7–6 victory.

So who won? The Buffalo papers, of course, sided with the local favorites. Wrote the *Buffalo Courier*, "Resurrecting the on-side kick from the football archives where it was laid by the lawmakers several years ago, the All-Buffalos defeated the Jeffersons of Rochester yesterday at Ryans' Park by a score of 7 to 6 in the final game of the year."[27]

The *Rochester Democrat & Chronicle* disagreed, writing, "Harry Irwin wasn't very well known [in Buffalo] before this afternoon. But he impressed his name very firmly upon local football annals when he caught a punt and ran eighty yards through a broken field to score the touchdown which gave the Rochester Jeffersons a 6 to 0 victory over All-Buffalo and took the state championship from here to Rochester."[28]

Neither team was backing down, and that indisposition could not be left unresolved as far as Lyons was concerned. His notes indicate that he met with referee Benzoni the Tuesday following the championship game but do not provide insight as to the nature or content of their conversation. Perhaps he felt he could convince Benzoni to reverse his decision of allowing the All-Buffalo touchdown or maybe make a definitive ruling as to the winner of the state title. That bit of information, unfortunately, appears to be lost to history.

Unsatisfied with things as they stood, Lyons devised a bold plan to resolve the matter once and for all. He decided to seek the counsel of none other than Walter Camp, the man considered the foremost authority on football matters in the country. Camp, the former head coach at Yale and Stanford, served on various collegiate football rules committees that developed the framework of American football and authored numerous books and articles on the subject. He is credited with the creation of the sport's line of scrimmage, the system of downs, the reduction of the number of players per side from 15 to 11, the standardized offensive configuration of seven linemen (two ends, two tackles, two guards, and a center) and four backs (quarterback, two halfbacks, and a fullback), and much more. Who would dare refute the man considered the "Father of American Football"?[29]

The next day, Lyons fired off a letter to Camp hoping he could adjudicate the legality of All-Buffalo's on-side kick and, ultimately, the winner of the big game. On Monday, December 11, Lyons received Camp's reply affirming the Jeffs' claim:

2. "Champions of New York State"

WALTER CAMP
NEW HAVEN, CONN.

December 8, 1916

Mr. Leo V. Lyons
Frost Avenue
Rochester, New York

Dear Sir—

Your favor of the 4th has been referred to the writer by H.W. Taylor, and I should be glad to be of service to you at any time.

If the quarterback and end were ahead of the kicker when he punted from behind the scrimmage line, when they were both offside and could not legally touch the ball until it had been touched by an opponent. If they touched it inside the ten-yard line it would go as a touchback to the opponents. If they touched it when offside out in the field of play it would go to the opponents at the spot where they touched it. Hence, the officials were perfectly right in calling the play you describe illegal, and the ball went properly to the Jeffersons.

Now, as to the rest of the matter, there is no provision or precedent so far as I know of continuing the game after a decision of this kind and then going back and beginning the game over again at such a point, after one side has left the field and discontinued play.

Yours very truly,
Walter Camp [signed][30]

Camp's word was law when it came to matters of the gridiron. The Rochester Jeffersons were the rightful champions of New York State!

A celebratory banquet was held December 19, with the team being presented a silver football-shaped trophy on which was etched "JEFFERSON FOOTBALL TEAM—CHAMPIONS OF NEW YORK STATE." The trophy was donated by Harry "Spike" Wilson, a local businessman and avid supporter of the team, and became one of Lyons' most prized possessions. He displayed it proudly in his office for the rest of his life and often carried it with him to public events and media appearances. The players presented coach Dutch Irwin with a silver loving cup for his four years of leadership culminating in the state championship.[31]

Letter from Walter Camp to Leo Lyons, December 8, 1916.

Winning the title was unquestionably one of Lyons' proudest moments, and although he had now taken the team to the football pinnacle of the entire state, he knew there were higher hills to climb. He had been reading about the great independent teams in Ohio such as the Canton Bulldogs, Massillon Tigers, Dayton Triangles, and Columbus Panhandles, as well as the Detroit Heralds in Michigan, the Pitcairn Quakers in Pennsylvania, and the Rock Island Independents in Illinois. How would the upstart Rochester Jeffersons of New York stack up against these grid goliaths? Leo Lyons was determined to find out.

Program from the celebratory ball held to honor the Jeffersons' New York State championship, December 1916.

The trophy awarded to the Rochester Jeffersons to commemorate the New York State championship of 1916 (photograph by Steven D. Desmond).

3

"I thought we were pretty good"
(1917–1919)

By 1917, Leo Lyons was becoming disenchanted with the limited competition his football team was facing Sunday after Sunday, year after year. Under his direction, the Jeffersons had expanded their scope outside of the greater Rochester area as far back as 1911, when they made the 60-mile trek to Lockport for a game. Since 1913, the Jeffs had taken at least one foray each year outside their normal sphere to face 11s in Lockport, Lancaster, or Buffalo. Winning the state championship in 1916 had unleashed Lyons' ambitions. He had been reading about the top out-of-state semipro squads and wondered how his team would fare against the best teams in the paid-football world. Just how would the Jeffs do against the best of the best, even those from Ohio, the recognized epicenter of the sport? He was going to find out in 1917.

As early as September 8, the *Democrat & Chronicle* was reporting Lyons' efforts at setting up a more ambitious schedule than in previous years, including prospective matchups against the Detroit Heralds and Cleveland Tigers. Although he was unsuccessful in securing either of those powers, Lyons eventually succeeded in arranging a game with the biggest plum in the pro football universe.

With the United States having entered the Great War earlier in the year, many grid teams—collegiate and semipro—were losing players to military service. The Jeffersons were no exception, losing two of their most valued members in Dutch Irwin and Dutch Mellody. Mellody was Lyons' closest friend on the squad as well as the Jeffs' longest tenured player, representing the last vestige of the team that existed prior to Lyons' arrival in 1908. Irwin had been occupying the dual positions of quarterback and coach since 1913. To fill his spot, Lyons promoted veteran tackle Pete Heinlein, whose tenure with the Jeffs went back to 1912.[1]

The Jeffs opened the 1917 season on the road against All-Buffalo at Buffalo Baseball Park. This was the team the Jeffs had defeated in the previous season's finale to claim the state title. But the All-Buffalo 11 evened the score, coming out on the good side of 21–6 win. A 0–0 tie with East Buffalo was followed by wins over Tonawanda (32–3) and then East Buffalo (20–0) in a rematch.

Lyons had an ambitious weekend planned for his team between Friday, October 26 and Sunday, October 28. Although playing two games in three days was not necessarily rare in pro football's rag days, it was still a taxing proposition for men engaged in such a strenuous pursuit. Lyons, however, was never one to let an opportunity pass him by, and he proved it more than ever on this particular weekend. First, he had the Jeffs scheduled to travel some 70 miles south for a rare Friday afternoon game against the grid team from Alfred University. The team was then slated to return home for a brief respite on Saturday before picking up the cudgel against the Buffalo Niagaras at Sheehan's Field on Sunday. Friday's plans were derailed, however, by a surprise snowstorm that dropped several inches in New York's Southern Tier, forcing the game's cancellation. The Jeffs then turned their focus to the Niagaras, but the next morning Lyons learned that that game was not going to be played either.

Having two games canceled on such short notice might have seemed like a setback, but it was to the Jeffs' good fortune that they were. Just as he was learning about Niagara's reneging on their contracted match, Lyons heard that the 47th U.S. Army Infantry—headquartered at Syracuse—was being deployed to North Carolina that week. It just so happened that a football team representing the 47th had a game scheduled against the Canton Bulldogs in Canton, Ohio, on the 28th. With that game now being canceled, the Jeffersons and the Bulldogs both had an open Sunday on their hands. Lyons wasted no time in springing into action.

"My Jeffs had played and beaten the available state professional teams and were searching for another opponent," he recalled. "I had read the Canton Bulldogs were claiming the title of World's Champs. I thought we were pretty good, so I wrote to Jack Cusack, the Bulldogs' manager, for at least one more encounter before the season's end. My challenge was accepted, and the eight-hundred-dollar guarantee seemed an attractive offer."

Now, trying to organize a sporting event nearly 300 miles away is hard enough, but Lyons discovered that patching his team together with practically no notice was going to take a herculean effort. Several of the Jeff players became unavailable to make the trip after coming down with the flu or having family members stricken. Others, such as Irwin and Mellody, were still in the service of Uncle Sam. With his roster reduced to ten healthy bodies, Lyons was forced to recruit players from other teams in the area, and he had to do it in a hurry.

"My intentions were really honorable," Lyons insisted, "for Tufts were playing at Syracuse University on Saturday, the day before the game in Canton, and I still had hopes of enlisting some players to give Canton a showing. This meant marching right into the locker rooms after the game. A tackle and a halfback were available from the Tufts team and Rip Flannery, a Syracuse halfback, agreed to take the tour to Canton for fifty dollars and transportation. Rip and I had to return to the locker room that night for his cleated shoes. The caretaker chased us across the campus and even fired a shot at a pair of fleet-footed broken-field runners."[2]

On the way, Lyons provided a quick tutorial in the team's signals. "These were very simple. Number eleven would mean the left half around right end. Twelve vice versa. Four the fullback up the middle, and so on. We'd start our charge on the count of three. No sense in getting complicated. Things would be confusing enough with these three strangers on the team."[3]

All this was happening at the same time the rest of the team was making its way to Ohio ahead of him. "The bulk of the Jeffs had departed Rochester for Buffalo on the train," Lyons recalled. "There they embarked on a passenger boat to Cleveland. Their remaining itinerary including the Wheeling and Lake Erie Railroad and a local streetcar to the Courtland Hotel in Canton. After a restful night in coach accommodations, the three ringers and myself joined the team on the morning of the game. We numbered sixteen men at this point."[4]

3. "I thought we were pretty good" 47

Signal drills were held in the hotel ballroom with the players running their assignments in stocking feet. Practice was held up at one point when quarterback Billy Bauer—on loan from the rival Rochester Scalpers—inadvertently tossed the team's only ball out of an open window.

Because the Bulldogs' originally scheduled opponent was forced to cancel on such short notice, the Canton papers simply began referring to the Jeffs as the 47th New York Infantry. The *Canton Daily News* even used posed photos of five Jeff regulars (Ward Fleming, Charles MacLellan, Walter Scheibel, Henry McDonald, and Art Webb, who was identified as "Adams") and referred to them as the "Quintet of Stars with Soldier Team." The misidentification was repeated in the game programs as well as the game accounts printed in the next day's paper.[5]

The Jeffs were greeted the following afternoon by a crowd of 3,000 Bulldog loyalists at League Park. As boos and jeers rained down on his squad, Lyons noticed that a stretcher had been strategically placed in front of the Jeffs' bench.

"We stopped for a look at the crowd and a man standing there asked, 'Is this your first team?'"

When Lyons confirmed it was, the man laughed, pointed toward the stretcher and declared, "We have a guy named Jim Thorpe. Last week he killed two guys playing against us."[6]

Halfback Henry McDonald recalled an incident that occurred just after the game had begun that illustrated Thorpe's authority over his fellow combatants. McDonald, all

Jim Thorpe pictured taking part in a kicking exhibition during halftime in the game between the Canton Bulldogs and Rochester Jeffersons. League Park, Canton, Ohio, October 28, 1917.

of 145 pounds, was making his way toward the sideline on a running play when he was shoved out of bounds with excessive force by a Canton player. According to McDonald, the Bulldog cocked his fists at the end of the play and said, "Black is black and white is white, and where I come from, the two don't mix!" McDonald, a former boxer, prepared to defend himself just as Jim Thorpe intervened.

"We're here to play football," Thorpe declared.

"I never had any trouble after that," said McDonald. "Thorpe's word was law on that field."[7]

Thorpe's kindness, however, stretched only so far. The Bulldogs took the first lead of the game when Milton Ghee connected with Earl "Greasy" Neale (playing under the assumed name of Fisher) on a touchdown pass early in the first, then rolled to an easy 41–0 victory.[8]

"The first time we played the Canton Bulldogs," Jeffs end Ray Witter recalled years later, "we were awfully curious to see what the famous Thorpe looked like, and let me tell you, he looked tough! I was playing offensive and defensive end that day and right away, he came toward my position. He was running an end sweep. I was able to drive him out of bounds and as we fell, my knee went into a water bucket and was twisted rather badly. At any rate, they beat our club because we didn't have the offense they had by any means. That man Thorpe was powerful! And I'll say this much, he was just as great defensively as offensively."[9]

"Neither the fans nor the Bulldogs frightened our team but they did defeat us," said Lyons. "With Thorpe a blurred streak skirting the ends and smashing the line, the Bulldogs romped to a forty-nine to nothing victory, sending my Jeffs back to Rochester bruised and believing that Canton did have the champions of the world."

Before leaving the field duly bruised, however, Lyons had an opportunity, albeit brief, to share a moment with the famed Olympian. Lyons half-stepped alongside Thorpe and suggested, "Jim, someday this game will draw like professional baseball." He replied, "The boys out here have been talking about it. I'll write you."

"Apparently, Thorpe realized the difficulties we faced in that game and respected our abilities enough to promise to contact me about the formation of a league."[10]

The trip to Ohio marked the beginning of a new era for the Jeffersons. Lyons had just witnessed what a top-tier football outfit looked like. He was more determined than ever to build a team that could compete respectably against the best teams in the game, regardless of which state they called home. Even though he had games already scheduled with sandlot clubs such as All-Geneva and the Oneida Northside Athletic Club, Lyons was busy thinking about the future of the sport. He concluded that imported talent needed to take precedence over the local players on whom the team had been built and sustained for nearly two decades. Big names were needed to draw crowds—star college players and, if possible, honest-to-goodness All-Americans.

Next up on the Jeffs' docket was a tilt with All-Geneva the following Sunday at Sheehan's Field. Due to an apparent miscommunication, however, the Genevans failed to show, disappointing the crowd that had already turned out to watch the game and adding to Lyons' frustrations with the local sandlot circuit.

"There was no message to the effect that they would not come," reported the *Democrat & Chronicle*. "The Jeffs never had an inkling on that score until Henry McDonald came in from Geneva about 3 o'clock. He said that he had seen the Geneva men in the street but without any suitcases and that it looked to him as if they were not coming here."[11]

No doubt dismayed at having to refund the admission fee to the fans who had paid to get in, Lyons could only try to put it behind him and move on. Since returning from Canton, Lyons had been burning the wires in search of star talent who might be willing to sign on with the Jeffersons. He was successful in securing the services of Colgate tackle Clarence Horning, a first-team All-American in 1916.

The man teammates and newspapers called "Steamer" made an immediate impact, contributing a touchdown in the Jeffs' 26–0 win over the Oneida Northside Athletic Club. That victory left the Jeffersons with a record of 3–2–1, good enough to qualify for a chance to defend their title as New York State champions against the All-Tonawanda Lumberjacks on Thursday, November 29—Thanksgiving Day. The Lumberjacks, despite a less-than-stellar mark of 2–3–1, had earned the right to face the Jeffs for the pennant after defeating All-Buffalo the previous Sunday.

The game was played on a snow-covered Baseball Park field on Thanksgiving Day before what the *Democrat & Chronicle* described as a "disappointingly small" crowd. It was a brutal game. Predictably, Henry McDonald bore the brunt of the visitors' abuse. Lyons seethed when one of the Tonawanda players taunted McDonald and called him "black boy."

"When Henry is called names," Lyons wrote incredulously, "he laughs. Some people make fun of Thorpe too—say he is a dumb drunk Indian wahoo. People are ignorant!"

McDonald might have been willing to laugh off the hurtful remarks, but when the Tonawandan uttered the slur a second time later in the game, Lyons had heard enough. He walked over and punched the offending opponent in the face. "[Referee] Benzoni looked and made no call. [The player] left the game with broken nose!" Lyons was not the only riled Jeff. "Chubby Brown, our boxer, walked over to the Tonawanda team and challenged them to fight. No takers!"

At some point, the combatants remembered they were there to play football. All-Tonawanda notched the game's first points with a touchdown in the opening frame, but the extra-point attempt was no good and the lead stood at 6–0. With the field blanketed in snow, it was difficult for the ball carriers to gain good traction. The Jeffs seized the lead in the third quarter when Ray Witter recovered a blocked punt in the Tonawanda end zone for a touchdown. Chubby Brown made good on the conversion attempt and the Jeffs had a 7–6 advantage. The Jeffs held on to the thin margin until the dying minutes of the fourth quarter when All-Tonawanda managed a 17-yard dropkick to win it.

Lyons felt good about his own performance, writing, "I had a decent game, 8 or 9 tackles, blocked punt." It wasn't enough, though, as the Lumberjacks prevailed in a 9–7 thriller and were awarded the state title.[12]

After the game, Lyons approached the offending player and demanded he apologize for his disrespectful behavior. "I wanted an apology and got one. He told Henry he was wrong." The Lumberjacks had won the football game, but the Jeffersons had won the battle for decency.[13]

The Jeffs convened one last time three days later for their yearly grudge match with the crosstown Scalpers. Despite Lyons' efforts to build a team capable of facing the best in the county on even terms, he never lost that underlying sense of provincialism. The Jeffs had faced the Scalpers at least once or twice every season except one since he joined the club in 1908. The games were a tradition as far as followers of the local grid scene were concerned and almost always determined the city championship. Since they had fallen short in their bid for the state championship, the Jeffs could at least look to the municipal title for consolation.

The Scalpers gave the Jeffs all they could handle in the first quarter, which ended in a 0–0 score. Fullback Bill Connell put the Jeffs ahead with a touchdown plunge midway through the second frame, but the extra point try failed and the bulge stood at six at the half. In the third quarter, Jeffs end Tom Gray intercepted a Scalper pass and ran 15 yards for a touchdown. Dutch Irwin's conversion extended the Redshirts' lead to 13–0. The score stood the rest of the way, and the Jeffs once again claimed ownership of the city pennant.

"The annual tilt, thought to be no longer of any importance because it seemed the Jeffs were growing away from the Scalpers," the *Democrat & Chronicle* reported, "will be looked forward to another year when the young blood on the Braves' roster gets more experience. Then the Reds will have to fight like the Scalpers did yesterday to hold their title."[14]

* * *

The conflict in Europe was still raging in the fall of 1918. The Rochester Jeffersons, like nearly every other American college and pro sports team, were negatively affected by the war since the vast majority of U.S. enlistees were men of football-playing age. The *Democrat & Chronicle* reported on October 6 that as many as 33 current or former Jefferson players were serving in the armed forces in some capacity.[15] Compounding matters at home and abroad was a worldwide influenza pandemic that restricted interstate transportation and resulted in the cancellation of many athletic activities, most notably the Stanley Cup finals of the 1918–1919 National Hockey League season.

Most football teams that opted to continue playing cobbled-together truncated schedules while others simply suspended operations altogether. Teams that were able to play did so with rosters composed of a handful of regulars playing alongside unfamiliar players of varying skill levels. The quality of play might have suffered, but the show went on.

Several Rochester regulars were lost for the entire season, including Joe Bachmaier, Nelson Lengeman, Pop Morrison, Dutch Mellody, Art Webb, and Jimmy Woods. Others, such as Bob Argus, Chubby Brown, and Dutch Irwin, returned after missing chunks of the team's abridged season.

Among the veterans available going into the campaign were end Elbert Angevine, guard Denny Cahill, fullback Babe Clark, end Dutch Dow, tackle Walter Frickey, tackle Pete Heinlein, guard John McCrohan, halfback Henry McDonald, tackle Mack Tarbox, halfback Bob Witter, and Lyons himself filling in where needed. New recruits included fullback George Schiller, formerly of the Pitcairn Quakers semipros, and center Pete Sullivan, formerly of Colgate.

"Rochester should be capable of supporting a strong team," Lyons told a reporter for the *Democrat & Chronicle*. "We could wind up the season on Thanksgiving Day with a game with a crack soldier team from Camp Dix. I have already begun arrangements for such a game through Bob Argus, last year's star halfback, who is at the camp in training. Some of the teams that may be brought here include All-Buffalo, All-Syracuse, Oneida, Onondaga Indians, Fort Niagara soldiers, All-Tonawanda, All-Watertown, Bradford and Erie, Pa."

Lyons had allowed his optimism to get ahead of him, considering he was able to schedule just five games for the Jeffs for the entire season and none would be against any of the teams he had listed. His desire to schedule games with out-of-state teams bore fruit, however, as he was able to arrange a game with the tough Detroit Heralds to open the season on Sunday, October 13, at Navin Field in the Motor City.

The players assembled at the New York Central train terminal on Saturday, October 12, and departed Rochester at 2:45 p.m. for the first leg of the long trek out west. Lyons noted his concerns as his depleted team settled in for what proved to be a disastrous trip. "Long train ride. Need QB & End. Too many players in war."

Playing with just enough men to comprise a proper 11, the tired Redshirts were overpowered in nearly every aspect of the game. The Heralds managed at least one score in all four quarters in rolling to an easy 37–0 win.

"BAD LOSS," Lyons wrote after the game. He also noted his concerns with the shape and size of the footballs being used at the time. "NOBODY can pass the ball. Need smaller football—too damn thick."

The train ride back to New York was no easier than the one that took them to Detroit. "Some players sick," he wrote. "Train conductor says back of train or no passage back to New York."[16]

It would be another three weeks before the Jeffs suited up again, this time against a team of cadets from the Kodak Park School of Air Photography at Sheehan's Field on Sunday, November 3. The Airscouts were a ragtag outfit, having played just one game since being assembled at the beginning of the current season. It appears there was never any intention for the school to have a football team, as no provision was made for uniforms or equipment. With no money available, a plea was sent out to other teams in the area to donate or lend spare or unwanted gear to the team. Lyons, always willing to help in any way he could to support the local football scene, lent 14 uniforms to the Airscouts in time for their inaugural game against the University of Rochester on October 27.

A week of good hard practice had molded the Kodak Park team into a respectable unit. They put up a tough fight, but the Jeffersons prevailed, 6–0, with Lyons scoring the lone touchdown on a one-yard plunge in the first quarter.

The Jeffs then defeated a team of sandlotters from Batavia Steel Products by a 13–0 score before a rematch with the Kodak Park cadets that resulted in a more lopsided 19–0 victory.

The season finale pitted the Jeffs against the Bausch & Lomb (Rochester) Senecas on Thanksgiving Day for the city championship. With regulars Chubby Brown, Bob Argus, and Dutch Irwin in the lineup, the Jeffs steamrolled their intracity rivals by a 35–6 count. Irwin and fullback Babe Clark scored two touchdowns each in leading the Jeffs to their third straight pennant.

The *Democrat & Chronicle* published an end-of-season summary of the city's gridiron scene. It had been a tough couple of years across the globe and the sporting world had not been immune. The *Democrat & Chronicle* expressed optimism as the hardships of 1917 and '18 were at last beginning to fade:

> Football fans who have followed local pro elevens can look back on the season just closed as one which served to keep the grand old game alive, even in the face of the fact that an epidemic, a war and financial troubles confronted the players all season. The rivalry and the quality of the game played were the redeeming factors of the season.
>
> Next year, with the boys back from France and the war frenzy spent, all sports should flourish and football should reap its reward for the work that was accomplished this fall. The

interest is present, only dormant, and when next October comes there should be some real football in this town.

The article included an All-Rochester team for the 1918 season, with 9 of the 11 spots on the first unit going to the Rochester Jeffersons. Leo Lyons, who had filled in ably at several positions during the season, was honored with the first-team nod at center. "Lyons, as in the days of old, shifted to center and proved he was the best pivot man in town."[17]

* * *

Hopes were high for the Rochester Jeffersons as they looked forward to the 1919 grid season. The previous year had been disrupted by a world war that robbed many semipro and college teams of their manpower and a worldwide pandemic that restricted travel and forced the cancellation of numerous sporting events.

Lyons was pleased to have several key players returning from military service including center and team captain Nelson Lengeman, lineman Joe Bachmaier, end Ray Witter, and old reliable Dutch Mellody. Among the mainstays returning from the abbreviated 1918 squad were Bob Argus, Babe Clark, Pete Heinlein, Henry McDonald, Pop Morrison, George Schiller, and Art Webb.

As he was assembling his roster for the upcoming season, there was one prospect Lyons had to forgo. It was a decision he would live to regret and yet another twist of fate that directed the course of events of professional football history as we now know it.

"In September 1919, I received a letter written on stationary [sic] from the Toledo Hotel," Lyons recalled. "It read: 'Dear Mr. Lyons: I am 6 feet tall, weigh 185 pounds, played end at the University of Illinois and on the Great Lakes Naval training team. I would very much like to catch on with your Jefferson football team. I am willing to come on and tryout [sic] at once and if I make good will accept $75 a week. The letter was signed 'George Halas.'"[18]

Believing he already had the end position sufficiently covered with Ray Witter and newcomer Harold K. "Butch" Clark (not to be confused with fullback Harold R. "Babe" Clark), Lyons ignored Halas' proposal. It was a decision he lamented for the rest of his days. While serving in the navy during the war, Halas played for the Great Lakes Naval Training Station football team that included future Hall of Fame players Paddy Driscoll and Jimmy Conzelman. He earned Most Valuable Player honors after leading the team to a 17–0 win over the Mare Island Marines in the 1919 Rose Bowl. The following summer, Halas signed on with the New York Yankees baseball organization. He appeared in 12 major league games before sustaining a hip injury that essentially ended his career. He then turned his attention back to the grid sport. After being ignored by the Jeffersons, Halas signed on with the Hammond Pros. A year later, he helped found the Decatur Staleys, which two years later evolved into the Chicago Bears.

The team experienced a minor upheaval just as the campaign was about to start when Dutch Irwin, who had served as the Jeffs' head coach since 1913, left suddenly to join the crosstown Senecas. To fill the void, Lyons brought back Jack Forsyth, who played for the Jeffersons off and on from 1910 to 1916. Forsyth was held in high regard by his teammates, having served as captain of the football team at West High and later at the University of Rochester.

The 1919 season kicked off at the Baseball Park on October 5 with the Jeffs facing a service team from nearby Fort Niagara. The field had been reduced to a quagmire by heavy rains, and this, combined with unseasonably warm temperatures, made for conditions the *Democrat & Chronicle* described as "suitable for anything but football. The pigskin chasers were under a severe handicap. On two occasions it was necessary to stop the game because the players were unable to stand the guff."[19] Bob Argus, however, managed to maintain his footing well enough to notch three touchdowns in pacing a 20–7 Jeffs win.

It was then on to Flint, Michigan, to take on a team representing the Champion Spark Plug Company known simply as the Flint Independents. Perhaps fatigued from the long trip, the Jeffersons managed just a single touchdown in losing 13–6.

The Redshirts returned home to face All-Syracuse at the Baseball Park and once again were able to muster just a single touchdown in a 6–6 tie. Even though it was not a win, it did start the Jeffs on a dizzying streak of seven games without a loss, including five wins and two ties. They skunked Fort Ontario (32–0) before knocking off the Lancaster Malleables (29–7) and destroying All-South Buffalo (69–0). The Jeffs then brushed aside the local rival Senecas (27–6) before defeating the Scalpers (20–0) to claim the city championship.

With their fine record of 6–1–1, the Jeffs had earned the right to face the undefeated Buffalo Prospects (8–0) for the championship of New York State. It would be the Jeffs' third appearance in the championship game in four years, having previously defeated All-Buffalo to claim the title in 1916 and losing it to All-Tonawanda a year later.

The big game was set for Thursday, November 27, at Rochester Baseball Park. Coach Forsyth held vigorous practices on Tuesday and Wednesday in preparation. In an effort to shore up the Big Red offensive line, Lyons reached out to tackle Steamer Horning about a possible return. Horning had not appeared with the Jeffs since playing a single game in the 1917 season. His current team—the Detroit Heralds—was going to be idle during Thanksgiving week, so the former Colgate All-American was eager to make the trip, along with a little extra cash.

The Rochester Jeffersons on offense against All-Lancaster, November 2, 1919. The Jeffs' lineup included center Joe Bachmaier (over ball) and right guard Art Webb (visible in line next to center's right shoulder) and backfield men (from left) halfback Bob Argus, fullback Babe Clark, quarterback Red Quigley (without helmet), and halfback Henry McDonald (courtesy Gary S. Maybee).

The teams were greeted by a crowd of 2,500 rooters as they trotted onto the snow-covered field, which made for tricky footing and dicey forward passing. Instead, the combatants relied heavily on the punting game in a battle for field position. The Prospects came close to taking the game's first lead early in the second quarter, marching all the way to the Rochester one-yard line. The Jefferson line stiffened, however, turning the Buffalo runner back and taking over on downs. The Jeffs had their best chance later in the same period when they drove the ball close to the Buffalo 20. On fourth down, Horning dropped back to the 30-yard line to attempt a dropkick. But the kick fell short and the game remained tied 0–0 until halftime.

The punting exhibition continued into the second half. Neither team managed to get into scoring position, and the scoreless tie, like the mud clinging to the players' uniforms, stuck until the final whistle.

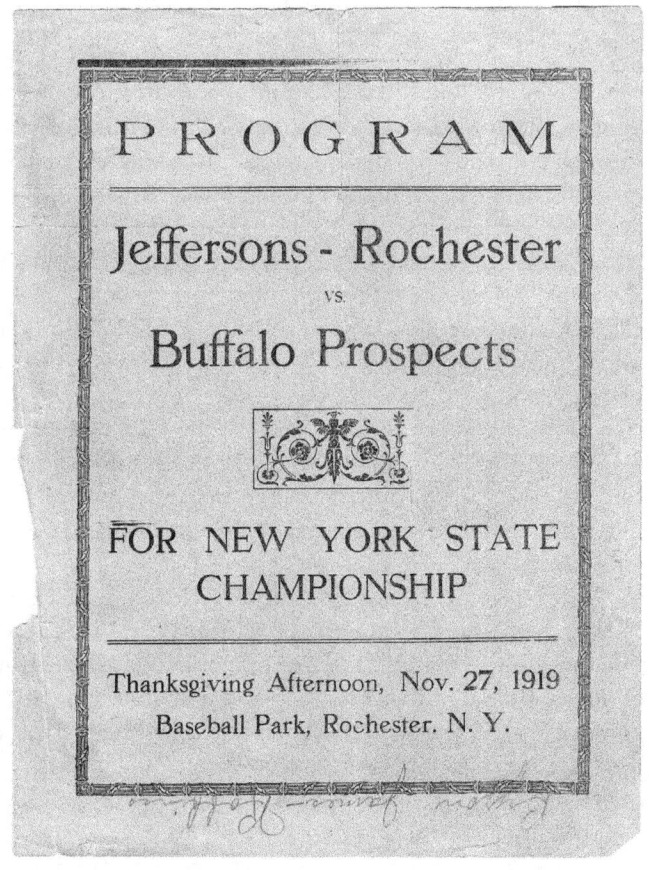

Program from game between the Jeffersons and the Buffalo Prospects, November 27, 1919.

Neither team was satisfied with the outcome. Owners Lyons of the Jeffersons and Doc Savage of the Prospects agreed to a second game, this time to be played at Buffalo's Baseball Park, three days later. Barring another tie, the winner would be crowned champion.

The Jeffs, accompanied by some 200 die-hard fans, boarded the train at the New York Central station at 9:55 a.m. bound for Buffalo. They arrived to find a steady snow blanketing the playing field while bitter winds "made the few thousand people in the stands cuddle close or stamp continuously to keep warm."[20]

The Jeffs took the field without their best player—Steamer Horning—who had returned to Detroit after Thursday's game. The Prospects, on the other hand, were fortified by several players who had not been in their lineup for the Turkey Day contest. Talented quarterback Austen Lake—longtime member of the Prospects—had missed the previous game due to an injury. End Joe Schwarzer and tackle Harry Segal, a pair of Syracuse University ringers, were new to the team, being recruited just for the occasion.

The Prospects broke the ice—both figuratively and literally—about five minutes into the first quarter when Lake connected with Schwarzer for a 35-yard touchdown pass. The conversion attempt failed, leaving them with a six-point advantage. They increased the lead to 13–0 in the second on a one-yard plunge by Watkins. The Jeffs' defense then tightened, holding the Prospects off the scoreboard until midway through the fourth quarter. Another Jeff drive was stopped deep inside Rochester territory, and center Hank Smith was called on to punt. The Jeff line failed to hold and the kick was blocked, with the Prospects taking possession inside the 20-yard line. Halfback Bill Gehring carried the ball over on the ensuing drive to extend Buffalo's lead to 20–0, and that was all, she wrote. The Prospects claimed the state championship before a home crowd of 2,000 frozen fans.

The next day's *Democrat & Chronicle* provided the following account:

IMPORTED STARS MAKE PROSPECTS TOO STRONG FOR JEFFS AND BIG RED ELEVEN IS DEFEATED, 20 TO 0

Combination of Colgate and Syracuse Players Put up Strong Game for Windy City Team; Smith Works Well for Jeffersons

Buffalo, Nov. 30—It may have been entirely by chance that the Prospect players were equipped with black gloves as an aid in resisting the piercing west wind that drove snow flurries across the Ferry Street ball park this afternoon while the local gridiron prides were battling with the Jeffersons, of Rochester, for the professional title of this section. Of course, it is possible that some one with a subtle sense of humor obtained the funeral hand coverings so that the Prospects might be at least partly in costume for the role of bearers at the burial of Jeff hopes. The Rochester boys gave everything they had, but they were helpless in the face of the remarkable attack and defense of the Prospects, who scored three touchdowns and won, 20 to 0.[21]

* * *

The 20th century's second decade was drawing to a close, and Americans were happy to bid adieu to the past couple of years that had brought home the pain and hardships of a devastating war and a global pandemic. The United States was entering a period of economic prosperity, and the focus turned from international and political affairs toward domestic concerns and individual pursuits that heralded the coming decade as the "Golden Age of Sport." Americans now had the time and money to pursue recreational activities thought decadent, unhealthy, or even unpatriotic just a few years earlier.

Professional football's reputation stood several notches below that of Major League Baseball, professional boxing, or college football. That negative public image impeded the sport's growth or capacity to elevate its economy beyond the sandlots on which the games had traditionally been played. By 1919, the strongest independent teams were crushing the weaker clubs and forcing many to simply fold. In the meantime, top players were demanding larger salaries for their appearances, leading to incessant team jumping as players sold their services to the highest bidder. Team jumping caused problems for marginal clubs who were prone to losing their best players to stronger, more financially stable teams. It was also a problem for promoters when advertising that certain star players were going to be in the lineup for an upcoming game, only to have that player not show up after getting a better offer from another club. Then there was the sin of inducing active collegians to come in on a Sunday and risk their eligibility if school officials discovered their transgression. Even players who had already graduated stood to lose their good reputation if they prostituted themselves to play the game for money.

To control costs and improve pro football's standing in the sports community, several team owners had been discussing the need to band together into a formal organization similar to Major League Baseball and the National Hockey League. One of those owners was Rochester's Leo Lyons, who was destined to play a major role in constructing a professional football association in the coming year and thus become one of the founding fathers of a league that eventually grew into the largest sports enterprise in the world.

4

"Hay had the good cigars"
(1920)

As far back as 1912, Leo Lyons had been dreaming of a nationalized pro football circuit similar to the major leagues of professional baseball. This dream seemed to be coming closer to reality in October 1917 after meeting Jim Thorpe and discussing the idea when the Jeffs traveled to Ohio to face the famous Canton Bulldogs. Lyons had maintained regular contact with Thorpe and Bulldog team managers Jack Cusack and then Ralph E. Hay—who had taken over from Cusack in 1918—with the hope that his team would not be forgotten by the supposed elites of the so-called Ohio League.

In early August of 1920, managers from several Ohio-based teams came to an agreement that the time had come for a formalized alliance of teams from Akron, Canton, Cleveland, and Massillon. As news of the planned league spread, representatives from still other cities, including Dayton, Ohio; Hammond, Indiana; Rock Island, Illinois; and two upstate New York cities, Buffalo and Rochester, sent letters expressing their desire to join. A meeting was scheduled for Friday, August 20, in Canton, but only four cities were represented: Akron (Art Ranney and Frank Nied), Canton (Ralph Hay and Jim Thorpe), Cleveland (Stan Cofall and Jimmy O'Donnell), and Dayton (Carl Storck). They agreed that a league was needed if the pro game were to rise above its current standing as the illegitimate offspring of the college game. To ease tensions that had been building between pro teams and officials at the university level, it was agreed that college players currently enrolled in their respective schools were off-limits. As a way of putting an end to the team jumping, the representatives agreed that current contracts would be honored and respected. A salary cap would be established to prevent teams from luring players away from other teams with offers of better pay. The league at this point was called the American Professional Football Conference. A second meeting, which they hoped would be better attended, was scheduled for September 17.[1]

Never one to let grass grow under his feet, Lyons was not content to wait for the next meeting to speak to Hay and Thorpe about the possibility of a game in Rochester between the Jeffs and Bulldogs. He wrote Hay in early September proposing a game and asking his terms. Hay responded with a letter dated September 9 in which he accepted Lyons' challenge and laid out his demands. To secure a game with the Bulldogs would require a guarantee of $3,500 plus a 45 percent privilege (of gate receipts).[2]

Thorpe, in the meantime, was biding his summer months as a member of the Akron Numatics International League baseball team. Lyons learned the Numatics were slated to be in the Flower City to play the Rochester Colts at the Baseball Park the same week as the next scheduled organizational meeting. Even though he was planning to attend the

Canton summit, Lyons decided to take advantage of Thorpe's trip to Rochester by reaching out to him and inviting him for a visit while he was in town. To his delight, Thorpe accepted the invitation and the two arranged to meet for dinner at Lyons' home at 343 Frost Avenue after his game on Monday, September 13.

After some initial chitchat about Thorpe's game that afternoon and his legendary feats in the 1912 Olympic Games, Lyons asked Thorpe if he was going to be in Canton on September 17. Thorpe told Lyons he was unsure whether he was going as he was either heading home to Oklahoma or playing ball in Akron. Lyons eventually came around to his primary reason for wanting to meet with Thorpe—the proposed game between the Bulldogs and Jeffersons. Thorpe reiterated Hay's need for a substantial guarantee, as they doubted there was enough support among football fans in the city of Rochester to justify the trip. Whether Lyons tried to negotiate is not known, but he eventually acquiesced. The *Rochester Democrat & Chronicle* reported that Lyons had agreed to pay the Bulldogs "the largest guarantee ever required for the appearance of a football team in Rochester." The game itself was arranged for Sunday, November 21.[3,4]

George Halas of the Decatur Staleys, considered by modern historians to be the "Father of the National Football League," was in a situation similar to Lyons'. As the manager of a team from outside of Ohio (Decatur, Illinois), he felt isolated from the more prominent teams of the Buckeye State. "I felt the Staleys had gone beyond this mobile situation," Halas remembered. "I wrote to various teams suggesting games. Replies were indifferent and vague. We needed an organization."

Having heard about the managers' meeting on August 20, Halas shot off a letter to Ralph Hay. "I mentioned our need for a league. He had already discussed the idea with Stan Cofall, a former Notre Dame star who was running the Massillon Tigers. They met with Frank Nied and A.F. Ranney of Akron and representatives from Cleveland and Dayton on August 20 in Akron. Hay was appointed temporary chairman. He called a meeting on September 17, 1920, at his automobile showroom in Canton."[5]

Lyons' notes—some scratched out in his journal and others on the cover of an old copy of the *Saturday Evening Post*—indicate he was in contact with at least some of the other invitees in the days prior to leaving Rochester for the great state of Ohio. He wrote, "Halas going from Decatur. Thorpe don't know. Doc going. O'Brien going. Ranney not going. Ball maybe. Flannegan yes. Massillon yes. Be in Canton by morning. Meet up with Halas and O'Brien. Buffalo not going Frank McNeil?" He also noted the location of the meeting: "Jordan and Hupmobile, 205 Cleveland Ave., SW."

Early in the morning of Friday, September 17, Lyons boarded a New York Central passenger car and settled in for the eight-hour trip to Canton. Once there, he booked a room at the Delmont Hotel, located at the corner of Cleveland Avenue and Second Street, almost directly across from the Independent Order of Odd Fellows building in which the Ralph E. Hay Motor Company showroom was located. There is no record of whether he was able to meet with Halas and O'Brien as planned or how he spent the afternoon prior to heading over to Hay's showroom. The meeting was scheduled to begin at 8:00 p.m., and there is little doubt the excited Lyons was prompt. With most of the expected attendees present, the meeting was declared open at 8:15 p.m., with Akron's Art Ranney recording the minutes.

The showroom, Halas recalled, was big enough to hold just four vehicles, so the men either stood or sat on the running boards of the automobiles. "Stood next to Halas," Lyons scrawled. "Nice guy." Bootleg beer, courtesy of Hay, was served in buckets. The group narrowly evaded trouble with the law when a couple of local constables happened by. "Lots of suds—almost sent to the hoosegow! Hay knew the police luckily! Had to hide the beer 3 times. O'Brien from Decatur looked nervous. Halas told him to drink. Hay had the good cigars."[6]

Despite the informal tone of the proceedings, the attendees were able to accomplish several important things. The group voted to change the name of its venture from the American Professional Football *Conference* to *Association*. Although no explanation was given at the time, historians have debated the reasons ever since. It is also worth noting that they did not use the word "league," which is what many of the founders—including Halas and Lyons—were seeking to create. At Ralph Hay's urging, Jim Thorpe was named the association's first president (forerunner to the NFL's modern-day office of commissioner). Hay took little time in convincing the conferees of the benefits of having the Olympic champion as its figurehead despite his lack of administrative experience. The Thorpe name would bring instant recognition and credibility to the venture. There were no dissenters. A membership fee was set at $100, though it has been accepted as fact that no team paid its dues at the meeting or at any time during the association's first season. A three-man committee was created to frame a constitution. To ensure franchise stability and keep players from jumping from one team to another, the founders agreed to honor existing player contracts. Each team was instructed to file complete rosters of players used during the season by January 1 so that the respective clubs would have first choice of a player's services for 1921. A motion was carried that all member clubs have stationery printed to include the words, "Member of American Professional Football Association [APFA]."[7]

Lyons jotted down several points he thought worth remembering, including, "No Massillon," as the Tigers opted not to join the association, and "Rules: 1 no college men. 2 can play non-league teams. 3 contracts honored." The ability to play nonleague clubs was good news for teams like the Jeffersons, which had long-standing regional rivalries with established semipro outfits from Rochester, Syracuse, and other nearby cities. This would allow such clubs to keep cash flowing by booking traditional adversaries on weekends when other APFA teams were unavailable.

News of the meeting was sent out on the wires the following day but was not published until Sunday the 19th when several major newspapers, such as the *New York Times*, finally found the space to run the story:

THORPE MADE PRESIDENT
Famous Indian Elected Head of Pro Football Association.

CANTON, Ohio, Sept. 18.—Jim Thorpe, famous Indian football player and coach of the Canton Bulldogs, a local professional team, has been chosen head of the American Professional Football Association, the only professional football organization in the country, according to announcement here today.

Representatives of eleven cities unanimously voted Thorpe to the Presidency, with Stanley Cofall of Cleveland Vice President and Art Ranney of Akron Secretary and Treasurer.

At the meeting held here were W.H. Fannigan [sic], from the Rock Island, Ill., Independents; L.V. Lyons of Rochester, N.Y.; E. Rall [sic] of Muncie, Ind.; George Hales [sic] of Decatur, Ill.; Charles O'Brien of the Chicago Cardinals, Cofall and Jimmy O'Donnell of the Cleveland Indians, Carl Storck of the Dayton Triangles, A.A. Young of Hammond, Ind.; Frank Nied and Art Ranney of the Akron Indians, and Mac Maginnis of Akron, but representing the Massillon Tigers.

A decision was reached to refrain from luring players out of college for the professional game.[8]

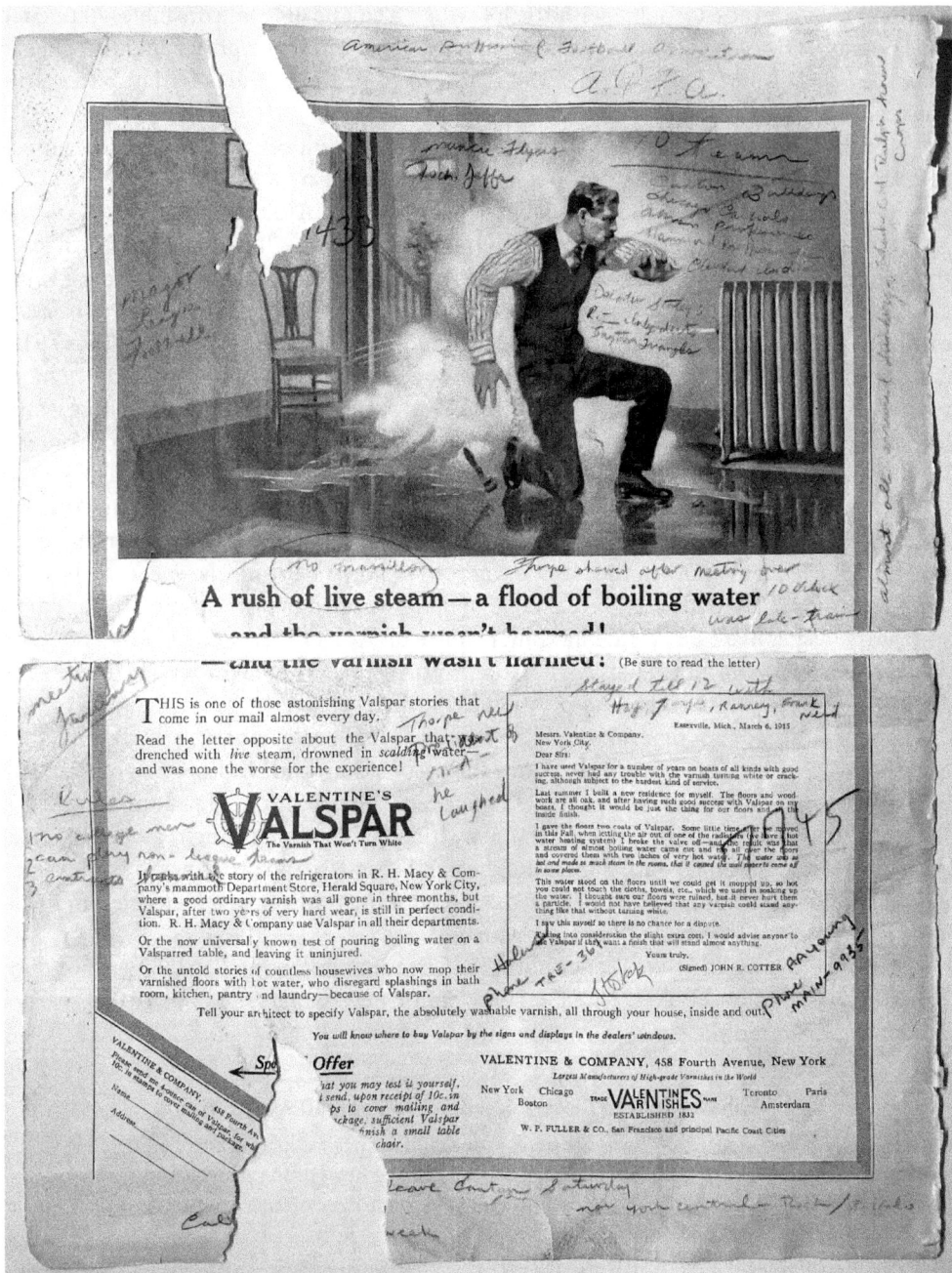

Page from a copy of the *Saturday Evening Post* on which Lyons jotted notes related to the APFA's organizational meeting held in Canton, Ohio, September 17, 1920.

Although some historians—including the oft-quoted Mr. Halas—have indicated that Thorpe was not present on September 17, Lyons' records state clearly that he did indeed show. The Olympian arrived, however, after the meeting had been adjourned and several of the attendees—Halas included—had retired for the evening. "Thorpe showed up after meeting over, 10 o'clock, was late—train," Lyons noted, adding that he was one of the handful still present when Big Jim finally appeared at Hay's showroom. "Stayed till 12 with Hay, Thorpe, Ranney, Frank Nied." When Thorpe was informed that he had been elected president of the new football association, "he laughed."[9]

Only the ten teams represented at the September meeting (Akron Pros, Canton Bulldogs, Chicago Cardinals, Cleveland Tigers, Dayton Triangles, Decatur Staleys, Hammond Pros, Muncie Flyers, Rochester Jeffersons, Rock Island Independents) are recognized today as charter members of the NFL, as the APFA became known in 1922. Four more teams joined the association over the next several weeks: Buffalo (nameless at this point), Chicago Tigers, Columbus Panhandles, and Detroit Heralds. Although recognized as APFA members that first year, they are not considered charter members.[10]

The long train ride back to Rochester gave Lyons plenty of time to reflect on how the idea he had been nurturing for nearly a decade was finally coming to fruition. The Rochester Jeffersons were no longer some far-flung, ragtag semipro football team from an upstate New York city some western teams refused to visit. They were now a recognized part of a formalized confederation of franchises. He hoped this was going to attract the big-name teams with star players that would bring in large crowds of paying customers.

Lyons also had time to think about the upcoming season, for there was plenty to accomplish before the Jeffs suited up for their first game as APFA members. Contacting the players he wished to bring back from his 1919 squad, recruiting new players and negotiating contracts, ordering equipment, contacting managers from other teams to book games, securing leases for the use of playing fields, talking to reporters from the local newspapers to generate publicity, and so much more.

It was around this time that Lyons made the regrettable decision to discard the familiar script "Jeffs" logo the team had emblazoned on their jerseys since 1915. "I decided when we joined the APFA that I would drop the Jeff emblem," Lyons recalled years later. "The team was originally named after Jefferson Avenue but it also was formed by the Jefferson Club. They were pro Democrat and was heavily involved in politics in our city and state. The last thing I needed was another reason for people not attending games, even though I would have loved the emblem on the uniforms. I thought all teams in our league should have an emblem."[11]

The team retained the red base color with white trim and numerals on the backs, though occasionally a player might still be seen wearing one of the old script logo jerseys if there were no plain ones available. These were, after all, pro football's "rag days."

* * *

The 1920 Jeffersons gathered for their first practice of the season on September 17, the same day Lyons was sequestered in Canton helping establish the new football league. Jack Forsyth, returning for his second year as coach after guiding the Jeffs to a 6-2-2 record in 1919, put the team through its paces. Lyons demonstrated he was serious about putting a competitive team on the field by securing the services of a number of former collegiate stars. End Joe DuMoe of Lafayette was a second-team Walter Camp All-American in 1919. Former Syracuse tackle Lou Usher was a first-team Camp honoree in 1918. John Barsha was a Russian-born rusher and former captain of the

Syracuse University 11. Halfback/fullback Jim Laird had been captain of the Colgate University team.

Returning to the Jeffs lineup were standby halfback Harry "Dutch" Irwin, end Hal "Butch" Clark, quarterback Gerald "Red" Quigley, guard Art Webb, guard Hank Smith, tackle Jim Woods, center Joe Bachmaier, halfback Otho "Babe" Clark, lineman Pete Heinlein, and Lyons' old friend Dutch Mellody, the longest tenured member of the Jeffersons now entering his 13th season with the team.

Yet for all the hubbub surrounding the formation of a major league for professional football, the Jeffs, along with nearly every other APFA team, faced a nonmember opponent in their inaugural game. In the first game recognized by the Pro Football Hall of Fame as featuring a legitimate APFA member team, the Rock Island Independents hosted the St. Paul Ideals at Douglas Field in Rock Island on Sunday, September 26. A sparse crowd of 800 saw the Independents roll to an easy 48–0 win. On October 3, the Akron Pros defeated the Wheeling Tigers by a score of 43–0 at League Park. Buffalo's new team, as yet unnamed, clobbered sandlotters West Buffalo 32–6 at the Canisius College Villa. Thorpe's Bulldogs hosted the Pitcairn Quakers at Lakeside Park and won handily, 48–0. The Decatur Staleys defeated the Moline Tractors 20–0 in front of 1,500 at Staley Field. The Dayton Triangles drubbed the Columbus Panhandles 14–0 at Triangle Park in Dayton in the first game played between two APFA member teams. Later that same day, Rock Island earned its second victory in as many weeks by knocking off the Muncie Flyers 45–0 in the latter's debut.

That same day, the Jeffersons played host to a familiar aggregation from the sandlots of Western New York called All-Buffalo at rain-soaked Rochester Baseball Park. Lyons' notes illustrate just how much planning went into preparing his team for its first whirl as an APFA team. "Need Benzoni to umpire game. Going to be muddy! Coach Forsythe 8 o'clock morning drills! Need all players on park by 8. Call Bell 1027." And something Lyons most certainly found disappointing: "Henry [McDonald, the former Jefferson] in lineup with Buffalo."

Lyons also listed the sundry items he wanted to be sure to remember and that now provide insight into all that was required to stage a "big league" football game in 1920:

- water pail
- clothes/rags
- first aid box
- footballs
- stopwatch
- lime for field lines
- benches
- ice block
- blankets
- hose
- board chalk
- tickets
- wood for goals
- rope
- lineups
- bathhouse soaps
- pencils, paper
- whistle

A meager crowd of 2,000 turned out to witness a bit of history as the Rochester Jeffersons played their first game as members of the new APFA. The Jeffs outclassed their nonmember opponents throughout the afternoon and walked away with a 10–0 victory despite completing just 1 of 15 passing attempts. Jim Laird scored the first points in the team's APFA era with a field goal in the second quarter. John Barsha scored the Jeffs' first-ever touchdown in the third, which provided a ten-point lead and the game's final score.

No doubt pleased with his team's opening-day performance, Lyons' postgame notes read, "Everybody played well. Baseball park—good crowd considering bad weather. Need better shoes in mud. Home games much easier! Laird—bruised hand. Henry treated well in Buffalo. Paid players ✓ All home ✓"[12]

The crowd size, however, was another matter. Lyons believed the team and league would be fine if they could get some good publicity and build up a loyal fan base, but they were going to need outside financial support as they struggled during the early, formative seasons. He had arranged another meeting with George Eastman to ask the great philanthropist for his help. If the Jeffs had the support of a wealthy benefactor such as Eastman, they'd be all set.

Lyons' notes provide the time and place the two were to meet: "Mr. Eastman. 1 o'clock. 343 State St. Main building. Mon Sept 27."[13] He gave the multimillionaire his best pitch, but the man was still not interested in supporting athletic endeavors.

"Trying to convince G. Eastman," Lyons wrote in his journal. "He says, 'Music is as far above football, baseball, running as the brain is above feet.' Must convince him otherwise."[14]

Eastman instead offered to donate a Johnson's No. 1 First Aid Cabinet, a metal case containing all of the essentials one might need in the event of an accident or emergency. Although the standard first aid kit had been around for decades by this time, the No. 1 First Aid Cabinet was considered state of the art because of its size, scope, and contents.[15] It had a retail price of $15 (approximately $230 in 2024). It might not have seemed like much of a consolation, but the kit became an item Lyons carried with tremendous pride throughout the Jeffs' time in the league. He mentioned the kit several times in his journal, whether for its application on the playing field or when some reprobate attempted to make off with it from the Jeffs' sideline.

The Jeffs continued to face nonassociation teams in their next three contests, knocking off a Buffalo-based service team (Fort Porter) with a 66–0 skunking, tying the Utica Knights of Columbus 0–0, then defeating the Syracuse Stars 21–7 to improve to 3–0–1.

It was then on to Buffalo on October 31 for the Jeffs' first matchup with an actual APFA member. This Buffalo team was the direct descendant of the Buffalo Prospects, which had defeated the Jeffersons the previous year to claim the championship of New York State. They were a formidable aggregation led by former Michigan quarterback Tommy Hughitt, who doubled as the team's head coach. Its lineup included several genuine Walter Camp All-America selections including Dartmouth guard Swede Youngstrom, Colgate halfback Ockie Anderson, Michigan fullback Pat Smith, and ends Murray Shelton of Cornell and Heinie Miller of Pennsylvania, making it one of the most aptly named clubs in league history now that they were being called the Buffalo All-Americans. Lyons' roster boasted several stars as well and was augmented for this game by the addition of army fullback Elmer Oliphant and Brown University quarterback Mike Purdy.

Lyons recruited Purdy after seeing him make some dazzling plays for the Syracuse 11 in the previous Sunday's game against the Jeffs. Purdy had been a second-team Camp All-American in 1916. Three years later, he was playing with the pre–APFA Akron Indians when he recommended they sign a diminutive African American halfback named

Fritz Pollard, with whom he had played at Brown.[16] Oliphant was one of the most famous players in the country after earning first-team All-America honors four times with two different teams (1913 at Purdue, 1915–1917 with the army).

Despite breaking away for several long gains, Oliphant could not break into the Buffalo end zone. Jim Laird accounted for all of Rochester's scoring, booting field goals in the second and fourth quarters in a losing effort. Final score: Buffalo 17, Rochester 6.

Unfortunately for the Jeffersons, this was to be Oliphant's only appearance in a Rochester uniform. Oliphant, like many other star players who followed him through the Jeffs' brief history, was too expensive to retain. Lyons recorded in his ledger that he paid Ollie $150 (along with a $100 signing bonus) for his single appearance but left other telling notes that seem to indicate there was more to the decision than money to not bring him back: "Head not in game," he wrote, adding, "going to be 29 years old, took much wear in college."[17]

A rematch with the Knights of Columbus team resulted in a 27–7 victory for the Jeffs, giving them an overall record of 4-1-1. Yet despite the team's on-field success, attendance for their home games had been sparse. For the Jeffs' contest with All-Tonawanda on Sunday, November 14, Lyons devised a one-time promotion he hoped would spur sales and generate sustainable interest. For this week only, Lyons was offering admission to kids for the low price of ten cents per ticket. The promotion was a success, according to the *Democrat & Chronicle*, which reported, "There were about 200 representatives of Young America on hand, ranging in ages from 6 to 16."

The bump in attendance was surely a welcome sight for Lyons, at least until the halftime whistle blew. It was then that some members of "Young America," taking advantage of a surprise storm that dropped several inches of snow on the Baseball Park field, "made themselves conspicuous between the halves by launching a five-minute snowball barrage on the adults in the stands."

Lyons seemed to take the merriment in stride, however. "Bad weather," he wrote. "Rain and snow. Snowball fight. Fans vs. kids. Everyone laughing, fun. 10¢ tickets, lots of kids."[18]

The game itself did not match the excitement in the stands, as the Rochester offense sputtered. The 6–0 final marked the Jeffs' first home loss of the season.

The Jeffs' slate of non–APFA competition continued a week later with a 16–0 defeat of the crosstown rival Scalpers. Three days' rest was all the Jeffs were afforded before having to suit up again for a Thanksgiving Day rematch with All-Tonawanda. Lyons learned the day before the game that he would be minus the services of both Mike Purdy and Lou Usher, the latter having sent a telegram to the Rochester boss declaring that he "is through with football for the rest of his life."[19] The Jeffs talent pool was already depleted after losing halfback John Barsha earlier in the season and failing to retain Elmer Oliphant's services after he had played a single game. It was not surprising that the Jeffs again failed to muster a viable offense against Tam Rose's Lumberjacks, managing just a field goal in losing 14–3.

That evening, the tireless Lyons took time away from family festivities to place phone calls to Messrs. Thorpe and Halas to discuss league matters.

"Talked to George," Lyons scribbled in his journal. "Decatur Staleys 6–0 vs Tigers. He is not happy with team except Sternaman, only scorer. Feels like they have chance to win title. Akron? Buffalo? George worried about weather in Dec. League Park Akron, Canton."

"Talked to Jim," he continued. "Canton backfield working well, Guyon-Calac-Thorpe. Jim not starting until later. Griggs at quarterback. Could use him! Pollard Akron, good runner."[20]

What Lyons did not memorialize was whether he and Thorpe discussed the reasons for the cancellation of the game the Bulldogs had scheduled at Rochester on November 21. The game had been agreed to when Thorpe visited Lyons' house on September 13. There was no mention in the papers as to why the contest was canceled, but the Bulldogs also backed out of a game scheduled at Rock Island a week later (November 28) "on the pretext of losing money" despite a $4,000 guarantee. Instead of traveling to Rochester on the 21st, the Bulldogs stopped off at Buffalo where they drew an impressive 9,000 spectators before skipping town with a 3–0 win.[21]

The Jeffs were able to schedule the Scalpers that day and won handily. Rochester's grid Goliaths met again on Sunday, November 28, resulting in a close 7–6 victory for the Big Red, allowing them to claim the title of city champions. Bob Argus scored on a ten-yard run in the second quarter to give the Jeffs a 7–0 lead. That score stood until late in the fourth quarter when the Scalpers finally found the end zone. The extra-point attempt failed, and the Jeffs held on for the one-point decision.

The Scalpers were not convinced. The 15th Warders challenged the Jeffs to one more game in hopes of redeeming their wounded civic pride. Despite winning the two previous games between the teams, Lyons accepted the challenge. But with the Jeffs short eight regulars and the field a sea of mud resulting from heavy early December precipitation, the game quickly devolved into a burlesque unworthy of the standards the APFA was seeking to establish for itself when first organized three months earlier.

The Rochester Jeffersons in action against the cross-town rival Scalpers, November 21, 1920.

"The game lacked a great deal in the way of brilliant plays and thrills and, in fact, showed little good football," reported the *Democrat & Chronicle*. "Fumbles were frequent and backlot tactics of other years occasionally crept into play. But it was a Scalper-Jeff battle of old and the crowd was satisfied."[22]

Rarely in the history of pro football has a game ending in a 0–0 deadlock left a crowd feeling satisfied. In this instance, however, it was an apt description. The brutal, bloody, mud-slinging clashes between these archrivals were the games Rochester grid fans enjoyed the most.

The first APFA season was now in the books. The Jeffersons posted a respectable final mark of 6-3-2, though only one game (a loss) was played against an honest-to-goodness APFA member team. It seems odd that Lyons, one of the most vocal exponents of a nationalized major league of professional football, was unable to schedule more league games for his team. To his credit, however, three scheduled games against APFA opponents (Canton, Columbus, and a second against Buffalo) were canceled for various reasons.

Despite their decent win-loss record, the Jeffs' first campaign was, like just about every other team's, financially disheartening. The Chicago Tigers and Detroit Heralds threw in the towel at the end of the season (though both would reorganize and return in 1921), while the Muncie Flyers did not even make it to the finish line.

The inability to retain high-priced star players like Oliphant, Barsha, Purdy, and Usher was both a blessing and a curse. Not having them on a regular basis certainly weakened the team on the field, but on the other hand, Lyons did not have to pay them when they were not there. The lack of support given by football fans in Rochester was no doubt disappointing, especially for someone so passionate not only about the game itself but also for his beloved home city. In the four home games for which attendance figures are available (out of a total of nine), the Jeffs averaged approximately 2,750 attendees. The money generated was not enough to cover player salaries, the visiting team's guarantee, field rental, equipment, and other expenses.

Yet perhaps the most disappointing thing for Lyons was the beating he took in his personal bank account. After ticket sales, he alone was responsible for every expense incurred by the football team. He did not have deep pockets like some of his APFA brethren, nor was he able to secure a major corporate sponsor. A look at his end-of-season ledger illustrates just how much of a financial thrashing Lyons sustained:

ROCHESTER JEFFERSONS FOOTBALL TEAM
LEO V. LYONS

1920 APFA FOOTBALL SEASON

EXPENCES [sic]	
PLAYER CONTRACTS	9,250.00
PARK RENT with insurance	454.20
EQUIPMENT footballs, med supp.	110.99
INSURANCE players	86.33
BONUS CASH FOR COLLEGE GRADS	signing 490.00

VISITING TEAM GUARANTEE	980.00
TRAVEL EXPENSES	85.63
MISC.	327.43
TOTAL OUT	11,784.58
GATE RECEIPTS	9,784.07
AWAY GAME	255.30
TOTAL IN	10,039.37
TOTAL LOSSES	1,754.21
LOAN FOR TEAM	802.00
	negative 2,547.21

MISC NOTES

	Signing NEG.
J. LAIRD COLGATE	75.00
E. OLIPHANT WEST POINT	100.00
M. PURDY BROWN	75.00
J. BARSHA SYRACUSE	75.00
L. USHER	75.00

5

"The finest Jeffs team to ever scar up a gridiron"

(1921)

The owners convened for their first-ever postseason meeting at the Portage Hotel in Akron, Ohio, on April 30, 1921. Club owners/managers present for this meeting were Art Ranney and Frank Nied (Akron), Frank McNeil (Buffalo), Ralph Hay and Lester Higgins (Canton), Chris O'Brien (Chicago Cardinals), Joe Carr (Columbus), Carl Storck (Dayton), Morgan O'Brien (Decatur), Doc Young (Hammond), and Leo Lyons (Rochester). Also present were Leo Conway, applying for a franchise for the city of Philadelphia, and Dr. Charles Lambert, who was present to advise the owners on game rules and procedures. Noticeably absent were Rock Island's Walter Flanigan and Decatur's George Halas, as well as Cleveland's Stan Cofall and Canton's Jim Thorpe, the association's vice president and president, respectively.

The first order of business was the awarding of the association's initial championship to the Akron Pros, which was decided by a vote of the owners. The Pros had finished the season with a record of eight wins, no losses, and three ties. Ties were not counted in league standings at the time, giving the Pros a perfect winning percentage. Decatur finished second at 10–1–2 (.909) and Buffalo third at 9–1–1. The Jeffersons' record of 6–3–2 was good for a seventh-place finish out of fourteen teams. To commemorate Akron's championship, team owners Art Ranney and Frank Nied were awarded a beautiful silver loving cup by the Brunswick-Balke-Collender Company.

The delegates then opened the floor for nominations for new executive staff. It was agreed new blood was needed to steer the association into the future. Thorpe was not the man to do it, but the one who could was already in the room. "The American Professional Football Association had many weaknesses," Halas recalled. "The great Jim Thorpe had served us well gaining publicity but, as we knew, he was no administrator, nor did he pretend to be. With the sport growing, we needed a man who could direct the development of our organization, help design rules and enforce them. Such a man was Joe F. Carr of Columbus, Ohio. He was a born organizer. He had organized employees at the Panhandle workshop of the Pennsylvania Railroad into powerful baseball and football teams. He had organized professional baseball in Ohio. He wrote sports for the *Ohio State Journal*."[1]

Carr was elected unanimously. Morgan O'Brien was elected vice president and Carl Storck reelected secretary-treasurer. The new president appointed a committee—composed of Storck, Ranney, and Dr. Lambert—to develop a league constitution and bylaws,

5. "The finest Jeffs team to ever scar up a gridiron" 69

something that had gone ignored during Thorpe's tenure. Carr directed the committee to have the documents ready for review by the owners at the next meeting.

The association reiterated its stance against using undergraduate players, resolving to disenfranchise any team violating this rule. It was agreed that all player contracts from 1920 would be respected by other clubs unless the player in question had received his outright release. League membership fee was set at $50. Applications were received from several cities including Cincinnati, Toledo, Fort Wayne, Minneapolis, and Louisville.[2]

Lyons also recorded the owners discussing the possibility of dividing the league into distinct regional groupings. "Discussed divisions, east-west. Would like to see divisions and in a playoff configuration. Clear champion of league." He sketched out how the proposed divisions would be aligned:

West	East
Rock Island	Rochester
Cleveland	Buffalo
Decatur	Canton
Chicago	Columbus
Chicago	Akron
Dayton	Muncie
Detroit	Hammond

(showed map to Joe—said will discuss next meeting)[3]

Twelve years before the NFL adopted George Preston Marshall's proposal of splitting into divisions, the founders were considering the possibility. The owners were always looking for ways to improve the game and enhance the fan experience.

The owners gathered again on June 18, but Lyons was not able to attend. It was at this meeting that the owners adopted the new constitution and bylaws submitted by the committee of Storck, Ranney, and Lambert. Several newspapers noted the inclusion of "a reserve clause, similar to that now existing in baseball" as an "outstanding feature" of the constitution, prohibiting players under contract with a member team from jumping to a contending team offering a higher salary. The reserve clause gave major league baseball teams the power to retain a contracted player's services for each season unless given his outright release. The adoption of the clause by the APFA was intended to put an end to the rampant team jumping by players seen during its inaugural season. This was welcome news for small-time owners like Lyons, who were most prone to losing their better players to teams in bigger markets.[4]

Meanwhile, Lyons had not given up on the idea of football trading cards which he had first conceived five years earlier. Now that his Jeffersons were part of a national professional football organization, he thought such a product could be effective in promoting the venture in much the same way cards were used to promote major league baseball. He took it upon himself to restart the campaign by sending new proposals to various companies whom he believed could help make the idea a reality, starting with George Eastman of the Rochester-based Eastman Kodak Company. Despite expressing skepticism about the future of pro football, the film and camera mogul left the door open to further discussion:

EASTMAN KODAK COMPANY
ROCHESTER, N. Y.

January 13, 1921

Mr. Leo V. Lyons
Rochester, New York

Dear Mr. Lyons:

I received your plans and proposals in regards to the card and chewing gum product. We are still carefully exploring the most viable and logistical way to accomplish this. The last time we delved into this, in 1917, the timing was not conducive to the task with the war in Europe. Though Mr. J.F. Bresnahan at American Chicle was a fine choice to make this possible, I still have strong doubts about football being popular enough to draw a consumer base to support this.

Now that American Chicle Company is no longer a Rochester business, Pulver Gum could support this but would have to hire more employees, not something Mr. Irl LaGrange was keen on.

I will be leaving Rochester for a while to get away from this chilly weather, packing up Sunday. I will consider this on hold til I return. I do have an associate looking into the best and most cost friendly card stock. I will call you when I return.

Yours very truly,
Geo. Eastman [signed][5]

The response received from Irl LaGrange of the Pulver Gum Company was similarly noncommittal. It was clear, however, that LaGrange and Eastman were taking the proposal seriously, as LaGrange's letter indicates the two had met to discuss the costs, logistics, and various methodologies of such an undertaking:

PULVER COMPANY, INC.
ROCHESTER, N.Y.

June 8, 1921

MR. LEO V. LYONS
Frost Avenue
Rochester, New York

Dear Mr. Lyons, we are in receipt of your proposals and have explored them fully. I believe that "Proposal 2" would work though product packaging may be a challenge. We here are currently experimenting on a way to package our chewing gum with the card that you have designed. We will work on this for a few more weeks, then we may still have to consider the coupon for card plan, if feasible.

Per our conversation last month, I have spoken to Mr. Eastman concerning his company producing the football cards. He was confident about the actual production but concerned about the cost and relative interest in the game of football, whether it be college, professional or regional.

Let us review the situation in a few weeks and we can all proceed accordingly. I am very interested in seeing this through to a successful conclusion.

Sincerely,
Irl E. LaGrange [signed][6]

Despite assurances they would continue talks "in a few weeks," there is no record that this proposal was ever again discussed with these key business figures. Lyons' notes show he also met with an official from Rueckheim Bros. & Eckstein, Inc., makers of Cracker Jack and other confections, at the company's Chicago offices in August 1921. That meeting proved more disheartening, as it appears the company rejected the idea out of hand.

"The Cracker Jack Co.," he wrote. "Met with Mr. F.E. Ruhling, sales manager. Not confident of idea—football. Only did baseball 2 years. Not cost friendly or overly popular (3 million $ in sales)."[7]

This series of setbacks was not enough to forestall Lyons in his quest to see football trading cards brought to market. His campaign carried on as he continued sending letters to officials of companies who might have even the remotest chance of helping make the dream a reality, from confectioners to paper and cardboard manufacturers to photographic and lithographic firms. His fellow owners were not spared of his exhortations either. Lyons continued to send letters or bend an ear of a co-owner whenever the opportunity presented itself.

* * *

Lyons was present for the association's third meeting of the year, this one held at the LaSalle Hotel in Chicago on August 27. The primary business conducted was the approval of four new franchises. Approved for admission were teams from Minneapolis, Minnesota (Marines), Evansville, Indiana (Crimson Giants), and Tonawanda, New York. The Tonawandans had been playing as an unaffiliated team for several years under the All-Tonawanda banner but were now official APFA members playing as the Kardex.

Also joining the association in 1921 was a team from the hinterlands of Green Bay, Wisconsin, sponsored by the Acme Packing Company. Under the leadership of its captain and star player Curly Lambeau, the team eventually evolved into one of the most successful franchises in the world of professional sports. As of this writing, the team that eventually morphed into the Green Bay Packers has won a record 13 NFL championships. This they accomplished without ever severing ties to their home city, which was the smallest in the association with a head count of just 31,643.

The owners also passed a motion that "season passes be sent from President's office to newspaper and prominent officials," as a way of promoting good public relations for the association. The savvy Carr was putting his experience as a newspaperman to work nurturing goodwill with fellow members of the Fourth Estate.

Lyons noted the delegates discussing an issue that was not recorded in Secretary Carl Storck's minutes. One or more of the owners brought up the idea of a "minor-major league format" for pro football. To that, he wrote, "Like my idea better." He then scratched out how he envisioned a league split into two divisions could work for the association. "Each team should be able to play another team from 'the other' league [division]. Why separate and limit schedule. East-West meet during season if so but a play-off format would keep division teams separate till they meet in 'Championship'—(Baseball)."[8]

It was a short meeting, taking just one day and Storck needing but a single piece of paper to memorialize the proceedings. It was a clear sign the owners felt they were heading in the right direction under new president Joe Carr. Carr reflected that confidence in a press release in which he predicted, "Within two years the big baseball leagues will be putting football teams into the field. Professional football last year drew crowds as large as many big-league baseball games did. With the popular interest already shown, and with the successful fight we are making on contract-breaking and other wild cat practices, we are confident of a big league standing before long."

Carr also addressed concerns expressed by officials at the university level of the sport. He pointed out, somewhat hyperbolically, that "more than half of the association's players are former All-American college football stars" and "99 out of 100 of them have been on college or university teams." However, he added, "This will not cause a conflict with college football by any means. No college student, whether engaged in, eligible or ineligible for athletics, can be contracted by any member club of the association."[9]

* * *

As the APFA's second season loomed, Lyons was actively pursuing top players to strengthen his team and keep the turnstiles spinning. On September 29, the *Rochester Democrat & Chronicle* reported that Lyons had re-signed two stars from the previous year, halfback Jim Laird and end Joe DuMoe. Laird, the team's captain and most consistent offensive performer in 1920, had been lured away by the Buffalo All-Americans at the end of the season. He was returning to the Jeffs after resolution of a contract dispute between Lyons and Frank McNeil, owner of the Buffalo franchise. DuMoe had shown great promise but missed much of the 1920 season due to injuries.

Newly signed were tackle Jim Barron, formerly captain of the Georgetown University football team, and Notre Dame/Fordham quarterback Jerry Noonan. Lyons' efforts continued to bear fruit as more stars joined the team throughout the season. Among the veteran sandlotters returning from the 1920 squad were halfback Bob Argus, center Joe Bachmaier, end Darby Lowery, guard Hank Smith, and lineman Jimmy Woods. Although there was no formal announcement, Dutch Mellody, the last link to the Jeffs' pre–Leo Lyons era, was not going to be returning after 13 years with the team.

Lyons announced that Jack Forsyth was returning to coach the team for a third season, though he was giving up his role as an active player. In a surprise move, Lyons signed three coaches to assist the 29-year-old Forsyth: Bob Bernhardt to coach the linemen, Dr. Raymond Brown (who doubled as the team's physician) to tutor the backfield men, and Dr. Graydon Long to oversee the ends. This gave the Jeffersons the largest coaching staff in the association and surely left some observers wondering how Lyons planned to cover the added expense.

That question might be partly answered by Lyons' next announcement, that he was naming an independent figure to assume the role of team president. John R. Powers, a well-connected member of the Rochester Chamber of Commerce and current assemblyman for Monroe County, was named to the post.[10] Although it was not clearly stated, Powers' role appears to have been to stir up interest and support for the team among the business community in the greater Rochester area.

The Jeffs opened the 1921 season on October 9 at Rochester's Exposition Park and made short work of the independent All-Buffalo 11 with a 41–0 win. Jerry Noonan paced the attack with three touchdowns and two extra points, while Jim Laird contributed two touchdowns and three conversions.

The Jeffs were booked to play the Staleys at Cubs Park in Chicago the following week. The Staleys had been based in Decatur, Illinois, during the league's inaugural season but had played just one game in that city in 1921, a victory over the Rock Island Independents on October 10. Just a few days earlier, A. Eugene Staley, president of the A.E. Staley Manufacturing Company, which sponsored the football team, had made Halas an offer he could not refuse. Staley offered Halas and his partner, Edward "Dutch" Sternaman, $5,000 to assume ownership of the team and move it to the Windy City. Staley's main caveat was that the team retain the company name for the remainder of the 1921 season. After that, Halas and Sternaman were free to use whatever name they wished. This game against the visiting Jeffersons was to be the first in which the team was identified as the *Chicago* Staleys.

Lyons was determined to give the people of Chicago a showing and spent the week burning the wires trying to recruit a number of former college stars to play for the Jeffs. He was able to attract only one big-name player, Howard Berry, the former All-America halfback from the University of Pennsylvania and current major league baseball player with the New York Giants.

"Berry was coaching the Hamilton College team in Clinton, New York, at the time," Lyons explained, "but he refused to answer my letters and wires. When I finally contacted him by long-distance phone, I invented the story that [Williams College All-American] Benny Boynton was anxious to play on the same team with him. I told him that Boynton said he was the greatest football player that ever stepped on a field. Prior to my call Berry had turned down Jim Thorpe and a number of other professional offers."[11]

Intrigued at the prospect of playing with Boynton, Berry advised Lyons his services would cost $300 plus travel expenses. This included taxi fare to Albany where Lyons was to meet Berry to accompany him aboard the 20th Century Limited for the balance of the trip to Chicago. And that was not all, according to Lyons. Berry insisted, "You better have a pair of Spalding Fleet Foot shoes at the Cubs Park, or I will not play."

Demonstrating his willingness to do just about anything to improve his chances of presenting a competitive team, Lyons complied with Berry's demands. "I met him in Albany and we rode the rails to Chicago, Illinois," Lyons wrote. "Long trip, but we talked a lot. He was very cocky but a good kid. Not sure if he is a long timer."[12]

He was eager to get to Chicago for another reason. Believing the game of football should be constantly progressing, Lyons was always looking for ways to improve the quality of play on the field and make it more exciting for fans. He recalled a conversation he had had with Jim Thorpe about improving the unwieldy shape of the football in use at the time, which was a descendant of the type used in the sport of rugby. In 1912, the ball was standardized to have a circumference on the long axis from 28 to 28½ inches when tightly inflated, 22½ to 23 inches on the short axis, and weighing 14–15 ounces. Referred to as a "prolate spheroid," the ball more closely resembled a watermelon than the football used today. Lyons believed the ball's shape was a hindrance to good offensive play. And since the home teams supplied the game ball, they were free to use whatever model—Wilson or Spalding—they had handy. As a result, there was no consistency in the quality of the ball from game to game.

"Spoke with Halas, early month, about trying the new football designed by the folks at Thomas E. Wilson & Co.," Lyons wrote. "Mr. Thorpe and I chatted about how difficult it is to pass with such a big, plump ball and how it is not easy to handle, passing and catching and carrying. I ran the idea to George H. during this spring. I figured he has some connections with Wilson there in Chicago. George says he talked to his 'connections' at WILSON and said we can meet up before our game at Cubs Park Sunday. It is a shame that great talented kids can't connect with their intended target because the ball is too hard to work with. And I certainly do not have the powers to make it happen on my set budget and clout."[13]

Halas' "connection" was Arnold Horween, a player with the Chicago Cardinals and employee of the Horween Leather Company. Founded in 1905, the Horween company provided Wilson with the leather the sporting goods manufacturer used to make footballs. Halas and Horween, though competitors on the field, had become friends over the years, and they too had had conversations about the quality of the balls in use at the time. Some time prior to January 18, Lyons and Halas were given an opportunity to examine a new ball being designed by Wilson. After a thorough going-over, Lyons jotted down his impressions:

> Notes—even though the new ball is easier to handle than the previous average ball, still not easy to play football with.
>
> MUST DECREASE SIZE
>
> A. Decrease circumference by 1 to 2 inches
> B. Must be streamlined for passing game
> C. Even though the J-5 is cheaper or more popular, Wilson is better quality ball overall
> D. If adopted—all teams should use same ball.

must be innovative to improve
let's be the ones to do it
Be Different—trade cards,
Make the news/advertise, improve ball and scoring.[14]

When Lyons' train alighted in Chicago at 9:00 a.m., Halas was there to greet him. "Met up with Halas when we arrived," said Lyons. "Let our team wash up and change at hotel apartments his players live at near field."[15]

The two then headed over to the Wilson Sporting Goods store at 42 South Wabash Avenue to meet with Horween and Halas' partner, Ed "Dutch" Sternaman. The four discussed their concerns with the current ball and ideas for improvement. Horween took their suggestions back to the Wilson company, which went right to work designing a ball more closely resembling the one the group envisioned.[16]

Prior to ending the meeting, Halas let Horween and Lyons in on a little secret. "The Staleys will be called Bears next year," he confided. Lyons, recognizing the significance, recorded the declaration in his journal. The news of the name change would not become public knowledge for another three months, when Halas finally made the announcement at the owners meeting on January 28, 1922.

Lyons had just enough time to make it down to a field on Michigan Boulevard near the lake where his team was going through its pregame signal drills. He had to feel confident about their chances against Halas' brutes seeing college stars like Joe DuMoe, Jim Laird, and Howard Berry prepping in bright red Jeffersons jerseys.

Berry was nothing short of spectacular in his debut with the Jeffs, starting with a 23-yard dropkick field goal in the opening frame to give them a 3–0 lead. Dutch Sternaman kicked a field goal to tie the game in the second, but Berry responded with an 85-yard return of an intercepted pass in the third quarter to put the Jeffs back on top, 10–3.

"It was at this point," said Lyons, "that George Halas, in shock, asked me, 'What the hell kind of team did you bring out here?'"

The Staleys closed the gap later in the same frame, however, when Ralph Scott fell on a blocked punt in the Rochester end zone, but the missed conversion attempt allowed the Jeffs to keep a one-point lead. Berry made good on a second dropkick in the fourth to extend Rochester's lead to 13–9, but Chicago fullback Ken Huffine bulled over late in the period to give the Staleys a thrilling come-from-behind victory.

"We won 16–13," Halas recalled. "The 7,500 fans went home happy and I walked to the hotel very, very content."[17]

Lyons, too, felt good about how his team had stood up against the eventual association champions. "I think it was the finest Jeffs team to ever scar up a gridiron," he reflected years later. "I was proud of those boys that day, even though we were defeated." Much of that delight was due to Berry's outstanding performance. Lyons had been looking for a stud ball carrier to complement Jim Laird since failing to retain either John Barsha or Elmer Oliphant the previous season. He was thrilled to have Berry on the team, though there was one thing about the All-American he found intolerable. He seemed genuinely surprised to learn that Berry was commonly referred to as "Nig" by friends and teammates, a racially motived nickname resulting from his dark Caucasian complexion. Lyons apparently had not noticed that newspapers had been using the nickname in stories about Berry as far back as 1917. He was genuinely appalled when he overheard some of the Rochester players using the epithet and Berry responding with seeming indifference. It reminded him of the times he witnessed Henry McDonald laughing off similar slurs a decade earlier.

"Players on the Jeffs and Berry himself think it's just a name, funny they say," wrote Lyons, vowing, "I will not call him Nig but Mr. Berry. Again, the color of skin issue. Don't understand and he isn't even black. I wonder if they called him that at Pennsylvania & New York."[18] Unfortunately, they did.

The team returned to Rochester to begin preparing for their upcoming meeting with the Buffalo All-Americans. Lyons' good mood received another boost on Friday (October 21) when he secured the services of Joe Alexander, center/guard from Syracuse University. Alexander had been selected to three consecutive All-America teams by Walter Camp, twice as a guard (1918–1919) and then as a center (1920). A graduate of Syracuse's medical school in 1921, Alexander had entered private practice prior to signing his first pro football contract. As a result,

Joe Alexander, All-American at Syracuse University (1918–1920).

he would carry the nickname "Doc" throughout his career, playing football on the weekends while practicing medicine during the week.[19]

Even with the addition of Alexander, the Jeffs had fewer All-Americans (three) than their opponent (seven), whose abundance of Camp selections provided the very nickname by which they were known. One of those All-Americans suiting up for the Buffalo 11 was former Jeff halfback Elmer Oliphant. After appearing in just one game for the Redshirts in 1920, Oliphant was now a regular in the Buffalo lineup. And although he was not able to find the Jeff end zone, he did pitch in with three extra points as the All-Americans rolled to a 28–0 triumph. Buffalo had 21 first downs while the Jeffs managed just 5. Buffalo completed 10 out of 15 pass attempts. The Jeffs completed 2 out of 11 aerials. Lyons could take some measure of satisfaction in seeing Ollie miss on all three field goals he attempted.

The Jeffs were scheduled to face the tough Akron Pros a week later, their third straight outing against an APFA opponent. Lyons was determined to give the defending champions all they could handle. During the week, he made a quick trip to the Keystone State in hopes of securing the services of one of the most famous names in the game.

"I drove to the Bethlehem Steel mill in Pennsylvania and signed All-American qb Benny Boynton," wrote Lyons, "right at his workstation." Although the bold act of entering the steel mill uninvited resulted in Lyons being "promptly escorted out of the plant by officials," Lyons succeeded in his quest of adding another great player to the Jeffs' lineup. In doing so, however, he incurred the wrath of the owner of the very team his team was set to play that coming Sunday.

"What I was unaware of was that the Akron Pros and Frank Nied had planned on signing him later that week. About a week later I received an unpleasant letter from Akron accusing me of 'poaching' his player. I responded by saying Boynton was unsigned by any team. I did what a manager does, scout talent, pursue talent and sign talent. He was under no commitment to you or your team. I wish you well!"[20]

Benny Boynton, All-American at Williams College (1917, 1919).

The Pros boasted several star players in their lineup, including fullback Rip King and ends Paul Robeson and Scotty Bierce. The brightest of them all, though, was halfback/coach Fritz Pollard, recognized by historians as the first African American head coach in league history. With Boynton calling the signals, the Jeffs kept it close for the better part of three quarters, going into the final frame down by a surmountable 6–0 score. But the Pros scored twice in the fourth to seal a 19–0 victory.

The Jeffs became part of a historical footnote when they hosted the team from the western New York city of Tonawanda on November 6. The Kardex, as they were now called, had been playing in the Buffalo area for several years as the All-Tonawanda Lumberjacks and had been a regular opponent of the Jeffs during that time. In 1920, competing as a non–APFA team, the Lumberjacks compiled an overall record of eight wins and one loss, with two of those victories coming against the Jeffersons. A year later, the team gained sponsorship from the American Kardex Company—a highly successful filing and index supply firm located in North Tonawanda—and assumed the company name.

As it had been in previous seasons, the Tonawanda roster was made up almost entirely of sandlotters, with one notable exception being their star halfback/manager Walter "Tam" Rose, the former two-time All-American from Syracuse University. So far this season, the Kardex had played just one game, a 0–0 tie with nonleague Syracuse. Two other scheduled games had been canceled.[21]

A reported crowd of 2,700 came out, though Jeffs center Joe Alexander recalled the assemblage being smaller—much smaller, in fact. "We had less than 200 people in the stands," he told an interviewer several years later. "It was obvious there wouldn't be enough to pay the visiting team. It was Tonawanda, and there would be peanuts for us. I gathered both teams at midfield and we agreed to play for nothing."[22]

The game itself was never close, as the Jeffs raced to a 21–0 lead by halftime, then scored 24 more in the final period en route to a 45–0 skunking. Quarterback Benny Boynton led the way rushing for one touchdown, kicking a field goal, and adding six extra points, while fullback Jim Laird contributed two touchdowns to the cause.

There was no more evidence needed to prove the Kardex were not ready for the big time. The club folded after this one officially recognized game, becoming the only team in NFL history to be credited with playing a single league game.

A game scheduled for November 13 against the McKeesport (PA) Olympics was canceled due to injuries sustained by McKeesport players in an earlier game. "Cancel day before game Sun," the frustrated Lyons wrote. "They played Duquesne day before and their players hurt. Already printed tickets and arranged players to play. Does not look good for fans. Try to book Scalpers? Bad management by them. Costs me!"[23]

Another cancellation, this one not directly involving the Jeffersons, worked to their benefit by allowing them to make up some of the money lost as a result of the McKeesport cancellation. The Union Quakers of Philadelphia were scheduled to host the Canton Bulldogs the following Saturday, but the game was called off due to a contract squabble between several members of the Quakers who were also members of the Buffalo All-Americans. These players had been playing with the non–APFA Quakers on Saturdays, then catching the overnight train to Buffalo to play Sundays with the All-Americans. Buffalo owner Frank McNeil complained to league president Carr, who met with Canton owner Ralph Hay on Friday and ordered him to nix the game scheduled for this weekend. Since the Quakers were not members of the association, they were not compelled to respect Carr's dictate. Five of the players in question chose to remain with the Quakers and bade adieu to Buffalo.

What transpired next was reminiscent of the time back in 1917 when Lyons took his team to Canton on a day's notice to face the mighty Bulldogs. After learning of the Canton-Union cancellation on Friday afternoon, Lyons agreed to have his team at Philadelphia the next day to take Buffalo's place against the Quakers. The Jeffs' indefatigable manager was able to get just enough players together—exactly 11—in time to catch the train bound for Philly that same evening.

The Jeffs, playing without stars Alexander, Berry, and Boynton, managed to go toe-to-toe with the Philadelphians through three scoreless periods. The Quakers finally broke the stalemate when Johnny Scott knocked a six-yard dropkick through to claim a 3–0 lead. The Jeffs tied it a few moments later when tackle Frank Morrissey sent a kick over from 47 yards out. The game ended knotted at three apiece.

The Jeffersons returned to Rochester immediately after the Quaker game for a contest against the Columbus Panhandles, a stalwart of the old Ohio loop featuring several members of the famous Nesser clan. This game marked the first trip to the Flower City for the Panhandles and their manager, APFA president Joe Carr.

According to the *Rochester Democrat & Chronicle*, Carr's visit served a dual purpose. The first obviously was in his role as manager of the club, a role he had been playing since 1907. His second was as association president in looking over the city of Rochester "as a prospective member of the proposed Eastern division of the Professional League next season. Tentative plans for this circuit provide for two divisions—one eastward from Cleveland and the other from Cleveland west to Chicago."[24] The idea of splitting the association into two divisions had been discussed at the owners meetings on April 30 and was obviously still up for consideration.

The Panhandles were headlined by the Nesser family of grid warriors, eight of whom played for the team at some point in their history (brothers Frank, Ray, Fred, Phil, Al, John, and Ted, and Ted's son Charlie). The brothers were all employed as boilermakers for the Pennsylvania Railroad, and in addition to each being notoriously tough and athletically gifted, they gave the team a novelty to exploit as a drawing card. Carr publicized the Panhandles as the "toughest team in professional football, led by the famous Nesser brothers." By 1921, however, the brothers were getting a little long in the tooth, with some retired and those still active now well into their 30s.

The Jeffs, having faced the Quakers the day before with just 11 healthy men, were bolstered by the return of Alexander, Berry, and Boynton. Still, the majority of the Jeffs appeared sore and tired in the first quarter, an obvious hangover after putting in such a valiant effort at Philly before hopping on the overnight train to make it on time for today's kickoff.

Columbus, with Frank, Fred, Ted, and Charlie Nesser in the lineup (one of nine games in which the father-son duo played in 1921), took advantage of the Jeffs' listless start by staking an early 6–0 lead on a pair of Emmet Ruh dropkicks. The Redshirts found their stride in the second period, with Jim Laird bulling over from four yards out to give his team a 7–6 advantage. The one-point bulge stood until the fourth quarter, when the Jeffs exploded for three touchdowns, with Laird, Ben Boynton, and Jerry Noonan all going over. The Panhandles responded with a touchdown of their own, but it was too little, too late, and the Jeffs claimed a 27–13 victory.

While Carr might have been impressed by the Jeffs' performance on the field, he must have been disappointed at the sparse crowd of 2,000 that passed through the gate.

Lyons noted, however, that the league president did not appear so. "Carr says he hopes Rochester continues on," he wrote, adding, "Likes Boynton."[25]

Carr also appeared unfazed at knowing the Jeffersons were employing an undergraduate in their lineup, a blatant violation of league policy. As an insurance measure, Lyons had recruited Syracuse fullback Bill Kellogg for this game. However, since Kellogg was still an active member of the school's football team, he played under the pseudonym Earl Ettenhaus.

"Joe knew I had a Syracuse player," Lyons wrote in his journal, "but didn't say anything."

The Jeffs faced the sandlot Syracuse Pros at the Baseball Park a week later to close out the home portion of their season. Heavy rains reduced the field to a quagmire and resulted in another disappointing crowd of 1,200. Runners found it difficult to get firm footing, while passing became almost impossible. It was not until the second quarter that Jerry Noonan was able to hit his stride and return a Syracuse punt 60 yards to give the Jeffs a six-point lead. Ben Boynton found his feet midway through the fourth, carrying the pigskin over on a reverse to extend the lead to 12–0, which proved to be the final score.

Lyons' charges then traveled to the nation's capital for a contest with the Washington Senators (or "District Pros" as they were called in that week's *Democrat & Chronicle*). He came ready with 16 men in tow, including his A-list players Alexander, Berry, Boynton, Noonan, and Laird. To his disappointment, however, a blinding game-day snowstorm had befallen the Capital District, resulting in a turnout of fewer than 300 hardy souls. Fearing there would not be enough ticket revenue to cover the Jeffs' $800 guarantee, Lyons asked for payment up front. Owner Tim Jordan balked, suggesting the Jeffersons instead play for a percentage of the gate.

"Jordan said he had about 100 of the 800 guarantee," Lyons wrote. "Not enough to get back to Roch." When Lyons declared his team was not going to play unless he received the guarantee money in advance, Jordan refused. At an impasse, Lyons pulled his team from the field. "Never been more mad! Wanted to slug him!" Since the Jeffersons were the ones who refused to play, the game was awarded to Washington as a forfeit. "Ref Metzger ruled for Wash. Jackass."

Those fans who braved the elements were refunded their money. The Jeffs, on the other hand, were on their own. "Had to scrap [sic] up money for train ride back," said Lyons. "No $ for food!"[26]

Although this game is still cited by some historians as the only forfeit in NFL history, it was ultimately declared a cancellation at the next owners meeting. Therefore, the game does not appear in either team's final standings for the season.

The Jeffersons finished their second season with a record of 4–3–1 (2–3–0 against APFA competition), good for a tenth-place finish in the 21-team association. Overall, this was the strongest team the Jeffs ever put on a field, with several college stars, including some who appeared on a fairly regular basis. Although inconsistent, the team performed extremely well in wins over Tonawanda and Columbus. They even managed to humble George Halas a little by nearly upsetting his Chicago Staleys on October 16. In two seasons, the Jeffs had put together an aggregate record of ten wins, six losses, and three ties, and even though their record against APFA competition was 2–4–0, Lyons had to feel very good about how his team had performed up to this point.

Lyons had another reason to feel sanguine at the end of the '21 season, as two members of his club were selected to an All-Pro team named by the *Buffalo Evening News*. Doc Alexander was picked for the center position, while Ben Boynton got the nod at quarterback. All things considered, 2 selections out of a total of 11 for a team with a 2–3 record is highly commendable. Only the 9–1–2 Buffalo All-Americans had more (3).

Signing Alexander was arguably the most important transaction Lyons made during the Jeffersons' APFA/NFL era. Not only was the former Orangeman an outstanding on-field performer; he brought credibility to the team that helped fuel newspaper coverage in every city the team visited. He manned the helm whenever Jack Forsyth's coaching commitment at the Mechanics Institute in Rochester prevented him from traveling with the team. With Forsyth moving on to coach full time at the school, Alexander was the logical choice to take over the post for 1922.

Lyons was plagued by the same issues in 1921 that befell his team in 1920. The inability to attract and maintain more top-level players made for inconsistent on-field performance. Attendance remained too low to cover player salaries, and once again Lyons took a financial beating. Fan turnout dwindled with each passing week after a promising 4,000 passed through the gate on opening day, then dipped to 2,700, followed by 2,500, and a mere 1,500 in the home finale, for a per-game average of 2,675 (75 fewer than in 1920).

APFA — 1921 — ROCHESTER JEFFERSONS

SEASON EXPENSES

PLAYER CONTRACTS (with bonuses)	10,659.54
PARK RENT AND FEES (ins. included)	387.07
EQUIPMENT AND MEDICAL SUPPLIES	204.40
INSURANCE — all	127.00
TRAVEL — CHI. AKR. PHIL. WASH. BUFF.	1,878.90
OPPONENT GUARANTEE CASH	896.00
TRAVEL EXPENSES	85.63
MISC.	906.30
***TOTAL EXPENSES	15,059.21
GATE RECEIPTS — IN ROCH.	5,292.90
GUAR. CASH AND PERCENTAGE — AWAY	5,875.33
Fundraisers — Car washes — Legion	300.50
***** TOTAL IN	11,788.84
TOTAL LOSSES	1,754.21
LOAN FOR TEAM	802.00
	3,270.37

5. "The finest Jeffs team to ever scar up a gridiron"

*WASHINGTON TEAM OWES TEAM DEC 4, 1921

                                                  contacted Joe Carr concerning
                                                  failure to pay by Timothy JORDAN

LEO V. LYONS
#343 Frost Avenue
Rochester, New York[27]

                        *   *   *

The owners gathered for their postseason meeting at the Courtland Hotel in Canton on January 28, 1922. Several important matters were addressed, including the official transfer of the Chicago Staleys franchise from A.E. Staley to George Halas and Dutch Sternaman. There was a glitch, however, in the form of a third party, Bill Harley (brother of Staleys halfback Chic Harley). Harley came to the meeting claiming a one-third ownership of the Staley franchise based on an agreement he had made with Halas and Sternaman while acting as agent for his brother. Halas disputed Harley's claim, declaring that the agreement with Harley had been nullified before the end of the 1921 season and insisting he and Sternaman were the sole owners of the franchise per the sale agreement with Staley. President Joe Carr, along with Halas, Sternaman, and others, telephoned Staley, who verified his desire to get out of the football business and confirmed the sale of the franchise to Halas and Sternaman the previous fall. The matter was then put to a vote, with Halas and Sternaman winning full control by an 8–2 count.[28]

Halas also took the opportunity to announce that his team was no longer going to be called the Staleys. From this point forward, the team was going to be known as the Bears. "I considered naming the team the Chicago Cubs out of respect for Mr. William Veeck [then president of the Chicago Cubs baseball club], who had been such a great help," Halas later recalled, "but I noted football players are bigger than baseball players, so if baseball players are cubs, then certainly football players must be bears."[29]

Next came the question of determining the championship for the 1921 season. Halas declared the Staleys were champions with a 9–1–1 record. Buffalo All-Americans owner Frank McNeil (who was represented by the team's coach, Tommy Hughitt) also staked a claim for the association title with a record of 9–1–2. The Staleys and All-Americans had played each other twice during the season, with Buffalo winning the first game (7–6) and the Staleys triumphant in the second (10–7). Tradition dictated that the outcome of the second game of the season series between two teams carried more weight than the first. It was also pointed out that the aggregate score of the two games was 16–14 in favor of the Staleys. McNeil insisted the last two games his team played—including the second Staleys game—were merely exhibitions. The matter was, by Leo Lyons' suggestion, referred to the executive committee for final action. The committee took little time in ruling in favor of the Staleys, giving Halas his first of six eventual championships.[30]

Carr and his fellow magnates then had to settle the issue of the Green Bay Packers, who were reported to have violated an association rule by using three Notre Dame players (Hunk Anderson, Hec Garvey, and Ojay Larson) in a game against the Racine Legion on December 4, 1921. Historians have identified Halas as the one who ratted out the Packers to the media in hopes it would give him a chance to sign Anderson, a star guard for the Fighting Irish. This type of skulduggery was certainly not beyond Halas, but there is no direct evidence it actually occurred in this case.

After breaking for lunch at Benders Tavern in downtown Canton, the meeting resumed with J. Emmett Clair, representing the Packers, taking the floor. He acknowledged that the team was guilty as charged and dutifully asked permission to withdraw from the association. The owners voted to uphold the Packers' withdrawal and return the team's $50 entry fee.[31]

The Packers, of course, were not the only ones who had been employing undergraduates. The Rochester Jeffersons had done so in their game against Carr's own Panhandles on November 20. That Carr aligned with George Halas in yet another issue was indicative of a growing bloc within the association. Fortunately for Lyons, he appeared to be—for the time being at least—sitting firmly in the Carr-Halas camp. The Rochester transgression was completely ignored. Bringing the matter up for open discussion would have put Carr in the awkward position of having to confess he knew about the incident at the time and did nothing. Lyons, too, was more than happy to let it go unmentioned, considering the price the Packers had paid for their offense.

The owners ruled in Lyons' favor in his dispute with the Washington Senators over money he insisted was owed as a result of the cancellation of their game scheduled for December 4 at Washington city. Lyons was happy with the decision but knew it was pointless. "$800 Washington must pay me or forfeit club," he wrote. "Never see it."[32]

It was then time to elect officers for the upcoming year. It came as no surprise that Carr was reelected president. John Dunn, owner of the Minneapolis Marines, was elected vice president, replacing Morgan O'Brien. Dayton's Carl Storck was reelected secretary-treasurer.

Each team was required to deposit $1,000 as a guarantee against the employment of college players. In addition to the loss of the bond, any offending team's franchise would be forfeited. The owners agreed unanimously that team rosters would be limited to 18 players, which was intended to help keep costs down. And in a move that received very little attention at the time, the owners decided to change the name of their organization from its original styling of the American Professional Football Association to the National Football Association (NFA). The new name was, of course, merely a place holder until the more familiar finalized version was adopted at the next owners meeting.[33]

* * *

It was well and good that the owners had taken a stand against the employment of undergraduate players at their most recent meeting. They had declared this position at every meeting since the association's inception in September 1920, but this was the first instance in which any meaningful action was taken against a team for violating the decree. The Packers were one of several teams using college men to augment their lineups but were nevertheless the only ones punished for it. And as far as college purists were concerned, the Green Bay incident was just the tip of the iceberg.

Followers of college football believed the sport instilled many admirable qualities in the undergrad player, including discipline, teamwork, sportsmanship, athleticism, and healthy habits while preparing them for careers in varied fields of endeavor. At the same time, it was commonly believed the only acceptable professional vocation related to football was coaching it, and then only at a high school or collegiate level. Playing football for pay was considered unseemly and unsportsmanlike by many of the game's most powerful coaches including Walter Camp, Amos Alonzo Stagg, Major Charles D. Daly, Fielding Yost, and many others. The professional game, some contended, led players down the path of wickedness and degradation. Pro football was seen as a gateway to gambling, drinking, and other forms of debauchery. Coaches went to great lengths to discourage their players from turning pro for fear of the demons that surely awaited them.

Still, countless players eschewed the patriarchal finger-wagging of their revered coaches and played for pay, many of them before having graduated. Some played under assumed names while others did not bother to hide their true identities.

"Our reworded ban on using collegians remained vague," recalled George Halas. "An ingenious manager could find loopholes in it."[34]

University officials knew it, too. Yet they were powerless to stop the practice unless irrefutable evidence gave them the leverage to expel players with remaining eligibility. At its founding meeting in December 1921, the American Football Coaches Association (AFCA), made up of 43 college football coaches from across the nation, declared its "opposition to professional football as a menace to collegiate sport." It went so far as to recommend that postgraduate players partaking in play-for-pay ball be stripped of their varsity letters.[35]

Everything came to a head, however, with the revelation of two scandals occurring during the 1921 football season. The first concerned the Green Bay Packers' use of college men in its game against Racine on December 4. President Joe Carr had demonstrated the seriousness of the association's stance by forcing the Acme Packing Company to surrender its franchise.

A second, more egregious incident occurred when two Illinois-based semipro teams employed several undergrad players in a game with a whopping $50,000 riding on the outcome. The game, featuring teams from Taylorville and nearby Carlinville, received widespread attention when it was revealed that not only was 50 grand at stake but also that both teams were paying as much as $200 to players from Notre Dame and the University of Illinois. Carlinville had as many as nine Notre Damers in its lineup while Taylorville used ten Illini. Joey Sternaman (Dutch's younger brother), kicked three field goals for Taylorville, leading them to a 16–0 victory and a handsome payday.[36]

Despite Carr's swift actions and the fact that the Taylorville-Carlinville game was outside the APFA's purview, officials at the college level were determined to take down the professional game altogether. Both incidents were part of the same nasty problem as far as they were concerned. Members of the newly established AFCA announced their intent to "break the professional football menace."

"I think the time has come for concerted action," declared Amos Alonzo Stagg, coach at the University of Chicago. "I have noted the danger for several years as the professional game grew, and have been ready to meet it."[37]

Fielding Yost, famed coach at the University of Michigan, added, "great menace of professional football to college athletics…. A healthy condition in college athletics has existed in Western Conference circles for the last 15 years, but the temptation offered by promoters of professional football is very strong."[38]

Art Ranney, comanager of the Akron Pros, rose to defend the APFA against the claims of the college men. "Stagg is wrong if he attempts to put the blame on the professional football association for this recent trouble. It's not professional football that is a menace to college football. It's unorganized semi-professional teams that are to blame, as the trouble in Taylorville shows. The game at Taylorville was thoroughly investigated and reviewed by our association at its annual meeting in Canton last Saturday. The promoters of the game are not members of this association and we have no more jurisdiction over them than the colleges have. So why blame us for the Taylorville incident?"

Ranney pointed to the association's action in ousting the Green Bay Packers as proof of the league's commitment to honoring the wishes of the universities. "At our meeting last Saturday we expelled one club owner when it was proven that he had used college men in his games. Does that look as though we are bucking the colleges? Further a resolution as passed asking that each owner place a $1,000 forfeit with the association. Club owners who then tamper with college players will not only be expelled from the association, but forfeit their $1,000."

He then made it clear the association was not going anywhere and scoffed at the AFCA's threats. "The idea that the colleges can kill professional football is absurd. What can they do—take away his letter? But they can't take away his football ability."[39]

Even Rochester's Leo Lyons had an opinion on the matter. "Two years ago the American Professional Football Association passed a rule prohibiting the use of college players who had not finished their college career. With the exception of one instance, that of the Green Bay Packers, who were dropped from the association last week, this code of ethics has been strictly adhered to. Never in its history has the pro game held such a high rank as it does at the present time, and surely the collegiate critics who are strong in their condemnation have nothing to fear from the pro game as far as the box office is concerned."

Lyons then turned the mirror back on the college officials to show their hypocrisy. "It is a harsh thing to say, but there are few colleges in the country that can hold their hand in the air and boast of real 100 per cent amateurism. If the collegiate bodies will confine their energy to the young athlete while he is in school, instead of telling him what he shall not do after leaving school, they will find they will be further ahead in the end. By all means keep the college game with its splendid spirit and morale free from any taint of professionalism, but to tell a college star that he shall not play pro football after he graduates is a narrow view, and one that will not work, but simply embitter the young athlete, who needs ready money, toward his alma mater. It is no more a crime to play professional football, if one has the ability, than it is to play major league baseball. The quick action of the National Football Association in ousting the Green Bay Packers from that organization for using players that had not finished their college career shows that the pro body means business, so why not accept the inevitable and keep both games clean."[40]

Unfortunately, the friction between colleges and the pros was destined to carry on for several more years.

6

"I nearly went broke a half-dozen times"

(1922–1923)

Leo Lyons and representatives from 17 other member clubs of the APFA gathered for their summer meeting at the Hollenden Hotel in Cleveland on June 24 and 25, 1922. After a reading of the minutes from the January 28 meeting, the executive committee met in separate session for the purpose of reviewing applications for teams from Racine, Wisconsin, and Youngstown and LaRue, Ohio. The LaRue franchise was to feature former Canton Bulldog and original APFA president Jim Thorpe coaching a team made up entirely of Native American athletes. The team eventually became known as the Oorang Indians.

A fourth application was received from Curly Lambeau, captain of the Green Bay Packers, the team that had been expelled at the January meeting after it was discovered they had used college players during a game the preceding season. Lambeau applied under the premise that the team was no longer affiliated with the Acme Packing Company, under whose auspices the franchise had been ousted. After making his pitch to the owners and forking over the $1,500 reentry free, Lambeau and the Packers were back in.[1]

Lyons reported to the group that he still had not received the $800 Washington owner Tim Jordan was ordered to pay to cover the guarantee owed the Rochester club for the canceled game of December 4, 1921. A motion was made that the Senators be expelled from the association for failing to comply. That motion was summarily rejected, and it was instead decided to give Jordan notice that the franchise would be forfeited if payment was not made within 30 days. Jordan apparently had no plans of returning to the association and ultimately ignored the order.

Some of the owners were voicing their dissatisfaction with the name the organization had adopted at the previous meeting (NFA). The topic was opened again for another lengthy deliberation, with several attendees expressing their opinions.

"I wanted Major League Football," Lyons wrote in his journal. "Carr wanted 'National.' Jimmy [O'Donnell of Cleveland] wanted National Football Assoc. Majority wanted NFA."[2] But as was becoming de rigueur at these meetings, the winning voice belonged to Chicago mogul George Halas.

"I lacked enthusiasm for our name," Halas wrote in his autobiography. "In baseball, 'association' was applied to second-class teams. We were first-class. The Chicago Cubs baseball club belonged to the National League, not the American League. 'Professional' was superfluous. I proposed we change our name to the National Football League. My fellow members agreed."[3]

For an event that now seems so momentous, it received very little attention at the time. Several newspapers included the name change in their reports of the owners meeting, but none thought it important enough to include in the story's headlines:

FOOTBALL MEN HOLD MEETING

CLEVELAND, June 24.—Representatives of professional football from Rochester and Buffalo, N.Y., Canton, Akron, Cleveland, Columbus and Dayton, O[h]., Louisville, Ky., Chicago, Rock Island, Ill., and Minneapolis met here today and voted to change the name of the American Professional Football association to that of the National Football League.

These Amendments were made to the constitution:

Each club must post a forfeit of $1,000 that it will observe the rules.

Engagement of a player still at college will entail a fine of $500. A second offense will bring expulsion.

Discovery that a man is playing under a false name will bring permanent expulsion.

Players' contracts will be similar to those of professional baseball, including the reserve clause.

The season will open the first Sunday in October and continue until the Sunday after Thanksgiving.

A decision was reached to refrain from luring players out of college for the professional game.[4]

As was his habit, Lyons jotted down several items he wished to remember. "5 hour notice before train depart—weather," he wrote in reference to the decision that in the event of a weather-related cancellation, home teams must provide notice five hours prior to the visiting team's departure or else be responsible to pay the guarantee. "Must play at least 7 games. No more 13. Football season begins 1st Sun in Oct to Dec 10." He also sketched out several possible NFL logos in his journal, including a couple that were based on the emblem Thorpe had worn on his track shirt in the 1912 Olympics, and very closely resembled the one adopted by the league in 1940.[5]

* * *

The Rochester Jeffersons of 1922 were led by Joe Alexander, the All-Pro center whom Lyons had tapped to coach the

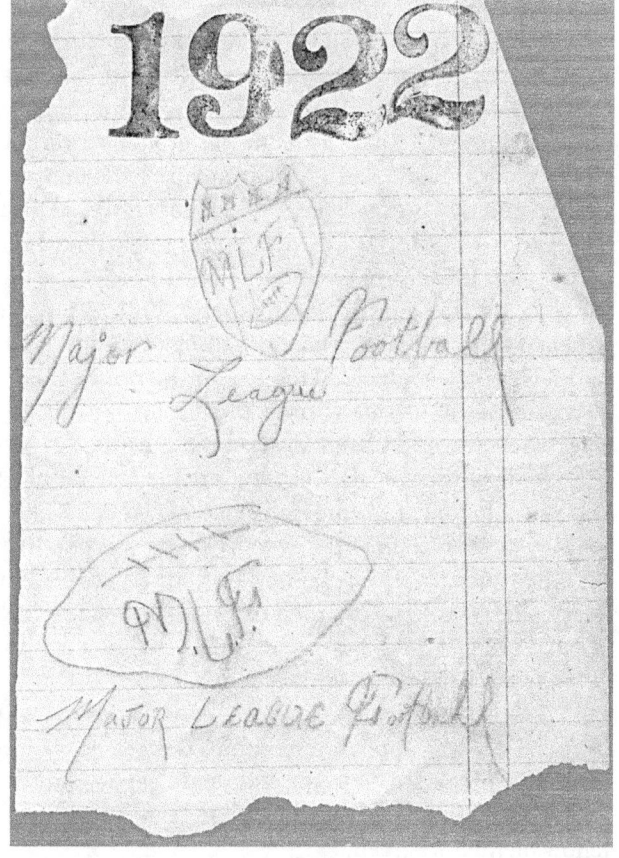

Examples of NFL emblems sketched by Leo Lyons at the time of the NFL meeting held in June 1922.

team at the end of the previous year. Alexander was able to use his considerable influence to recruit several of his former teammates from Syracuse to join him with the Big Red, including guards Frank Matteo and George "Tiny" Thompson, halfback Larry Weltman and tackle John Dooley. Two Orangemen from the 1921 Jeffs—backs Cliff Steele and Ray Witter—were retained.

Lyons and Alexander were very pleased to have Ben Boynton returning as well. Even though Boynton had been credited with playing in only three league games with the Jeffs in 1921, he was a spectacular performer whenever he was in the lineup. Rounding out the roster were returning veterans Bob Argus, Joe Bachmaier, Darby Lowery, Elmer "Spin" Roy, and Hank Smith, along with newly signed lineman Ralph Henricus, who had previously toiled as a member of All-Tonawanda.

While cobbling together the schedule for the upcoming season, Lyons reached out to Jim Thorpe about bringing his new Oorang Indian team to Rochester. Although the two were friends, Thorpe had no interest in visiting the Flower City. He remembered the puny crowds that had come out for games when he came through as a member of the minor league Akron Numatics.

"Jim says no to Roch.," Lyons wrote. "Roch. no good for sports of any kind," Thorpe said, adding something of which Leo had become painfully aware over the past two seasons: "Fans not interested—no money at ticket gate."

He couldn't argue Thorpe's point. Expenses consistently outpaced revenue from ticket sales at Jeffs games, causing Lyons to lose his shirt on a weekly basis. Football fans in Rochester—what there were of them—seemed more interested in local players and sandlot games than they did the famous teams with big-name players. Highly paid stars like Alexander, Boynton, Howard Berry, or Elmer Oliphant had little appeal to the average Rochester football enthusiast. Despite having come to that realization, Lyons continued to recruit the big names in hopes he could turn the tide.

* * *

Lyons had to be disheartened by the crowd that turned out—or perhaps more appropriately, *didn't* turn out—for the season opener. He had tried to give the locals everything they could have wanted but to no avail. He had his two biggest stars—Boynton and Alexander—returning to the fold. The remainder of the roster was an attractive mix of players from nearby Syracuse University and the sandlots of Rochester. He had kept ticket prices for Jeffs games lower than any other team in the league (50 cents for bleacher seats and $1 for grandstand).[6] The game itself was a matchup with traditional rival All-Syracuse. Even the weather, an unseasonably warm autumn afternoon, gave Lyons cause for optimism. He was certain this game was going to have fans breaking down fences to get in.

Sadly, a mere 600 souls passed through the Baseball Park turnstiles, easily the smallest assemblage in the Jeffs' 14 home games since joining the league in 1920. Lyons had done everything he could. The city of Rochester just did not seem interested in major league football.

Despite his disappointment, there was still a game to be played. The Jeffs took a 7–0 lead in the first quarter on a touchdown run by Larry Weltman. Bob Argus extended the lead to 13–0 in the third. The game devolved into a defensive struggle in the fourth with neither team able to score, and the Jeffs held fast for the 13-point win.

Considering the paltry turnout for the season opener, Lyons was more than happy to be leaving the home city for a road trip that would last nearly two months. Since there was no money to be made in Rochester, the Jeffs could take their chances on guarantees as a visiting team in other cities.

First up was a jaunt to northeast Ohio for a meeting on October 8 with the Akron Pros. At some point during the week leading up to this game, Lyons caught wind of some derisive remarks made to the local press by Frank Nied, co-owner of the Akron club. Nied was still sore at having lost a bidding war to Lyons for Ben Boynton's services the previous season and decided to go public with his grievances.

"Unusual week," wrote Lyons. "Nied speaking bad about me and my team in papers. He has disliked me since I signed Boynton away from him last year."

Rather than become upset, Lyons decided to use the opportunity to employ a bit of skulduggery and stoke some controversy, maybe get a little free publicity for the league. "I wrote him a letter that I signed Miller, Little, Wray, French to see what he would put in paper. Stir it up."

The Jeffs departed Rochester Saturday the 7th aboard the overnight train destined for Akron. When they arrived the next morning, they learned that heavy rains had rendered the gridiron at Elk's Field unusable. Rather than cancel, the teams agreed to postpone until Thursday the 12th. This caused problems for some of the players, who had work and family commitments back east.

"Spent Sunday calling players families and work bosses to see if they could miss work," Lyons wrote. "Half the team traveled back to Roch because of work—Weltman, Dooley, Roy, Smith, Argus. Half the team remained in Akron with me—Joe A, Thompson, Matteo, Lowery, Steele, Sawyer (had to bribe many of their bosses)." Those who remained in Akron during the week held workouts at the field whenever possible. Lyons recorded that the players also spent time visiting local schools to "talk football with their teams."[7]

The downtime in the Rubber City afforded Lyons the opportunity to peruse some of the local newspapers, and he liked what he was seeing. The *Akron Beacon* reported an eyewitness account of Nied receiving Lyons' mendacious telegram the day before the Jeffs' arrival:

ROCHESTER JEFFS SIGN THREE ALL-AMERICAN "GRID" STARS
Heinie Miller, Lud Wray and Lou Little of All-American Fame to Be Here Sunday—French of West Point Also Added to Jeff's Lineup

A TELEGRAPH BOY rushed up to Frank Nied, owner of the Akron Pros, and handed him a telegram.

Without opening it, Nied said, "Well, I'll lay you two to one that this is from that bird in Rochester."

Turning the envelope over, he continued, "He's got a lotta nerve sending telegrams with the team he's got. When we get through with those birds tomorrow, he won't have the price of a telegram. Ha, ha!"

Nied rambled on with his talk and started opening the telegram. He unfolded it before him and started to read.

He stumbled back a few feet almost in a faint, shuddered and made a weak cry for water. He shoved the telegram over to the writer.

It read like this:

"Have just closed contracts with Lud Wray, Heinie Miller, Lou Little and French. Will be with me Sunday in Akron."

It was signed by the manager of the Rochester Jeffersons.

Nied quickly recovered and for the next few minutes the air was blue, while the Pros owner took pains to explain his idea of the Rochester Jeffs, omitting no details in his explanation.

"Wow, get Brewer," he shouted. "Get Coach Brewer. For the love of mud, what'll we do? What if they beat us? That big bum."[8]

"It worked!" Lyons recorded in his journal. "My plan to create attention for game—paper full of pregame summary in Akron here. League needs more controversy—needs headlines more than just stats! Bad press not bad! Bulldogs coming to watch now. This league needs more headlines!!! Use newspapers—more pictures of games interesting players and story lines give fans something to look forward to on Sundays."[9]

Weather conditions had not improved much by the time the teams took the field on Thursday, which resulted in a disappointingly low turnout. However, the 2,000 hardy souls who did venture out to Elk's Field that day were treated to a whale of a game. The teams traded blows through a scoreless first quarter, but the Pros took a 6–0 lead in the second when Red Daum hit Scotty Bierce with a forward pass in the Rochester end zone. The Jeffersons stormed back in the third quarter, going up 13–6 on touchdowns by Bob Argus and Spin Roy. It appeared Rochester had the game in hand until six minutes left in the final frame. The Pros stopped a Jeff drive deep inside Rochester territory, forcing a punt. The Rochester kicker backed up behind his own goal line and received the center snap. Al Nesser broke through the Rochester forward wall, blocked the punt and fell on the ball in the end zone, closing the Jefferson lead to a single point (13–12). Untz Brewer's extra-point attempt was blocked, but an official ruled Spin Roy had jumped offside prior to the snap. The point was awarded to Akron, and the game ended in a 13–13 tie.

Lyons was livid. "Sloppy game," he wrote, adding, "bad call—calls Roy offsides. Get kick to tie game. Should have won game. Team hungry to win."[10]

Tying Nied in such a fashion wasn't the only thing that stuck in Lyons' craw that week. The Akron magnate earned an additional last laugh when he shamelessly signed quarterback Cliff Steele away from the Jeffs shortly after the game. Steele had started in Boynton's place in the Akron tilt and made a favorable impression on Nied and Akron's head coach Untz Brewer. He had been playing for Rochester without a contract, which essentially made him a free agent. He didn't hesitate when Nied offered him one with the Pros.[11]

Things weren't going to get any easier for the frustrated Jeffs as they moved on to Chicago where they were scheduled to face the Bears three days later. The Bears won the league championship in 1921, but the Jeffs had played them on even ground when the teams faced off on October 16. Despite coming up on the short end of a 16–13 final, Lyons remembered that Jeff team as the finest he had ever assembled. With a roster at least the equal of the 1921 aggregation, he had to like his team's chances in this year's matchup.

Meanwhile, Chicago-based Wilson Sporting Goods had been working on the new ball design discussed by Lyons, Halas, Dutch Sternaman, and Arnold Horween the previous October. The company delivered one (or more) of its A-5x prototypes to Cubs Park in time for this contest, giving Halas and Lyons an opportunity to have some of the game's elite players put the ball through its paces. Lyons noted gathering several players from both teams before the kickoff to take part in a skills test to see which model—the A-5x or the standard Spalding J-5—performed the best. He drew a chart in which he listed the individual players trying their hand at four basic football tasks, which included passing, catching, carrying, and kicking. Four Bears (George Halas, Pete

Stinchcomb, Joey Sternaman, and Dutch Sternaman) and five Jeffersons (Ben Boynton, Bob Argus, Joe Alexander, Chris Lehrer, and Lyons) took part. Lyons did not record how many trials each player had; his chart only providing each player's preference for a ball as it corresponded to each task.

Spalding J-5 — Wilson A-5x prototype
Practice before game Chicago
Comparison

	PASS	CATCH	RUN	Kick
Halas	S	W	S	S
Stinchcomb	W	W	W	S
J. Sternaman	S	S	S	S
E. Sternaman	W	W	W	S
Boynton	W	W	S	S
Argus	W	W	S	S
Alexander	S	W	W	W
Lehrer	W	W	S	S
Lyons	W	W	W	

The chart shows the majority of the group preferred the narrower Wilson prototype for passing and catching. The plumper J-5, the most common ball in use at the time, was preferred for kicking. One can only imagine the spectacle that would be made of such a pregame event in today's NFL, having star players displaying their individual talents and giving their opinions on football equipment. In 1922, however, it didn't even merit a mention in any of the papers reporting on the game. But if any of the 7,000 fans who passed through the turnstiles on this balmy autumn Sunday arrived early enough, they were treated to what amounts to an early version of the modern-day Pro Bowl Skills Competition.

With all that talent on the field, fans were assured that a barn burner was in the offing. They weren't disappointed. Just as they had one day shy of one year ago, the Bears and Jeffs stood toe-to-toe for three solid quarters. It was a defensive struggle, with neither team able to get within striking distance of the other's goal line until Chicago broke through late in the fourth. With time winding down, the Bears drove deep into Jeffs territory. At the Rochester four-yard line, the Bears went into a spread formation that flummoxed the Jeff defenders. Halfback Pete Stinchcomb took a lateral and plunged through for the touchdown. Joey Sternaman booted the extra point to give Chicago a 7–0 lead, which stuck as the final score.

The Jeffersons entrained the next day for Rock Island, Illinois, which was the western-most city in the league at that time. Upon arriving late Tuesday afternoon, coach Alexander trekked over to nearby St. Ambrose College to arrange use of the school's field for team practices. He also arranged for the St. Ambrose team to scrimmage the Jeffs during the week.[12]

6. "I nearly went broke a half-dozen times"

With Cliff Steele gone and Ben Boynton's status uncertain after suffering a severe charley horse in the Bears game, Lyons hit the wires in search of another quarterback. It was a close call, but Lyons managed to sign Dick King, the former Harvard All-American, on Saturday, barely 24 hours before Sunday's scheduled kickoff. King had been a first-team selection by Walter Camp in 1915 and later played professionally with several teams, including the Hammond Pros (1919–1921) and Milwaukee Badgers (1922).

A drizzling rain soaked the field at Douglas Park and made for precarious footing, which seemed to affect the visitors more adversely than the home team. The Islanders managed touchdowns in the second and third quarters and two in the fourth in rolling to a seemingly easy 26–0 win. It was a brutal game with players from both squads getting hurt.

"Lots of injuries at game," Lyons wrote in his journal. "Hank S. carried off field. Hurt bad. Talked to Conzelman, Flanagan—nice guys. RI used my J&J kit [Johnson & Johnson first aid kit]. J. Conzelman said he wants one of those!"

Chart drawn by Leo Lyons marking each player's preferences during a skills test prior to the Jeffs-Bears game held at Cubs Park in Chicago, October 15, 1922.

The leg injury wasn't the only misfortune Smith suffered that afternoon. "Hank hit with beer bottle in back of head from stupid guy after game. One of the Independents players ran over and knocked guy out cold before anyone else got over there."[13]

The 26-point loss was the worst the Jeffs had suffered since losing to Buffalo 28–0 the previous October.

It was then up to the western shores of Lake Michigan for a matchup with the Racine Legion. The Legion were in their first year in the NFL after spending several years as an independent outfit. They were entering this game at 1–3, their only win coming against the Green Bay Packers three weeks earlier. The Jeffs traded blows with their hosts throughout the first half and shared a precarious 0–0 tie at halftime. The defensive struggle continued into the second half, with neither team able to find the other's end zone. The Legion, however, were able to take advantage of three successful field goals by captain Hank Gillo and claim a 9–0 triumph.

After a month on the road and having only two substitutes available for this outing, the Jeffs were just plumb tuckered out. Lyons' observations after the game tell the tale of his road-weary team.

"Jeffs no depth. Can't afford depth like other teams. Players tired by 2nd half of games—playing both sides of line—no breaks. Other teams can rest top talent."[14]

The grueling schedule was set to continue at Cleveland the following Sunday, but that contest was canceled after the Cleveland management failed to post its forfeit guarantee with the league, leaving the Jeffs with an open weekend. A game scheduled a week later with a semipro team from Youngstown, Ohio, was also canceled.

Even though the open dates meant no revenue for the Jeffs, it did give the players time to rest and tend to their personal lives. In the meantime, to fill the void left by the Youngstown cancellation, Lyons tried to set up a game in Buffalo against the semipro Prospects. Lyons was asked by a reporter from the *Democrat & Chronicle* why the Jeffs seemed to be avoiding games in their home city.

"I am afraid to take a chance," he replied bluntly. "Rochester is dead as far as football is concerned—especially when placed against the smaller cities of the west."

He pointed out that smaller cities like Rock Island, Kenosha, and Racine, all with populations in the 50,000 range, regularly drew 3,000–7,000 to a game. "I nearly went broke a half-dozen times trying to play football here for the fans will not turn out. Maybe later in the season."[15]

A funny thing happened on the way to Buffalo, however. Since the Jeffersons were a member of the NFL, they needed the blessing of the Buffalo All-Americans to play a nonleague team in their home city. League president Joe Carr advised Lyons that he had no objection to the Jeff-Prospect contest so long as the Buffalo management was agreeable. But Chester McNeil, representing the All-Americans in the absence of his brother Frank, refused to waive his team's territorial rights. McNeil argued that the All-Americans had a meeting of their own pending with the Jeffs and the outcome of the Prospects game could adversely affect attendance for their game. Despite Lyons' pleas, McNeil would not relent, and the Jeffs' game with the Prospects was nixed.

The Jeffs resumed their road trip the following weekend with two games on the itinerary. The first stop found them in southeast Pennsylvania on Saturday, November 18, to face the Conshohocken Athletic Club, the self-proclaimed state champions. A fair-sized crowd of 3,000 turned out in a drizzling rain, only to see the locals surrender a 6–0 defeat to the invaders from New York.

It was then on to the nation's capital to face the Washington Pros, the former APFA member team managed by Lyons' nemesis, Tim Jordan, with whom he had apparently reached some type of settlement. Jordan had opted to let his franchise lapse after the 1921 season and continue on as an independent team. The Pros' star player all year had been none other than Ben Boynton, the one and the same who was in and out of the Jeffersons' lineup much of the past two seasons. However, the former Purple Streak of Williams College was nowhere to be found this particular Sunday afternoon.

Despite an impotent offense that was averaging a mere three points per game, the Jeffs had usually managed to remain competitive with a stingy defense that was yielding—aside from the Rock Island drubbing—a little more than seven per game. And so it was against the Pros as the teams battled through three scoreless quarters before the Jeffs broke the stalemate late in the final frame. The Pros found themselves hemmed deep inside their own territory and prepared to punt. The kick was blocked and rolled into the end zone. Rochester tackle Hank Smith fell on the errant pigskin to give the Jeffs a six-point lead. Dick King added the extra point to make it a 7–0 score. The Pros responded on their next possession, resorting to the forward pass to move the ball quickly to the Jeffs' 30. From there, halfback Dutch Leighty connected with Bullets Walson in the Rochester end zone, pulling the Pros to within a point. The try for the extra point failed, and the Jeffs escaped with a narrow 7–6 triumph.

The Jeffs stood at 2–0 in the second leg of their road trip but were now heading back to the Keystone State for a tilt with the high-flying Frankford Yellow Jackets. The Jackets were an independent team representing a neighborhood in the northeastern section of Philadelphia. Their roster comprised an abundance of former college stars, including several players who had deserted the Buffalo All-Americans midway through the 1921 campaign after a financial dispute with team management. So far this season, the Yellow Jackets had compiled a record of eight wins and no losses while outscoring their opponents by a combined 235–9.

Ten thousand Philadelphians made their way out to Brown's Field for the game, easily the largest gathering the Jeffs had seen the entire season. They kept it close, but the Yellow Jackets were just too much, sending the Jeffs packing with a 20–7 defeat.

The exhausted Redshirts made their way back to Rochester and prepared to play the first game in their home city since October 1. Lyons had tentatively booked his club to play against the All-Americans at Buffalo on November 19, but the game was never made official by the league. The All-Americans instead hosted Akron that day, forcing the Jeffs to spend the weekend on the road at Conshohocken and Washington, D.C. There was no love lost between the teams to begin with, and McNeil's efforts at scuttling two games from the Jeffs' schedule (November 12 with the Prospects and November 19 with the All-Americans) only compounded the dislike.

A crowd of 2,200 came out to witness the grudge match. Even Rochester Mayor Clarence D. Van Zandt made an appearance, having been invited to boot the ceremonial kickoff prior to the game. Noticeably absent, however, were Alexander and Boynton, both of whom were advertised to be in the lineup. As a result, the Jeffs were forced to start the contest with the bare minimum of 11 players on the field. They never stood a chance but made a game of it, limiting the powerful All-Americans to just three touchdowns in going down to a 21–0 defeat.

The crowd, already displeased by the no-show of the team's biggest stars, grew more unruly as the game progressed. Lyons noted in his journal, "Drunks on field. Needed city police. Mayor NOT HAPPY. Argus crushed one guy for coming on field. Police stopped one fan. Had gun—was arrested. Need better barriers to protect field." The last notation emphasized Lyons' greatest concern: "Looks bad for league."[16]

The loss to Buffalo brought the Jeffs' third season to a close. The 0–4–1 record posted against fellow NFL clubs was easily their worst yet, good for a second-to-last finish out of 18 teams. The Jeffs' offense averaged a paltry 2.6 points per game, which was also the second-worst among teams having played at least five games, while the defense gave up an average of 15.2 points.

Despite the team's poor record, Doc Alexander and Ben Boynton repeated as All-Pros (Boynton even though he was credited with playing just one league game).[17]

The indifference demonstrated by the people of Rochester had grown from troublesome to chronic. In fact, it was so bad that after drawing just 600 to the season opener, Lyons took his team on an extended road trip that ultimately lasted two full months. When they returned home for the finale against the Buffalo All-Americans, a game that should have drawn a large crowd, only 2,200 turned out. While Lyons was quick to attribute the lack of local interest to loyalty toward sandlot and regional teams, a writer for the *Rochester Democrat & Chronicle* placed the responsibility squarely of the shoulders of the team's owner.

"Each year the Jeffersons try to crop out on the professional football field as a regular eleven," the editorial began, "but Rochester fans still have to find out that they have a pro team in this city. Usually, the Jeffs just flop down and die and no one gives a bang, for few people go to the games."

The writer did not mince words as he laid out his case: "Leo Lyons, manager of the team, is to blame for the condition existing in pro football in Rochester, and no other. He has had backing—especially last season—but he has failed to come through with the promises that he made at the start of the season." The writer cited Lyons' optimism at the beginning of the season and pronouncements of star players signed. "But when the multitude goes to the games the stars are missing. Why? No one seems to know why and most persons don't care, except the few who go to the games who claim that they have been gyped [*sic*] out of their money."

The season finale against Buffalo was given as a prime example. "The Jeffs played the Buffalo All-American team the same day that the University of Rochester and Hobart College played last fall; the attendance at the game was around 2,500 while the varsity drew about 5,000. Joe Alexander and Benny Boynton were booked to play with the Jeffs. When game time came around no one could discover Boynton or Alexander on the field and a yelp went up: 'Where's Boynton? Where's Alexander?'"

"Mr. Lyons was standing on the sidelines with a morose look on his face, looked up with a startled expression when reporters asked him about the two stellar lights who had been booked to play, and finally said: 'Look here.' He showed a telegram from Benny Boynton saying [he] was unable to play football for the rest of the season because of an illness. Yet Boynton played with the Frankford Yellow Jackets the next Sunday—two days later."

"'Where's Alexander?' was the next question hurled at Lyons. 'I don't know,' was the reply. 'I thought he was going to be here.' It developed later that Alexander had taken a team to Binghamton to play a pro eleven there, and he explained then that he wasn't sure of his money in Rochester, but he was in Binghamton, that's why he left the Jeffs flat."

The writer then offered some unsolicited advice he felt Lyons should follow if he wished to make a serious go of major league football in his beloved home city. Whether the writer had a basic understanding of economics is not known.

"If Lyons is going to make pro football a sport which can be enjoyed by thousands, he will have to follow different tactics this season [1923]. He will have to bring these stellar players here and pay them what they ask, so that there will be no quibbling; he will have to take his losses like a man, and they may amount to $5,000 or $6,000 for the season; if he lives up to his promises he probably will have enough support next season so that he will be able to make a little money."

It was clear the writer was also not aware of Lyons' efforts to bring in marquee teams (the Canton Bulldogs and Oorang Indians, for example), only to be rebuffed for concern there was no money to be made in Rochester. "Some strong pro teams must be brought here if Lyons hopes to attract football fans of Rochester. Outside of the Buffalo All-Americans last fall, there has been only one real pro football team brought to Rochester, and that was the Columbus Panhandles, a team which has finished near the bottom of the professional league each year. If Lyons would bring Dayton, Canton, Rock Island, Cleveland or one of the Chicago or Milwaukee teams here this year—maybe several of them—he probably would get patronage—provided, also, that his own advertised stars showed up for each game."

The editorial also addressed Lyons' assertion that the team had not received an appropriate amount of publicity from the local press. "Why is that? Simply because he advertises stars and they do not appear here. Not once has this happened but a dozen times. Lyons need not be worried that he will not receive enough newspaper publicity—unless he follows the same tactics that have been used in other years. He will be accorded full support—but he must live up to his advance agreements."[18]

Lyons responded with a letter of his own, which appeared in the *Democrat & Chronicle* a week later. As to claims of false advertising, he explained, "I have managed the Big Red team of the Jeffs for a matter of about ten years and during that time have striven with might and main to give Rochester real football. There have been times when players have failed to appear when their names were used but in all my connection with football I have never used a player's name if I was not sure he was going to appear. Lou Usher had a habit of turning over in bed on Sunday morning in Albany where he was to catch a train at 6 A.M. and then sending me a wire later in the morning that he had missed the train. After pulling this trick on two different occasions he was released."

With regard to Boynton and Alexander's nonappearance at the November 30 game against Buffalo, Lyons argued that money had nothing to do with it, as the players were fully compensated. Instead, he attributed the no-shows to misinformation.

"Last Thanksgiving Boynton and Alexander failed to appear in the game against the Buffalo All-Americans and I have since found out that fraternal influences kept them out of here owing to the feeling that was aroused among local college men by statement of an afternoon paper that 'the Jeffs had thrown down the gauntlet and were going to see whether Rochester would support pro football or college football.' Such a statement was of course nonsensical because while I believe that five years from now pro football will be on a plane with major league baseball, I never expect to see it even compare with the college game in matter of spirit because the two are as far apart as the two poles. Boynton and Alexander received their full compensation last season. I handled over $16,000 last fall in two months and while I did not make any profit, I did not lose anything and the players received their money."[19]

While the quarrel seems to have ended there, it could not have looked good in the eyes of the local fans Lyons needed so desperately to come out to the games. With attendance by this time averaging in the neighborhood of 1,400 per game, however, Lyons saw no alternative but to schedule an increasingly fewer number of home games for his team.[20] Within three years, the Jeffs would be playing exclusively as a road team. Road games, if nothing else, provided guarantees that home games could not.

Still, no matter how outside observers saw it, the bottom line was, Lyons had tried everything to attract fans to the games with no success. When attendance didn't generate enough income to cover expenses, it was Lyons who bore the loss. He was not an independently wealthy businessman like some of his fellow owners, nor was he able to attract a reliable corporate sponsor to underwrite costs. He had tried a number of times to enlist George Eastman, the founder of the Eastman Kodak Company, to back the team. The famous entrepreneur and philanthropist simply was not interested in supporting athletic pursuits.

It seemed Lyons was more concerned with the financial footing of his beloved Jeffs than he was with maintaining blissful domesticity. He struggled with the concept of prioritizing, often placing concerns of the team ahead of his family. There was no question that he was willing to work hard and sacrifice to make ends meet, which he demonstrated time and again. In addition to managing the football team, Lyons pulled double duty working as a clerk at Rochester City Hall and as a laborer with the local telephone company. To keep household expenses at minimum, Leo, Catherine, and their two young daughters continued to live with her family on Frost Avenue in the city's 19th Ward. Meanwhile, he was offering star players contracts he couldn't afford, taking time off from work to accompany the team on road trips, spending money on trains and accommodations while attending league meetings, and footing the bill for any other expenditures incurred by the team.

He had to find another source of income or his team was finished.

"Again—need better players," he had written after the season-ending loss to Buffalo, adding, "more bootlegging."[21]

Wait. What was that? Bootlegging? Yes! With money in constant short supply, Lyons was at the point where he was willing to do just about anything to raise the funds he needed to keep the dream alive. Prohibition, in the form of the 18th Amendment to the U.S. Constitution, which banned the manufacture, transportation, and sale of intoxicating liquors, went into effect in January 1920. Once the domain of legitimate business, the liquor, wine, and beer industries had been taken over by organized crime syndicates, Appalachian moonshiners, and any number of everyday private stock producers seeking to make a buck on the sale of illicit spirits. It provided ample opportunity for daring young men (and women) who were willing to transport the contraband from town to town and still to speakeasy for a cut of the action.

Leo Lyons was one such young man. Although there is no record of exactly when he became involved in the running of bootleg booze, Lyons recalled that his career as an outlaw lasted for a five-year period between 1921 and 1925.

He committed the memories of his desperado days to paper in 1952:

> Made a lot of extra dough rum running along Lake Ontario during the 20s. The pickup point was exactly 13 miles from the shore in Webster. Our navigator always got us to the particular spot. There would be a larger sized vessel ready to unload its cargo. The money was already paid and we loaded up the various spirits and headed to Irondequoit. About a mile offshore was the "watch area." There would be 2 or 3 boats lurking about from agents from FBI, Coast Guard and various police agencies. We would slowly make our way toward shore, using binoculars. We would, depending on the site or feel, head to either Ides Cove or Oklahoma Beach. Ides Cove or Secret Cove could either be a dropoff to boathouse or simply unload everything into the shallow water along the edge. Other option was sneak into boathouse on Webster sandbar where we could unload in garage with trap door. We were shot at twice by agents but escaped both well.
>
> Our crew of 6 included different players from different years 1921 to 1925. One player worked at a brewery which made things easier: Distribution. I, along with a few players, had

friends in high places from working at City hall. We were caught twice and escaped incarceration because of friends. Other associates and fellow bootleggers were not so fortunate. It seemed most agents were lax except for a certain 3 men. If they got you, you were caput. We always made sure they were not anywhere near me or the boys. Looking back now, I should not have done it, the risks outweighed the reward. But the money was hard to ignore.[22]

Just how much Joe Carr was aware of Lyons' extracurricular activities is not certain, but even the notoriously straitlaced league president knew it was necessary to turn a blind eye to questionable behavior if it benefited the organization in the long run. As an example, when Chicago businessman Charles Bidwill purchased the Cardinals franchise in 1933, he was already known to have ties to notorious gangster Al Capone.[23]

"In truth," observed author Jeff Davis in his book *Papa Bear*, "when Carr realized in 1925 that his National Football League was ready for the big time and needed a New York team, he didn't blink when a bookmaker and horseplayer named Tim Mara came up with the $500 franchise fee. The same held in 1933 when another racetrack sharpie named Arthur Rooney cashed in a huge parlay bet worth several hundred thousand dollars after a great day at Saratoga to buy the new Pittsburgh Pirates franchise."[24]

Carr had also looked the other way when he knew that Lyons was using an undergraduate in a game against his own Columbus Panhandles. It is possible that Carr, who, like Lyons, was the owner of an ever-struggling franchise, saw a little of himself in the man from Rochester. There is no denying their willingness to do whatever it took to make their teams and, more important, the league successful. Sometimes it was necessary to bend the rules and take a few risks.

One fellow owner who was fully aware of Lyons' dabblings in the underworld was George Halas. The two had become good friends in the short time they had been acquainted, usually finding themselves in lockstep when it came to league matters. Doing business in the mob-ruled city of Chicago, Halas was all too familiar with the dangers that surely awaited his Rochester counterpart if he continued down the path of vice. The well-connected Papa Bear offered Lyons an opportunity not only to get out of the rum-running racket but also to earn a better living than he did working his legitimate jobs with the city and the telephone company.

"Halas in '22 introduced me to 2 men with the Hockaday Paint Co.," Lyons recalled in 1936. "George wanted me to find safer extra work, bootlegging not so safe. He said it was a lucrative business and Hockaday was looking for someone to sell and market their washable wall paint in N.Y. After the 22 season ended in Dec., I met with George at the Hockaday Co. on Carroll Avenue in Chicago. Also present were 2 men with Hockaday, Thompson and Haas (I think). I agreed to attend several classes there during the winter months."[25]

Lyons had no way of knowing at the time that Halas was setting him on the path by which he would build a very successful business and provide for his family for years to come.

* * *

The annual owners meeting was held January 20, 1923, at the Hotel Sherman in Chicago. Lyons, doubtless unable to get away from his day job(s) and mounting responsibilities at home, did not attend. Among the highlights of the meeting was the reelection of President Joe Carr, Vice President John Dunn, and Secretary-Treasurer Carl Storck and the Canton Bulldogs being named champions of the 1922 season. The

Rochester Jeffersons 1923 National Football League membership certificate.

league voted to place a maximum admission fee of 50 cents for children under the age of 16. It was hoped the lower fare would allow more young men to attend games and build sustainable fan bases across the league. For the first time in its short history, the league took steps to regulate uniforms as a committee was appointed with the purpose of examining "the colors used by various clubs in their jerseys and socks, on account of confusion in the past." With most teams wearing dark jerseys, it became nearly impossible to tell which teams players were on in games played in bad weather or muddy fields.[26]

* * *

The year 1923 was transitional for the Rochester Jeffersons. The lack of capital prevented Lyons from signing well-known college men like Howard Berry, Doc Alexander, Elmer Oliphant, and Ben Boynton. As a result, more than half of this season's lineup (11 players out of 21) was comprised of men who never played a down on a university gridiron. The only new signees with college experience were halfback Tom Kasper, formerly of Notre Dame, and Alfred "Shag" Sheard, a triple-threat quarterback from St. Lawrence University in Canton, New York.

The campaign opened with a meeting at the Baseball Park against a sandlot squad from Hornell, New York, a small city about 70 miles south of Rochester. In front of just 680 paying customers, the Jeffs rolled to an easy 46–0 victory. Newcomers Sheard and Kasper led the way, scoring two touchdowns each.

The Jeffs then hit the road for what could only be described as a complete disaster of a trip, as the team was outscored by an aggregate 149–0 in the first three games alone. The first drubbing came at the hands of Chris O'Brien's Chicago Cardinals.

When the Jeffersons arrived at Chicago's Normal Park prior to the game, they found a field that Lyons described as "half grass-dirt, looked like a sandlot." The Cardinals, however, with a lineup that included famous All-American backfield men Paddy Driscoll and Arnold Horween (playing under the pseudonym A. McMahon), seemed to have no problem finding their footing on the rough terrain.

"Outplayed badly," Lyons wrote after the game. "Couldn't stop Driscoll."

Driscoll was indeed a one-man wrecking crew, scoring 27 points on four touchdowns and three conversions in leading the Cards to a 60–0 romp. It seemed the only time the Jeffs were able to slow down the hero of the 1919 Rose Bowl was when at one point they drove him into the stands with a particularly brutal tackle.

"Driscoll knocked out of bounds into crowd," Lyons observed. "Think he killed a fan. Fence did not fare well. The umpires shirt was red with blood from fan. I think someone fired a gun at one of the houses overlooking the field—play stopped!"[27]

It was then on to Rock Island, where the Independents gave the Jeffs a 56–0 thrashing.

"Embarrassing!!!" wrote Lyons. "56–0. Never again."

As a result of cancellations and open weekends, the Jeffs did not play again for nearly five weeks, but when they returned to action, it was more of the same. The time off had given Lyons a chance to do some recruiting, but the only name player he was able to sign was tackle Stan Keck, a two-time All-America selection from Princeton.

The Jeffs traveled to Philadelphia to face the always tough Yellow Jackets, who featured former Jeff head coach Doc Alexander in their lineup. The Hornets were rolling through another successful campaign, standing at 5–0–2 after seven starts, with their two ties being 0–0 deadlocks. The Jeffs never stood a chance, suffering a third straight skunking, 33–0.

A day after the Frankford defeat, the Jeffs traveled 100 miles north to take on another independent aggregation called the Wilkes-Barre Panthers. Led by hard-driving backfield man Tony Latone, more than half of the Panthers roster consisted of players from the very same Yellow Jackets the Jeffs had played the day before, including Butch Spagna, Lou Little, Johnny Scott, Pat Smith, Bull Lowe, and Bunny Corcoran. Somehow, the Redshirts were able to make a game of it this time, coming out on the short end of a 10–3 decision.

The Jeffs returned home from their ill-fated trip with no game scheduled the following weekend. Lyons was not about to let a potential payday pass by, however, so he went right to work in trying to secure a game for his team. On Thursday the 22nd, after exhaustive wheeling and dealing over the wires, Lyons announced that he had arranged to bring the Toledo Maroons to Rochester that Saturday. The timing worked well for the Maroons, who were already scheduled to meet the Buffalo All-Americans on Sunday. They could simply leave Ohio a day earlier than planned and play two games in the area instead of just one.

The timing was fortuitous for the Jeffs as well, as there were no other college or sandlot games scheduled for that day, leaving them as the only option for lovers of football in the Flower City.

"The absence of other big grid games in Western New York makes the game of much more interest as it gives Rochester sport lovers a chance to see these men at no sacrifice to the teams that they usually follow," read the *Democrat & Chronicle*. "Syracuse and Cornell are not scheduled for the region and the great number of fans that trek to the bulwarks of these teams will have nothing to do but go down to the horse show paddock in order to see this exhibition."[28] There was more good news for Big Red fans as Lyons announced the signing of tackle Jim Welsh and end Jim Leonard, star players from Colgate University. The pair had just completed their college eligibility the previous week after leading Colgate to an upset victory over Syracuse. They arrived Friday evening and would be in the lineup for Saturday's game.

The Maroons took the game's initial lead in the first quarter with a touchdown pass from Dutch Lauer to Si Seyfrit. The extra-point attempt was no good, leaving the visitors with a 6–0 advantage. Shag Sheard then took control of the proceedings, interspersing long runs and nifty passing to put the Jeffersons in scoring position midway through the second period. With the ball resting deep in Toledo territory, Sheard flipped a short pass to end Hal Clark, who tumbled into the end zone to tie the score. The conversion attempt failed, and the teams retired to the locker rooms with the score knotted at six apiece. The Jeffs moved the ball well in the third quarter and were within striking distance of the Toledo goal line before a fumble turned the ball over to the Maroons. Tillie Voss returned the pigskin all the way to the Rochester 30, setting up a touchdown run by Cowboy Hill that put Toledo ahead by six. The Jeffs never recovered, however, and the Maroons held on to win, 12–6.

Despite losing, the game had been a hit with local fans. With no other games being played in the vicinity that day, the team had the city's undivided attention. The Jeffs played well and all of the men advertised to be there actually were there. Suddenly, the city was abuzz with Jeff fever.

It was no secret that the Jeffersons had never enjoyed the community support or fiscal advantages of, say, the Bears, Cardinals, or Packers. Lyons himself was not a businessman or skilled promoter. Prior to the 1921 season, he brought in the well-connected Rochester entrepreneur and politician John R. Powers to act as team president in hopes that he could drum up support for the Jeffs. That experiment, however, failed to bear fruit and the Jeffs continued to—quite literally—wallow in the red. Lyons continued to seek support from the city's local businesses, and it appears the success of the Toledo game was enough to finally convince some of his well-heeled friends that the Jeffs were an important community asset. With "Do it for Rochester" as its rallying cry, a group of prominent sports enthusiasts met on Tuesday, November 27, with the intention of creating a stock company to support and promote the football team. The group was led by John W. Jardine (vice president of the Genesee Valley Trust Company), Joseph Scanlon (Mohawk Tire Company), and Percy Durnherr (One Piece Paper Box Company), all of whom Lyons was familiar with through his involvement in the Knights of Columbus, Rochester Chamber of Commerce, and other civic organizations.

The *Democrat & Chronicle* reported:

ROCHESTER GRID FANS PLAN TO BACK PRO FOOTBALL HERE
Local Business Men Meet Today to Discuss 1924 Campaign—May Play on Saturday

Professional football made so many friends in Rochester last Saturday by its great exhibition between the Toledo Maroons and Rochester Jeffersons that a number of business men in this city will organize a stock company at a meeting today for the express purpose of promoting a game here on Saturday if a suitable opponent can be found for the Jeffersons. The company will then elect officers and take in a limited number of prominent lovers of the gridiron sport who are located in industrial firms of Rochester for the development of next year's team.

The game on Saturday will probably show the Akron Pros or the Buffalo All-Americans here if either one of those elevens can be booked. Arrangements will be made today or tomorrow for the appearance of one of these two leading teams of the National Professional League. The Buffalo All-Americans tied the Toledo Maroons on Sunday in Buffalo, 3 to 3, in a game that was featured by great defensive playing of both forward lines.

Big Plans for 1924

Next year, the organizers of the new movement for the development of a team to represent Rochester in the Professional league will place players of reputation in good positions in the industrial firms of the city so that these men will not be recruited for each game but will be able to attend daily practice under tight supervision of the team's management. This method is practiced by the Canton Bulldogs, the Chicago Cardinals and other teams in the league, and results in the fans of those cities receiving the best football attractions offered by the pro game.

Rochester already has a large number of men who are capable of playing in the fastest of gridiron circles and with the addition of enough men to round out a good squad of practice sessions and substitutes, the city could be as well represented on the football field as in other lines of sport, which have brought renown in the city, and advertised it throughout the country.[29]

The new group showed initial promise when it arranged a game with the Buffalo All-Americans for the following Saturday. It would be the second prominent pro team to visit Rochester in two weeks. The All-Americans were no longer the team that finished with back-to-back 9–1 records just a couple of years before, but they were still one of the league's better performers, coming into this contest at 4–3–3. Despite going 0–3 against the All-Americans in three NFL seasons, their proximity to Rochester had made them the Jeffs' archnemesis among NFL teams.

The inspired Jeffs put up a tough fight, recording eight first downs and holding Buffalo to just one, but too many errors proved their undoing. Buffalo took a 3–0 lead in the first after recovering a Jeff fumble in Rochester territory, which led to a 25-yard field goal from Frank Morrissey. A Rochester fumble early in the third led directly to another 20-yard field goal from Morrissey, boosting Buffalo's advantage to 6–0. The All-Americans extended their lead later in the quarter after forcing the Jeffs to punt from their own end zone. Just as the ball left Shag Sheard's foot, Buffalo end Scotty Bierce grabbed the pigskin and touched it to the ground for the touchdown. The All-Americans held on the rest of the way for a 13–0 win.

For the second straight year, the Jeffs finished at the bottom of league standings, posting a record of 0–4–0 versus league competition (1–6–0 overall). Offensively, the team managed a single touchdown for the entire season to average 1.5 points per game (down from 2.6 in 1922). They gave up 141 points for an average of 35.25 points per game, easily the worst in the league. Things ended on a high note, however, as the Jeffs performed admirably in their final two contests against league teams (Toledo and Buffalo) and enjoyed a surge in community support, which included efforts toward the creation of a stock company to back the team. Just how long and to what extent that movement would go remained to be seen, but it at least provided a sense of optimism as Lyons began thinking about the 1924 football season.

* * *

Lyons made the 600-plus-mile trek to Chicago for the owners' traditional season postmortem, held on January 26 and 27, 1924, at the Hotel Sherman. The Canton Bulldogs, with a final record of 11–0–1, were awarded the championship of 1923—their second straight pennant. Not surprisingly, Joe Carr, John Dunn, and Carl Storck were all reelected to their respective offices. The owners then revisited the idea of splitting the league into divisions and voted unanimously to direct President Carr to appoint a five-man committee to study the idea further.[30]

Racine manager George Ruetz, at whose urging the matter was reopened, argued that having teams within divisions facing off against one another for the first half of the season would cut down on travel expenses, while the division winners would play off for the overall league championship. The proposal created a western division (Rock Island, Hammond, Duluth, Milwaukee, Green Bay, Minneapolis, St. Louis, Racine, Chicago Bears, Chicago Cardinals) and an eastern one (Buffalo, Rochester, Cleveland, Dayton, Toledo, Akron, Canton, Columbus, Louisville, Oorang Indians). After much discussion, however, the proposal was defeated, primarily by owners from teams from larger cities for whom travel was not as much of a concern as it was for smaller market clubs like Racine and, of course, Rochester.[31]

7

"We never played a game expecting to lose"

(1924–1925)

Lyons' mind never wandered far from football matters during the offseason following the 1923 campaign. Meetings and communication continued between him and the "Do it for Rochester" group that had pledged its support of the Jeffersons back in November. A concerted campaign began during the summer in which the group canvassed the business community and any known high-profile backers in an effort to renew interest in the city's major league football team.

"The Rochester American Legion will back professional football here this Fall," reported the *Rochester Evening Journal and the Post Express*. "Two hundred letters have been mailed out to various parties who are interested in football. The following are sponsors for the meeting: Charles E. Bostwick, Joseph Scanlon, Dr. Ray Brown, Leo F. McSweeney, Fred Bloom, William F. Love, George Bartold, Percy Durnherr, John W. Jardine, Frank J. Smith, Carl S. Hallauer and John R. Powers."[1]

However, when the time arrived for the luncheon scheduled on Friday, July 25, only 25 of the prospective 200 supporters turned out. Still, it was progress and a plan of action was initiated. "The moving spirit behind the meeting was Leo Lyons, who has been manager of the Jeffersons for years," wrote the *Rochester Herald*. "Leo thinks he has sufficient people interested this year to make a success of the team. Committees have been appointed in the different industrial plants and banks of the city to dispose of tickets, and it is thought that by the time football starts there will be plenty of cash on hand. It is planned to sell season books for bleachers, reserved and box seats, with the bleacher seats selling for $1, the reserved seats for $1.50, and the box seats for $2."

Immediately following the meeting, Lyons boarded a train bound for the NFL owners' summer meeting being held that weekend at the Hotel Sherman in Chicago.[2] The *Herald* reported that Lyons "was to take $1,000 with him to be deposited in the Dayton City Bank as a guarantee of the good faith of the Rochester team and to guarantee that he would use no college players still in their alma maters. Each team in the league posts such a guarantee, which is refunded to them at the close of the season, provided they have lived up to the rules. Leo was not certain just where he was going to get the $1,000."[3]

The meeting was rather uneventful, its main purpose seemingly to resolve small matters prior to the start of the 1924 season. One of the more pressing issues addressed was the adoption of a tentative schedule, which would require a few minor tweaks before the planned start date of September 27. Those tweaks were necessary with the admission of new teams from Kansas City (Cowboys) and Philadelphia (Frankford Yellow Jackets). Additionally, the league approved the transfer of the Buffalo franchise from Frank J. McNeil to Warren D. Patterson and Tommy Hughitt. With four teams leaving (Louisville, St. Louis, Toledo, Oorang Indians), the league was down to 18 franchises. The owners also voted to increase roster sizes from 16 to 18 players (after a team's third game), which provided teams extra manpower in the event of injuries occurring during the season.

Lyons was fairly active during the two-day meeting, making two motions that were supported by the group. On Saturday, Lyons made a motion that the league president appoint a Resolutions Committee. The motion was seconded by Frank Nied and carried. On Sunday, Lyons suggested the next league meeting be held in Cleveland. That motion was seconded by Sam Deutsch and carried. Whether Lyons paid the $1,000 guarantee was not recorded by Treasurer/Secretary Carl Storck, but it can be assumed he did, considering the Jeffersons were active in the 1924 season.[4]

Whether the subject was broached at this meeting is not known, but Lyons had not given up on his idea of football trading cards. He continued to press his fellow moguls, primarily George Halas, Carl Storck, and Joe Carr, to invest in the concept as a way to promote the league. Perhaps directed by President Carr to finally get Lyons off their collective backs, Secretary Storck sent a letter advising Lyons that the matter was being shelved until the league was in a better financial state:

The National Football League
OFFICE OF THE SECRETARY

March 21, 1924

Mr. Leo V. Lyons
Rochester, New York

Dear Leo,

Happy belated birthday my friend, trusting you kept yourself out of trouble. You need to take up golfing during the off season, you are getting old.

Joe read your recent plan for the creation of football card type collecting pictures like the ones in baseball. I think it is a risky but good proposition, however, Joe feels it is too early on in our league to pursue this at the present time. I am sure he brought up the fact that the [?] baseball league has been around for "some" years. Unfortunately, the league finances can not support this and I know George and you spoke to the Wrigley folks to no avail. It always comes down to money, something you and I are always short of.

Good luck this season. See you this summer at our meeting, your friend Halas wants it in Chicago, I know we would of preferred an Ohio location.

Very truly yours,
Carl Storck [signed][5]

"Had several phone conversations with Joseph Carr and Carl Storck about a possible National Football League trade card set that could be offered with either Wrigley or Cracker Jack products," wrote Lyons. "It would be a great way to promote our new league. Create a fun collectible piece that combines a tasty confection with an item used for amusement and hobby. I only received lukewarm sentiment from Carr and Storck, saying too early for this and lack of funds make it impossible."[6]

It was obviously an idea in which Lyons strongly believed, but the owners clearly had more pressing issues to address at this early stage.

* * *

In mid–September, Lyons announced that former Jeff quarterback Jerry Noonan was returning to the club as player and head coach. The former star quarterback at Notre Dame and Fordham had spent parts of the 1921 and 1923 seasons with the Big Red but was now returning in a full-time capacity. Lyons was also pleased to have Benny Boynton returning to the fold after spending a season with the Washington Pros.

On September 23, the *Democrat & Chronicle* reported that Lyons had signed former Rutgers All-America tackle Bob "Nasty" Nash to play for the Jeffs. Nash had spent the previous three seasons with Buffalo, including an All-Pro campaign in 1921. Rounding out the lineup, Lyons had a reliable core of veteran players returning from the previous year, including Bob Argus, Joe Bachmaier, Butch Clark, Darby Lowery, Frank Matteo, Spin Roy, Shag Sheard, and Hank Smith.

As the team prepped for the season opener against the Frankford Yellow Jackets, rumors were circulating that Boynton's contract with the Jeffersons was being disputed by Warren D. Patterson, the new owner of the Buffalo Bisons, who claimed Boynton had signed a contract with them. Lyons was approached by a reporter from the *Democrat & Chronicle* asking whether Patterson's claim had any merit. The Rochester magnate was resolute in his belief that Boynton was legally bound to the Jeffersons. He reported that he had received a wire from the Williams grad accepting terms for the season and that league rules state an acceptance by wire or letter is a valid contract.[7]

Boynton was in the Jeffs' lineup when they took the field at Frankford. Also suiting up for the Jeffersons was Joe Alexander, who had appeared unannounced. Fans were treated to a melee which erupted when Alexander took exception to what he felt was a cheap shot.

"Joe A. and Darby fight Stein and Thomas," Lyons wrote. "Joe mad because of hit to his knee." Yet even with the former college stars in the lineup, the Jeffs failed to generate an offense and were defeated 21–0.

Upon returning to Rochester, Lyons received a communiqué from league president Carr informing him of Patterson's contention that he had a contract bearing Boynton's signature and his belief that this document superseded the telegram in Lyons' possession. It was common in the early days of the NFL for a player to sign a contract with one team, only to sign another after being offered more money by a second club. There were reports that Boynton had given Lyons an ultimatum that he was not going to stay with the Jeffersons unless steps were taken to strengthen the offensive line. When Lyons failed to sufficiently upgrade the line, Boynton scoffed at his agreement with the Jeffs and accepted an offer from the Bisons.[8] Lyons contended that Boynton was protected property, having been placed on the Jeffs' reserve list since leaving the team to play for the independent Washington Pros two years earlier. Patterson was not backing down, claiming that the actual contract Boynton signed with Buffalo should take precedence over an agreement made by telegraph.[9] Carr ultimately sided with Patterson and Boynton became a permanent member of the Bisons.

"Sad day," Lyons wrote in his journal. "Boynton contract with Buffalo. Money once again. Last game for Benny."[10]

A crowd of 1,200 turned out at Edgerton Park the following Sunday to watch the Jeffersons take on the Akron Pros. With Alexander and Nash still in the lineup, the Jeffs put up a strong fight, but a second-quarter field goal by Paul Hogan gave the Pros all the points they needed for a 3–0 triumph.

The loss against Akron was a costly one, as it was learned Bob Nash was going to

Edgerton Park, home field of the Rochester Jeffersons, 1923–25.

be lost for the balance of season after sustaining an arm injury. The Jeffs also learned that Joe Alexander was going to be unavailable for a while, further weakening the team's permeable forward wall. Lyons rolled up his sleeves and went right to work in search of new talent. He was able to secure several new players in time for Sunday's encounter with the Columbus Tigers, including three men with previous pro experience, fullback Fred "Fritz" Foster and tackles Roy Martineau and John Dooley. Foster had played briefly with the Jeffs in 1923 and played alongside Martineau with the Buffalo All-Americans that same year. Dooley, another former Jeff, appeared in a handful of games for the team in 1922. He had spent the 1923 season in the employ of the Milwaukee Badgers. Martineau and Dooley provided much needed heft to the Rochester line, weighing in at 210 and 224 pounds, respectively. Also signed were three first-year men in Syracuse end Reaves Baysinger, Colgate guard Elmer Volgenau, and a fullback out of Iowa, Clem Nugent.[11]

The Columbians were no longer the team once dominated by the famed Nesser clan, as all had either retired or moved on to other clubs by 1924. Joe Carr had sold the franchise after the 1922 season to concentrate solely on league matters. The new owners made several changes, including renaming the club the Tigers. The new lineup responded by recording the franchise's first winning season since 1916, finishing with a 5–4–1 record, good for an eighth-place finish in league standings. They had opened 1924 the previous week with a 13–0 loss at Buffalo.

The Tigers took the game's first lead in the opening frame when Shag Sheard was tackled by Boni Petcoff in the Rochester end zone for a safety. Bob Rapp extended the lead in the second period by catching a scoring pass from Sonny Winters. The extra-point attempt was unsuccessful, leaving the Tigers with an 8–0 advantage they held to intermission. Winters and Rapp combined for another touchdown in the third quarter, giving Columbus a 15–0 lead. The Jeffs finally responded late in the fourth when

Jerry Noonan smashed over on a short run, but it was not enough. Final score: Columbus 15, Rochester 7.

Rochester football fans received a jolt on October 17 when they opened the *Democrat & Chronicle* and read that Leo Lyons was selling his beloved football team. The group that had pledged its support at the end of the previous season was now reportedly buying the team outright. The paper stated that the group, which comprised city power brokers John W. Jardine, Joseph Scanlon, and Percy Durnherr, now included real estate mogul Edward Schlegel and John R. Powers, the entrepreneur and county assemblyman who had served briefly as Jeffs team president in 1921. Johnny Murphy, well known locally for his heroics primarily on the hardcourts at the University of Rochester, was assuming day-to-day management of the team.

JOHNNY MURPHY TO MANAGE ROCHESTER FOOTBALL TEAM
Basketball Coach and Player to Direct Club Under New Organization; Lyons Out.

The management of the Rochester football club has changed hands again. The franchise of the outfit in the National Professional Football League was sold to a group of young Rochester business men who will succeed Leo Lyons in directing policies of the club and who have obtained the services of Johnny Murphy, Central basketball coach and star guard. The new organization directed last Sunday's successful game with Columbus.

The taking over of the club franchise by Murphy means that Rochester fans will be assured of seeing some of the best teams in the country here in games and that players of high-class caliber will be hired for all games. Murphy's experience in the professional basketball game will hold him in good stead for this work and will help in molding a stronger team for the local fans to watch in action.

For the game in Buffalo on Sunday, the players will practice this afternoon at Edgerton Park, and tomorrow morning and afternoon at the same place. From now on players will be forced to attend all practice sessions or there will be no pay for the games. This rule was decided on between Coach and Captain Jerry Noonan and Murphy as soon as it was definitely known that the club franchise would be transferred.[12]

The sale of the Jeffersons, however, was no more than sleight of hand. The team never fully changed ownership but was merely placed under the illusory management of the syndicate, fronted by Murphy. Despite his total lack of football experience, Lyons was banking on Murphy's celebrity to spur interest in the team, and the influence of the others to draw support from the city's business community. He had laid out the plan in a letter to the Rochester Chamber of Commerce in August 1924:

Johnny Murphy
John Powers
Ed Schlegel
Members of the Rochester Chamber of Commerce

It is a plan to save the Jeffs.

They have agreed to "take over" the team but it is only for public. Their names will help sell tickets to those that otherwise would not have an interest. Already several city businesses in the food and clothing sectors will now sell tickets and advertise the games. The newspapers already have me out the door for God sake. This deal is on a trial run. With Johnny's reputation in Rochester sports and John Powers with his business acumen and name should help. I am tired of running around the country to sign All Americans only to watch them join another team is beyond old. So many games lost by a touchdown or less, those one or two players would have changed the outcome.

Need to call Carr about the situation. Will be at office by 9.[13]

Although Murphy was identified as the manager of the Jeffs for the balance of the season, Lyons remained fully involved behind the scenes in all the team's decision-making. His notes clearly show he accompanied the Jeffs on their road trips and was present on the sidelines at the games. There is, in fact, no evidence that he ever relinquished even a small percentage of ownership in the team.

Meanwhile, the recent dispute over Ben Boynton's services deepened the sports rivalry that had existed for over a decade between the cities of Rochester and Buffalo. The feud made for good copy, and the local papers ran with it.

"To say that the rival factions will have blood in their eyes is putting it mildly," wrote the *Buffalo Evening News*. "The Benny Boynton controversy has not helped to clarify matters and the decision favoring Buffalo, in the warfare conducted over his contract, is still rankling in the hearts of manager Leo Lyons and his cohorts."[14]

The *Buffalo Enquirer* reported, "The sports rivalry between the cities has been greatly intensified by the recent Benny Boynton controversy and arrangements are being made in Rochester to literally take Buffalo by storm. A special excursion will be run over the New York Central and indications are that the record of three years ago when close to 900 Rochester fans came to Buffalo for the memorable clash with the Buffalo All-Americans, will be broken Sunday."[15]

Among the crowd who came out to witness the grudge match was the man who had decreed Boynton's services to Buffalo, league president Joe Carr. No record survives as to how many of the 3,500 in attendance were imported from Rochester, but there is no doubting all who turned out that day were left awestruck by Boynton's electrifying performance.

After a scoreless first period, Boynton put the Bisons up by three early in the second with a 14-yard dropkick field goal. Boynton then caught a ten-yard touchdown pass from Chick Guarnieri and added the extra point himself, giving Buffalo a 10–0 advantage. The Purple Streak increased the Bisons' lead to 13 before the half with another dropkick field goal. Boynton pulled off the most exciting play of the day early in the third quarter when he returned a Rochester punt 80 yards for a touchdown, making it 19–0 in favor of Buffalo. But he was not done. In the fourth quarter, Boynton tossed a five-yard touchdown pass to Guarnieri for the game's final score. All told, Boynton had caught a touchdown pass, returned a punt for a touchdown, kicked two field goals, kicked an extra point, and thrown for a touchdown. He was a one-man wrecking crew!

Despite Lyons' misery in having to watch Boynton lay waste to his team, the two shared a couple of brief moments that Lyons committed to his journal. "Benny at quarterback," he wrote. "Met before game. Said 'sorry' after he scored. I shook my head."[16]

With the Boynton controversy—and game—now behind them, the Jeffs moved on to Cleveland to face the undefeated Bulldogs (2–0–1). The Bulldogs were a new team born from the ashes of the former Canton Bulldogs and Cleveland Indians. Canton had won the two previous league championships but fell on financial hardships in the process. Sam Deutsch, owner of the Cleveland Indians franchise in 1923, purchased the kennel from Ralph Hay in August 1924 for $2,500. Deutsch then combined the two teams to create the new Cleveland Bulldogs, retaining Canton player-coach Guy Chamberlin, who had guided the 'dogs to their back-to-back titles.

The Jeffs played tough in the early going, surrendering just two field goals to give the Bulldogs a seemingly tenuous 6–0 bulge at the end of the first quarter. But things turned ugly for the Jeffs in the second stanza as the Bulldogs extended their lead to 33–0 with halfback Dave Noble running for three scores and fullback Ben Jones adding a fourth. Chamberlin showed mercy as the third quarter started, inserting a bunch of second stringers who managed to score another touchdown before the starters were reinserted to start the fourth. The 'dogs found the Rochester end zone three more times in the final frame to run up the score and humiliate the Jeffersons with a 59–0 final tally.

Undaunted, the Jeffersons returned to New York State to meet up with the Utica Knights of Columbus at Athletic Field in Utica. With a mere 500 fans in attendance, the Jeffersons finally got off the schneid with a 6–0 vanquishing of the independent Knights. Quarterback Shag Sheard scored for the Jeffs on a six-yard run in the third quarter, providing the margin of victory.

The team had now played three games since John Murphy was named manager on October 17. Since that date, his name in connection to the Jeffs in Rochester newspapers was almost nil. His level of involvement with the team is highly questionable, considering the number of games he had actually attended in that time frame, as well as his seeming indifference when finally pinned down by a reporter from the *Rochester Evening Journal and the Post Express.*

"The newspapers are busy," said Murphy. "I see I am impresario of the Jeff eleven and am planning to operate a court team in Syracuse. Well, I've seen the Jeffs play once this season, and that's all I know about them."[17]

This statement seems a clear indication that Murphy's position with the team was merely as figurehead. One wonders how the manager of a team could credibly assess that team's on-field performance or offer any meaningful input with regard to personnel moves or strategy, not to mention the scheduling of games, travel arrangements, and other tasks that required a greater level of attention. Clearly, the Rochester Jeffersons were not high on Murphy's list of priorities.

Perhaps buoyed by the victory at Utica, the Jeffs performed well in their next outing against the Providence Steam Roller, losing by a narrow 3–0 score. They then made the 700-mile journey to play the Columbus Tigers the following Sunday, losing 16–0.

The recent string of futility was more than team management—represented publicly by Murphy—could take. With the powerful Buffalo Bisons due in town the upcoming weekend, the team announced some major changes were being made. The first was the dismissal of the head coach, who had led the Jeffs to a dismal 0–6 record against league teams while producing just a single touchdown.

"While Buffalo is known to have a strong eleven," reported the *Democrat & Chronicle,* "the locals will not be weak, according to Murphy who is planning on several changes in the lineup for Saturday's game. Jerry Noonan is gone and will not return. His place will be filled by a capable player."[18]

No immediate replacement was announced, but it appears that captain Shag Sheard was left in charge of the team's on-field affairs for what was left of the regular season.[19] The Jeffs sent another shock wave through the local fan base two days later when it was announced that they had signed veteran backs Cecil Grigg and Lou Smyth to contracts. The two provided much-needed experience, having both played for the Canton Bulldogs and helping them to win back-to-back championships in 1922 and '23. Smyth was considered one of the top forward passers on the pro scene. Neither had played thus far in 1924 and would be available for this weekend's matchup with the Buffalo 11.[20]

The Jeffs were in Buffalo on October 16 for the year's first meeting between the clubs and were trounced 26–0 as Benny Boynton ran wild. The Bisons were coming to the

Flower City for the rematch, which the Rochester faithful hoped was going to be a more competitive outing based on the recent changes made by team management. Unfortunately, it was more of the same as Boynton played another spectacular game, registering a touchdown, a field goal, and an extra point in pacing a 16–0 Buffalo victory.

The Jeffs found themselves in the state of New Jersey a day later to face an independent squad called the Atlantic City Roses. Newcomer Lou Smyth booted an 18-yard field goal in the third quarter to provide the margin of victory in a 3–0 final.

The victory was assumed to be the team's season finale. Before allowing the players to resume their offseason lives, however, Lyons accepted a challenge from John G. "Doc" Striegel, a Pottsville, Pennsylvania–based surgeon and owner of the independent Pottsville Maroons, to play one more game.

"Our regular season had ended," Lyons recalled years later. "The Pottsville coach was searching for a game. He was looking ahead to playing Chicago for the league championship and wanted to play us on an open week in his schedule 'just to keep my boys in shape.' He figured to kick the stuffing out of us and build up his team's confidence."[21]

The Jeffs reconvened at the Yates Hotel in Syracuse and practiced on a field on the Onondaga Indian Reservation. En route to Pottsville, the team made a special stop at Wilkes-Barre to pick up star center Joe Alexander, who was going to be needed.

The Maroons were a formidable team, having posted an impressive 12–0–1 record to claim the championship of the so-called Anthracite League of eastern Pennsylvania. Their lineup included several standout players, including former NFL All-Pro Gus Sonnenberg at left tackle, hard-hitting halfback Tony Latone, quarterback Johnny Scott, and right tackle Wilbur Henry, the former Canton Bulldog and future Pro Football Hall of Famer. In 13 games played so far this season, the Maroons had outscored their opponents 281–7!

"No one in that town expected us to win that day," said Alexander. "The Jeffersons were a bottom team and Pottsville was one of the very best."

"When we arrived in Pottsville," said Lyons, "there were eight thousand people in the stands. The field was at the base of a mountain and the ground was a little bit soggy from melting snow, but it was a good day for football." It was a good day for the Jeffersons.

Lyons' inspired charges came storming out of the gate, driving deep into Pottsville territory on their opening drive and coming away with a field goal from fullback Dick King for a 3–0 lead. The Maroons responded with an impressive drive of their own that stalled at the Rochester 20. Johnny Scott, the former Buffalo All-American, backed up to attempt a dropkick.

"I rushed Scott and the kick hit me in the air," remembered Alexander. "It bounced off my thigh and into my hands, and I ran eighty yards for a touchdown."[22] King booted the extra point, and the Jeffs now led by ten.

The stunned Maroons never recovered, unable to breach the Rochester goal line until late in the final quarter. It was not enough. The Jeffersons held on for a thrilling 10–7 upset win.

"We just surprised them," said Lyons. "There was no weather alibi for Pottsville. We were winless, they were undefeated, but we never played a game expecting to lose."

Flush with victory—and cash from the gate—the Jeffs enjoyed a celebratory meal at a local eatery before heading back to New York. "Oh, were we ever a happy bunch," Lyons recalled. "We celebrated after the game at a little lunchroom a block from the

Pottsville field. Darby Lowery, a superb player who loved to make noise, shouted, 'We did it, boys. We knocked Pottsville out of a shot at Chicago for the championship!' The lunchroom owner didn't like the sound of that at all. He jumped over the counter, pulled out a roll of money that would have choked a cow and said, 'Take this and come back next week. We'll whip you twenty to nothing.' But we'd proved our point."

The train ride back was jubilant, no doubt. But when Lyons learned several years later that the league did not count the win in its official standings, he was not pleased. "The only thing that gets me about that game," he related in a 1975 interview, "is that we never got credit for an official victory in the record book. We should have. Pottsville asked us for the game, Joe Carr approved it, and it hurt Pottsville's prestige enough to cancel the showdown with Chicago." Unfortunately, since the Maroons were a non-league team, the Jeffs' victory remains unrecognized by the NFL.[23]

While the triumph over the powerful Pottsville club might not have redeemed a winless campaign for the Big Red, it provided a positive note on which to end the year. The Jeffs, at 0–7–0, were one of three teams that finished the season without a win against league competition (Kenosha 0–4–1 and Minneapolis 0–6–0). However, averaging a single point per game offensively (one touchdown all season) while giving up 22.3 points per game (worst and second worst, respectively), the Jeffs bore the distinction of finishing dead last for the second straight year.

* * *

The postseason owners meeting was held at the Hotel Statler in Cleveland on January 24–25, and for the first time since joining the league, Lyons was not alone in representing the Rochester Jeffersons. Accompanying him on this trip was Percy Durnherr, one of the principals of the group Lyons had enlisted to help save the team from financial ruin. Lyons left no notes relative to this particular meeting, so the purpose of Durnherr's presence is not clear. It seems likely, however, that he was there to abdicate any claims to ownership or management of the team. It was important to know there was going to be no challenge to control of the franchise like the one Chic Harley made against the Chicago Bears in 1922. There was some discussion regarding the fate of the team carried on between Lyons, Durnherr, and other owners, as evidenced by the motion made on the second day by Mr. Ness of Minneapolis and seconded by Mr. Gentry of Frankford that "the Rochester Jeffersons Football Club be transferred to the Rochester Football Association, with Mr. E. Schlegel as President." The motion was carried.[24]

Lyons had written in his journal on Thursday the 22nd, "Ed in, Percy out."

What did all this mean? It is clear Lyons never actually sold the team in whole or in part to the group of Jeffersons backers, contrary to reports published in the *Rochester Democrat & Chronicle* on October 17. The Jeffersons were still his property. The *Democrat & Chronicle* got it wrong, but it was merely publishing misinformation provided by the man himself. Lyons had written that the "take over" of the team was "only for public" as far back as August.[25] The ruse, like nearly every other scheme hatched by the Rochester mogul, proved an abject failure.

With regard to Schlegel's role, there is no documentary record indicating that Lyons had sold him the club prior to the January owners meeting. Lyons stated in later interviews that he passed ownership to Schlegel in 1925, though never gave an exact date of the sale (normally an inveterate notetaker, Lyons left no solid clues for future historians to follow). However, the naming of Schlegel as president was a signal not only to the

NFL owners that the team was going to be stable financially, but it also provided Lyons with connections that Durnherr et al. could not. Schlegel was acquainted with some of Rochester's wealthiest men, and his access was going to be needed when Lyons initiated his greatest scheme later that season.

* * *

The NFL held its summer meeting on August 1–2 at the Hotel Sherman in Chicago. After attending the winter meeting accompanied by Percy Durnherr, Lyons was once again flying solo, a clear indication that he was the one—the only one—calling the shots for the Jeffs. Among the significant matters attended during this meeting were the approval of four new franchises—the Detroit Panthers, New York Giants, Pottsville Maroons, and Providence Steam Roller—and the welcoming back of an old one, the Canton Bulldogs.

The city of Canton was returning from a year's hiatus after the Bulldogs' franchise was sold to Sam Deutsch and merged with the Cleveland Indians to form the Cleveland Bulldogs in 1924. Deutsch was now selling the former Bulldogs franchise to a Mr. Herbert Brandt of Cleveland, who planned to bring the team back to Canton. The league also awarded several former Bulldog players back to the reconstituted team, including, among others, All-Pro tackles Link Lyman and Pete Henry, guard Duke Osborn, and back Harry Robb, the prospective head coach.

The city of Detroit was making its second foray into the league after the failed efforts of the Heralds/Tigers of 1920 and 1921. The Panthers were being organized by one of the game's biggest stars, Jimmy Conzelman, who was serving not only as the team's owner but also its quarterback and head coach.

The Pottsville Maroons were the best football team outside the NFL in 1924, winning the so-called Anthracite League championship with a 12–1–1 record (their only loss, of course, coming against the Rochester Jeffersons on November 30).

The Steam Roller (alternately known as the Steam Rollers) were another strong independent team, having been around since 1916. They finished 1924 at 12–3–1, with an impressive 3–2–1 mark against league competition (including a 3–0 defeat of the Jeffs).

There had been an NFL team called the Giants in New York City before, though its tenure was brief indeed. It was commonly referred to as "Brickley's Giants" in deference to Charles Brickley, the former Harvard luminary who coached the team. That franchise lasted less than one full season (1921) while playing just two league-sanctioned games (both losses). The new New York Football Giants bore no relation to that old team, though Joe Carr had tried to convince Billy Gibson, the boxing promoter and owner of the defunct Giants, to buy back in. Gibson was not interested. Instead, he introduced Carr to his friend Tim Mara, a well-heeled New York bookmaker. Mara knew next to nothing about the game of football, but his friend—Dr. Harry March—was a fan. March had been the team doctor for the pre–NFL Canton Bulldogs and convinced Mara there was money to be made in the sport. Mara ponied up the $500 franchise fee, and the Big Apple was back in the business of professional football.[26]

The delegates also spent a large amount of time discussing the need for an official game ball. The league did not have an "official" ball up to this point. The balls used since the dawn of the APFA (as the NFL was known in 1920 and 1921) were typically the model used in the college game, adopted in 1912. This ball had a circumference on the long axis from 28 to 28½ inches when tightly inflated, on the short axis from 22½ to 23 inches, and weighed 14–15 ounces. Referred to as a "prolate spheroid," the ball was difficult to grip with one hand, making it hard for players with smaller hands to execute a credible forward pass. In truth, the ball more closely resembled a watermelon than the football used today. Lyons had met with George Halas and Arnold Horween in 1921 to discuss the need for a standardized ball that was streamlined to make it easier to carry and throw, but nothing had ever come of that meeting.

During the course of the two-day league meeting, the owners gave both Wilson and Spalding the opportunity to present their cases to become the exclusive ball supplier of the NFL. Mr. Wyle of the A.G. Spalding Company presented their ball on August 1. This was the J5 model, which he advised would cost the league $6.75 per unit in lots of 20 dozen or more. These balls would bear a league stamp. Mr. Whitlock of the Wilson Company gave his pitch the next day. The Wilson A5 ball could be provided at a cost of $7.25 each. These footballs came with a new feature—guaranteed shape. As an added incentive, Wilson offered to provide a trophy to the league champions at the end of the season.

After some deliberation, the owners voted to go with Spalding, and on August 2, 1925, the J-5 model became the NFL's first official game ball. Although the league did not adopt the ball with dimensions approximating those today's players and fans recognize (28 to 28½ × 21 to 21¼) until 1934, this action demonstrates that the league's founders were always looking toward the future and ways to improve their game.

* * *

The league released its tentative schedule for the upcoming season on September 15. The schedule showed the Jeffersons had only a handful of league games set up as the season drew near. The one thing these games had in common was that none of them were taking place in the city of Rochester. Figuring his team could do just as well financially on the road with guarantees as they could playing at home to near-empty bleachers, Lyons had determined the Jeffersons were going to be a traveling team, plain and simple. To that end, he arranged for the Big Red to open its season on Sunday, September 27, at Canton. The other games on the itinerary at this point were at Buffalo (October 4), Providence (November 1), New York (November 11), Pottsville (November 15), and Detroit (November 22). He continued to work feverishly to add more games—mostly nonleague—to the schedule throughout the season.[27]

The Jeffs had a good number of players returning from 1924, including quarterback Cecil Grigg, whom Lyons had appointed the team's head coach. Grigg was joined by ball-heaving halfback Lou Smyth, end Spin Roy, guard Darby Lowery, tackle Frank Matteo, halfback Shag Sheard, end Ham Connors, end Butch Clark, tackle John Dooley, and center Hank Smith. Also returning was halfback Bob Argus, entering his 12th season with the Jeffs, making him by far the longest-tenured player on the roster. Lyons also announced the return of Syracuse halfback Bill Kellogg, who had spent some time with the team back in 1921 under the alias Earl Ettenhaus. Newcomers included veteran center Tex Kelly (who previously played with the Toledo Maroons and Buffalo Bisons) and rookie ends Dave Ziff (Syracuse University) and Eddie Lynch (Catholic University of America).

Lyons arranged for the Jeffersons to travel to Canton's Lakeside Park to open the season against the reconstituted Bulldogs. Although several of the old Bulldogs were awarded to the Canton franchise when it was reinstated at the owners meeting in

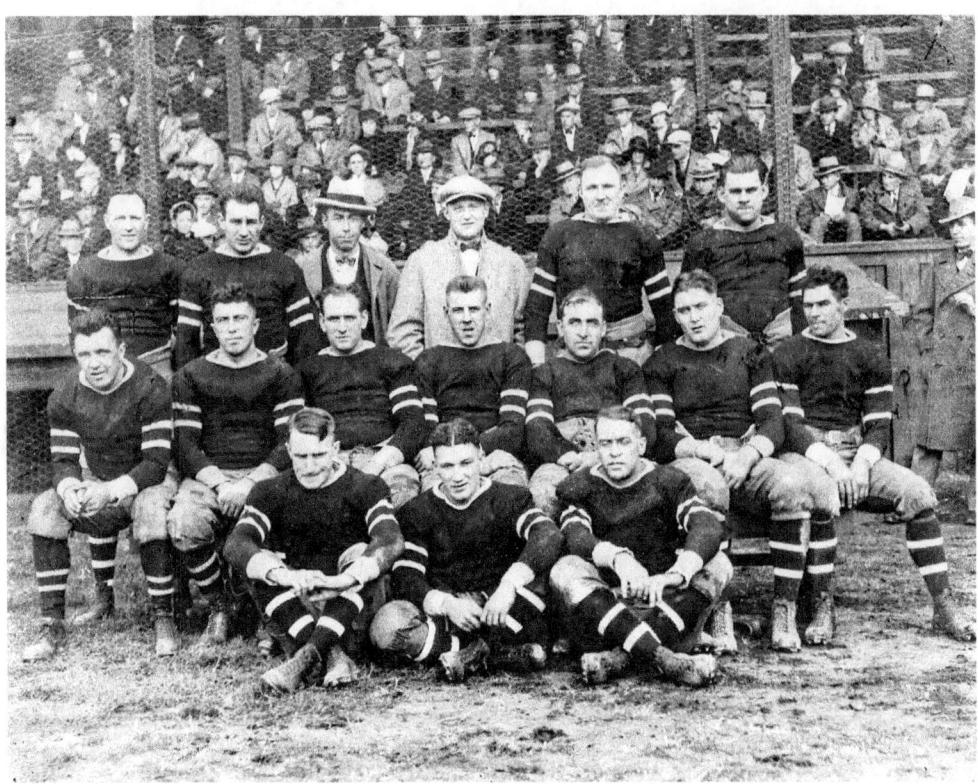

The Rochester Jeffersons, 1925. Back row (from left): Butch Clark, Bob Argus, Leo Lyons (manager), Ed Schlegel (president), Tex Kelly, Lou Smyth. Middle row (from left): Ed Lynch, Frank Matteo, Roy Martineau, Hank Smith, Darby Lowery, John Dooley, Gene Bedford. Front row (from left): Shag Sheard, Jake Hoffman, Cecil Grigg.

August, Jim Thorpe—the player most commonly associated with the team—was not among them.

"Bulldogs without Jim strange," Lyons recorded in his journal. "Talked to him last week. Doing OK. Wishes he was young again! Hopes someone with money will support the Jeffs. Said I deserve better for all the work I've done. Keep collecting, he said, football 'junk.'"[28]

Thorpe had been busy playing baseball with the Zanesville Greys of the Eastern Ohio League and making movies in Hollywood and so had not yet signed with an NFL team.[29] In truth, there were few teams willing to give the 38-year-old, out-of-shape, former Olympian a contract commensurate with his once-considerable fame. The fledgling New York Giants, however, looking for a big name to help draw crowds, came calling a couple of weeks later and added Thorpe—though briefly—to their roster.

Twenty-five hundred fans turned out to welcome the Bulldogs home, and they were rewarded with a victory. After a tightly played first quarter that failed to produce any points, the Bulldogs broke the stalemate when wingback Giff Zimmerman scored on a short run. Pete Henry's extra point made it 7–0. A touchdown run by fullback Ben Jones later in the quarter, along with another conversion by Henry, pushed the Canton lead to 14–0. The Jeffersons played a strong game, keeping the Bulldogs off the scoreboard the rest of the way. They pulled to within a touchdown in the fourth quarter when Shag Shard scored, but it was too little, too late. Final score: Bulldogs 14, Jeffersons 7.

Back in western New York a week later, the Jeffersons invaded Buffalo's Bison Stadium for a contest with their archrivals from New York's Queen City. It was the season opener for the Bisons, who were welcoming home native son Walter Koppisch as the team's new head coach. Koppisch had led Buffalo's Masten Park High School to a pair of city titles before going off to Columbia University, where he earned back-to-back All-America selections from Walter Camp (1923 and '24). At barely 24 years of age, he was one of the youngest head coaches in NFL history, before or since. As expected, his signing with the Bisons caused an immediate sensation with the locals. A crowd of 5,000 frenzied fans turned out for Koppisch's home debut, which was preceded by a parade, presentation of a congratulatory floral horseshoe, and a ceremonial kickoff from Buffalo Mayor Francis X. Schwab.[30]

"Some ceremony before game," Lyons wrote. "Big crowd. Everyone here rooting for W. Koppisch."[31]

Although Koppisch was able to break away for a few nice runs, the Jeffs defense managed to keep the local hero at bay through most of the game. Despite registering nine first downs, the Bisons never got closer than 12 yards from the Rochester end zone. The Jeffs' offense was even more impotent, never mustering a serious threat to the Buffalo goal line, while managing just two first downs. Still, a 0–0 tie was the best outcome the Jeffs had managed against a Buffalo team in six previous outings.

A week later, the Jeffs invaded Brassco Field in Waterbury, Connecticut, to take the field against that city's pro 11, which called themselves the Blues. The Blues were a strong team led by quarterback Harry Stuhldreher, one year removed from his membership as one of the famed Four Horsemen backfield that had led the University of Notre Dame to the national championship in 1924. Anchoring the Blues' offensive line was end Ed Hunsinger, one of Notre Dame's so-called Seven Mules who paved the way for the Four Horsemen's heroics. So far this season, the Blues had won three out of three starts, outscoring their opponents by combined 73–3.

The Blues struck first when Hunsinger recovered Cecil Grigg's fumble at the Rochester 45 and raced unmolested for a touchdown. Stuhldreher made good on the conversion attempt and the Blues were out in front 7–0. Lyons recorded a humorous first-half incident in which Waterbury fullback Dutch Forst lost his jersey while being tackled by an unidentified Rochester defender. "Player for Waterbury lost his blue shirt, ripped off," Lyons wrote in his journal. "Everybody whistled—funny."[32]

The Redshirts were poised to tie the game in the third after Lou Smyth connected with Lynch on a 40-yard scoring pass, but the kick failed and the Jeffs remained a point behind. And that was as close as the Jeffs could get, as the Blues held on for a hard-fought 7–6 win.

The weekend of Sunday, October 25, was originally left open after Lyons failed to arrange an opponent for that date during the scheduling session at the summer owners meeting. His perseverance paid off, however, when he managed to secure the Green Bay Packers, who also happened to be open that weekend after their originally scheduled opponent, the Racine Legion, withdrew from the league.

Lyons left a detailed record of the trip, which began with boarding the New York Central at 7:00 a.m. on Saturday. Total cost for tickets for the first leg (approximately 600 miles from Rochester to Chicago) was $132.60 ($6.63 for 20 passengers). From Chicago to Green Bay (approximately 200 miles), the total cost was $15.00 ($0.75 for 20 passengers). The train arrived at Green Bay at 9:00 a.m. Sunday. The players were put up at the Beaumont Hotel at a cost of $30.00 (20 rooms at $1.50 each). Meals came to a total of $40.

Lyons was busy as usual the morning of the game. He planned to meet with Packers head man Curly Lambeau at 10:00 a.m., then catch up with the team for practice at 11:00 a.m. Game time was 2:15 p.m. At some point, he was advised there was no one available to function as timekeeper for the game. "Oh boy," he wrote. "Official game timers—Me (Roch). Abrams (GB)." Fortunately, Lyons always carried his trunk of essentials to every game. "Hope my old stopwatch still has legs."

With a disappointing crowd of "less than 2,700" on hand, the teams battled through a scoreless first half. The Jeffs put a brief scare into the Green Bay faithful early in the second quarter by driving from their own one-yard line all the way to the Packers 26. They were relieved when Darby Lowery's field goal attempt fell short, leaving the score knotted at 0–0 going into intermission. But things changed drastically in the third quarter as the Packers scored on a short forward pass from Charlie Mathys to Marty Norton, giving the host team a 7–0 advantage. The Jeffs threatened again when Lou Smyth intercepted a Mathys pass and raced 90 yards toward the Green Bay goal line, only to trip over his own feet at the five-yard line. The Packers were awarded possession at their own three moments after a Rochester pass fell incomplete in the end zone. A punt gave

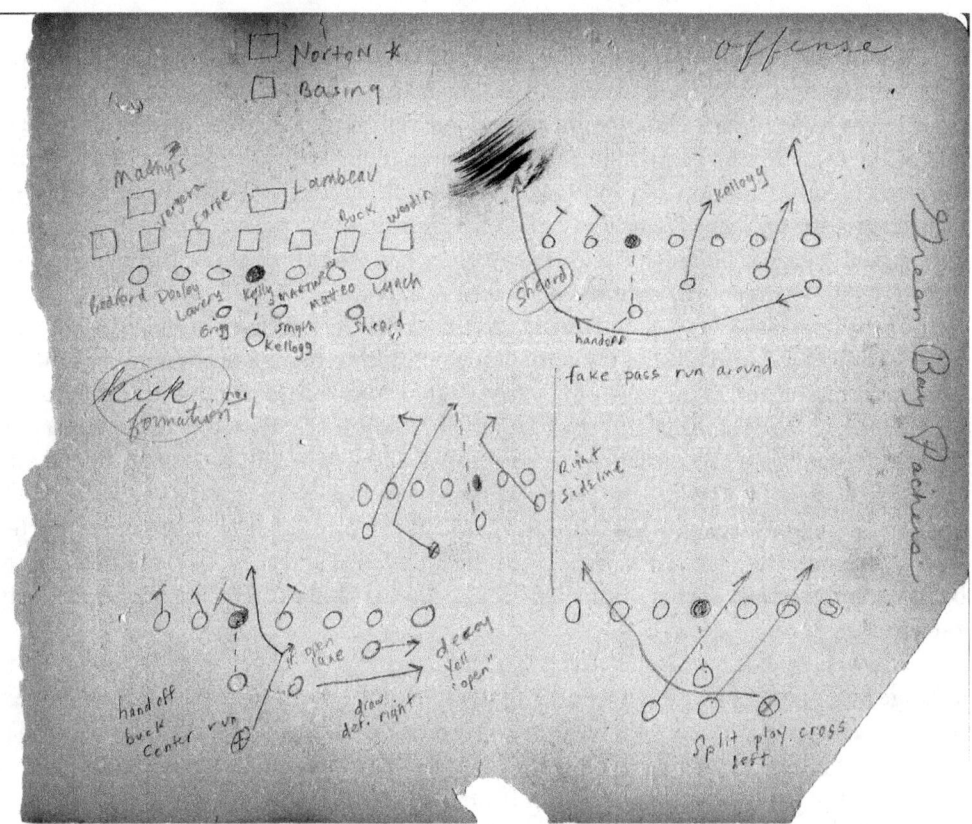

Sketches drawn by Leo Lyons during the Jeffersons' game with the Green Back Packers, October 25, 1925.

the ball back to the Jeffs, but Norton intercepted a Smyth pass and returned it 60 yards to paydirt, extending the Packers' lead to 13 points. Lambeau intercepted a Jeffersons pass to blunt Rochester's ensuing possession, then hit Dick O'Donnell from 15 yards out, and the Packers led 20–0. The Jeffs employed their passing game on their next drive in a desperate attempt to close the gap. They marched as far as the Green Bay 20, from where Smyth connected with Kellogg for the score. Grigg's extra point closed the gap to 20–7. The Packers widened their lead to 26–7 on their next possession when Lambeau hit Myrton Basing with a 45-yard scoring strike. The two teamed up again for another scoring aerial midway through the fourth, this time from 60 yards out, making it 33–7, Green Bay. The Jeffs were not going down without a fight, however. A late drive took the Big Red deep into Green Bay territory, and Kellogg finished it off with a six-yard run, bringing the final score to a more respectable 33–13.

It was a tough loss, but the Jeffs were clearly no match for the well-coached and well-stocked Packers. "We need better, faster players to compete," Lyons observed. "More depth needed like GB."

Most impressive was Lambeau's brilliant performance, which included three touchdown passes. "Stop Lambeau," wrote Lyons. "Curly can't have time to throw. Too much time. Curly could throw touchdowns from a tractor."

The teams had occasion to mingle and enjoy a cold one after the game. "Several Packers players had beers with us after game," Lyons wrote. "Nice fellows," adding, "Curly gave me Packers gate money box. Has bad latch—still can use it. Waterproof." That money box remained a memento Lyons kept on his office desk for the rest of his life.

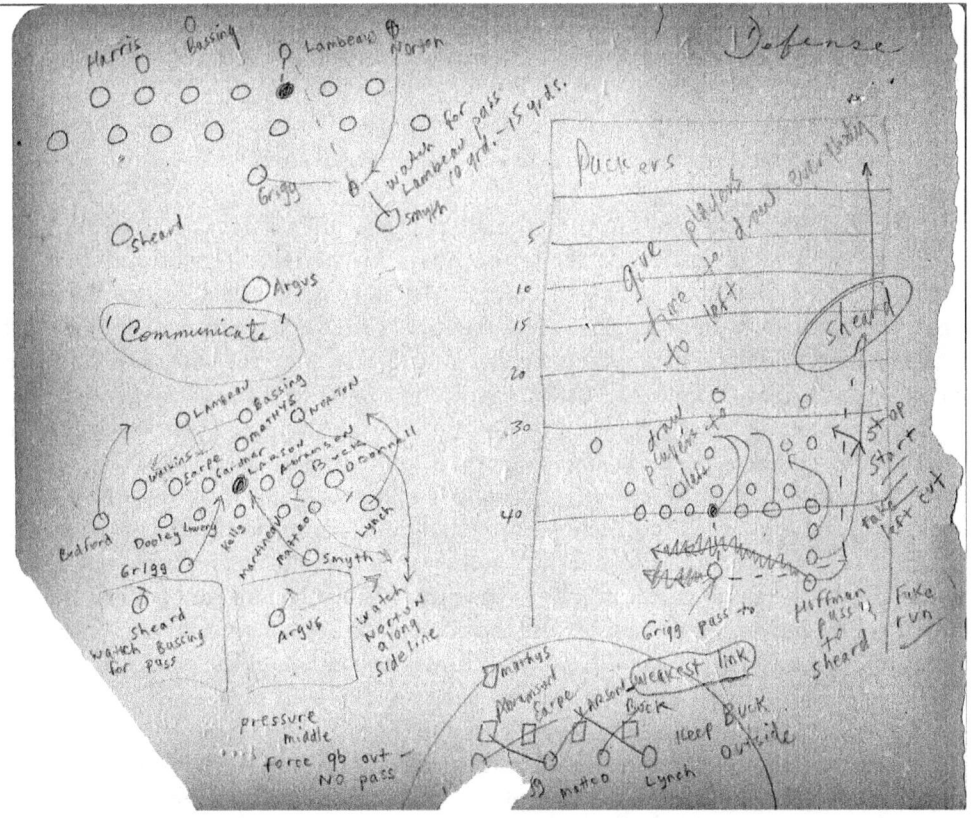

Lyons' ledger shows the Jeffs' return trip to Rochester cost a total of $147.61. The total paid out to the players was $750.00. The guarantee received from the Packers was $800.00. For the trip, Lyons ended up losing about $315.[33]

The following weekend found the Jeffs in Providence, Rhode Island—a distance of over 1,100 miles from Green Bay, spanning eight states along the way—for a matchup with the Steam Roller at the Cycledrome. Once again, the Jeffs played their opponent through a scoreless opening period, but the Steam Roller took a 2–0 lead in the second quarter when Shag Sheard attempted to pick up a punt at his own one-yard line before being tackled in the end zone for a safety. The Rollers then made it 8–0 when a Sheard punt from his own 30 was blocked by guard Lloyd Young. Fullback Jack Spellman picked up the bounding ball and scooted 18 yards to paydirt. Halfback Cy Wentworth gave Providence a 14–0 lead with a 20-yard touchdown run in the third quarter. Reserve halfback Fred Sweet closed out the scoring with a 22-yard field goal in the fourth, giving the Rollers a 17–0 triumph.

A third foray into the state of Connecticut had the Jeffs helping the former Waterbury Blues inaugurate their new home facility, Clarkin Field, in the city of Hartford on Sunday, November 8. A driving rain that resulted in a disappointing crowd of 2,000 diehards left the field a sea of mud from start to finish. The game was a rough one, with the Hartford papers reporting several instances of excessive roughness by the visitors. Harry Stuhldreher took the opening kickoff and headed upfield. He had not gotten far when Rochester tackle Roy Mackert nearly decapitated the erstwhile Horseman by grabbing him around the head and spinning him to the ground. Stuhldreher, badly shaken up, stumbled to his feet but had to be helped from the field.

"Mackert knocked Stuhldreher out!" Lyons wrote. "Went to hospital. Blues after Mack!" Stuhldreher was taken to a local infirmary, where it was determined that he had suffered a concussion.

Mackert then reportedly set his sights on Dutch Forst, leading with his hands to Forst's face while a teammate hit him low. Forst emerged from the pile with a broken nose.

The miserable field conditions and rough play precluded offensive fireworks, leaving the game scoreless until late in the second quarter when the Jeffs put together a drive that took them to the Hartford 20. Lou Smyth picked up a muffed center snap and hurled a pass to Bill Kellogg, standing alone at the one-yard line. Kellogg stepped into the Hartford end zone, and the Jeffs suddenly had an all-too-rare lead. The extra-point attempt failed, so the score stood at 6–0. The Blues responded later in the period when they had the Jeffersons pinned back on their own five. Cecil Grigg attempted a forward pass, but Ed Hunsinger pilfered the aerial and returned it to the Jeffs' two. On third down, Forst dived over the line to tie the score at six apiece. The teams slugged it out through a scoreless third period, but the Blues' defense provided the winning points late in the fourth. The Jeffs had recovered a Hartford fumble at their own five and began a drive they hoped would lead to the game-winning score. However, a Grigg run around left end on first down profited only a couple of yards. He then called for the same play around the other side, directly in Ed Hunsinger's direction. Hunsinger sealed off the end and, aided by guard Hugh McGoldrick and fellow Notre Damer Hec Garvey, sacked Grigg behind the goal line for a safety. It was all the Blues needed to claim an 8–6 victory.[34]

The New York Giants were one of four new teams joining the NFL in 1925, and it seemed every team wanted a chance to play a game in the nation's biggest city. During the league scheduling sessions held the previous summer, Giants owner Tim Mara had arranged a whopping 11 games for his team, 8 of which were scheduled to be played at the legendary Polo Grounds, the Giants' home field. Every Sunday was booked from October 11 through November 22. Mara knew the Jeffersons were not a big draw, but Lyons, eager for a shot at the hefty payday that surely awaited any team visiting the Big Apple, was willing to take whatever was available. They settled on Wednesday, November 11—Armistice Day.

The Giants were on a roll, winning three straight games after getting off to a 0–3 start. They were led by star fullback Jack McBride, tackle Century Milstead, and center Joe Alexander, the former Rochester Jefferson. Jim Thorpe had been signed earlier in the season but was let go after just three games after failing to live up to his enormous legend.

It was the Jeffs' first visit to New York City, and perhaps a bit nervous about the scope of the trip, Lyons wrote a list of items he wanted to be sure not to forget:

Bring:

- med kit
- footballs
- towels
- chalkboard
- megaphone
- stopwatch
- chalk
- equip. box
- clothes

He had arranged to meet with Mara before the game to inspect the field. "Meet with Mara and Alexander 10 o'clock," he wrote. "Should be large crowd." Later he added, "Field not good."

Giants halfback Heinie Bankert about to be brought down by a swarm of Rochester defenders after a long gain. Polo Grounds, New York City, November 11, 1925.

The Gothamites scored first, taking a 7–0 lead in the opening frame on a 25-yard strike from McBride to end Lynn Bomar, followed by McBride's successful conversion kick. Moments later, the Giants extended the advantage to 10–0 with a 35-yard field goal by Dutch Hendrian. Hendrian made good on a second field goal in the second quarter, and the Giants had a 13–0 lead they held to intermission. The Jeffs found their footing in the second half, holding the Giants off the scoreboard. Cecil Grigg made a spectacular play to open the second half, taking the kickoff 60 yards to the New York 30. The effort was squandered a few plays later when Grigg was intercepted at the New York one. The Jeffs' next best opportunity to prevent a shutout came on the game's final drive. Grigg connected with Shag Sheard on a beautiful 40-yard aerial that took them to the enemy's 15, but time expired before they could get off another play. The Giants prevailed 13–0.

Lyons' postgame notes revealed that big-city venues such as the Polo Grounds are prone to fans finding their way onto the fields just as they had at the small parks where the Jeffs had played since the very beginning. Once again, his prized first aid kit was the target of a pair of would-be thieves.

"Johnson and Johnson box taken by 2 fans," he wrote. "3 Jeffs and 1 Giant player ran them down and put a whipping on them."[35]

Next up, a return to the coal mining region of eastern Pennsylvania and a game with the powerful Pottsville Maroons. The Maroons had been champing at the bit for a chance to redeem the embarrassing defeat they received at the hands of the inspired Jeffersons at the end of 1924, which had cost them an undefeated season.

"According to information received from Leo Lyons, manager of the Rochester Jeffersons," wrote the *Pottsville Republican and Herald*, "he will bring a team here to the county seat that will administer the same fate to them as last year's club."[36]

A Giants runner is brought down after a short gain. Jeffs defenders identified here are Lou Smyth (12) and Ed Lynch (15). Polo Grounds, New York City, November 11, 1925.

7. "We never played a game expecting to lose"

There was little chance the Jeffs were going to be able to surprise the Miners in this rematch, but fatigue might be another issue. Pottsville owner Doc Striegel had scheduled his team to play the tough Frankford Yellow Jackets in Philadelphia on Saturday, the day before they were slated to play Rochester. A game with the Yellow Jackets was sure to be brutal and just might result in an advantage for the Jeffs.

Things did not turn out as hoped, however. Despite suffering a 20–0 pounding at the hands of the Yellow Jackets, the Maroons came ready to take down the team that had blemished their otherwise perfect record the year before. The Jeffs started strong as usual, holding Pottsville to a 0–0 tie after the first quarter. The Maroons found the end zone in the second stanza after Walter French put them in scoring position with 40-yard punt return and a run for 15 more. With the ball resting on the Rochester three, Tony Latone crashed through, and the Jeffs found themselves down 7–0. The Jeffs pulled to within a point later in the quarter after end Eddie Lynch took a forward pass 30 yards down to the Pottsville 20. On the next play, Lou Smyth found Shag Sheard in the end zone. The point-after attempt failed, leaving the Jeffs trailing by a single point. The Miners extended their lead to 14–6 early in the second half as Latone sprinted into the Rochester end zone from ten yards out. The Jeffs relied on the passing game the rest of the way but were unable to get near the Pottsville goal line, and the Maroons held on for a 14–6 win.

It was yet another gloomy train trip back to Rochester for Leo Lyons and his football team. All these road miles were the harsh result of being based in a city that simply would not support its team. Lyons' effort toward maintaining big-league football in Rochester had been met repeatedly with indifference and disappointment. He had brought in several star players over the years (Ben Boynton, Joe Alexander, Howard Berry, Bob Nash) only to see them leave for more money from more successful clubs. But there was at least one more star Lyons thought might save his moribund franchise if he could somehow get him to agree to play professional ball for the Jeffersons. That man was Harold "Red" Grange, star halfback from the University of Illinois.

The Wheaton, Illinois, native was a three-time consensus All-American and had led the Illini to a national championship in 1923. His fame skyrocketed after running for five touchdowns against the University of Michigan on October 18, 1924. The Wolverines were favored, but Grange returned the opening kickoff 95 yards for a touchdown and then scored three more times on runs of 67, 56, and 44 yards—all in the first 12 minutes of the first quarter. In the second half, Grange scored a fifth touchdown on an 11-yard run and then threw a pass for a score. The Galloping Ghost, as he was famously known, was arguably the only player in the nation more famous than the Four Horsemen of Notre Dame.

"This is what NFL needs," Lyons wrote. "A star—big crowds."

And the more he thought about it, the more he wondered, "Why not Rochester?" He had been ruminating the idea for well over a year. Lyons knew there were other team managers who were coveting Grange, especially George Halas, who wanted the Ghost for his Chicago Bears. Papa Bear had sent Grange a handful of letters and even shared one phone conversation with him but could not get a commitment. It appeared all his efforts might be in vain after Grange suffered a season-ending injury in a game against the University of Minnesota on November 16. Lyons, too, expressed concern in a journal entry in which he mentioned Grange's name for the first time.

"Grange injured, torn ligaments—arm/shoulder. Zuppke. Illinois." He then added, "Halas wants Grange for Bears. So do I! Hope he is ok!"

Lyons began to put his plan to sign Grange in motion while in Chicago in early January 1925, first attending a convention of the Hockaday Paint Company there. After visiting with Halas on January 7, Lyons traveled 130 miles south to meet with a school chum of Grange's named Marion "Doc" Coolley, who at the time was acting as the star's quasi-manager. Lyons' notes show he met with Coolley in the latter's hometown of Danville on January 8 and then with Lyle Grange, Red's father, the next day at his home in Wheaton. According to Lyons, he was prepared to offer Red a contract for $5,000 plus 40 percent of the gate receipts. He was advised, rather disingenuously, that because Red was still enrolled at Illinois, he was not allowed to talk to anyone about going pro.

Two weeks later, on the eve of the January 25–26 owners meeting at which Ed Schlegel was named president of the Rochester Football Association, Lyons wrote, "Ed has backers with $ for Red." On Sunday the 26th, Lyons wrote, "Ed will have money for Red come this fall."

Fast-forward to the league's summer meeting. Lyons left Rochester a few days ahead of the gathering scheduled for the weekend of August 1–2 in Chicago. He had set aside some time in which he planned to have further conversations with Coolley and the elder Grange.

"Mr. Lyle Grange," Lyons wrote in his journal on July 28, "115 Main St. Wheaton. 2 o'clock." On July 29, he wrote, "Marion 'Doc' Coolley, 2274-J or 2915 telephone. 1 o'clock." The next day, Lyons scribbled, "call Eddie" and "call Boscarino."

The Boscarino to whom Lyons referred was Alfio Boscarino, a prominent underworld figure and Rochester's reputed "King of the Bootleggers." It was reported that during the city's Prohibition era, Boscarino made millions while at the same time surviving eight attempts on his life.[37] It was Boscarino who was going to provide the money Lyons needed to make the offer to Grange. Both Lyons and Schlegel were acquainted with Boscarino, but Schlegel's presence gave the appearance that he was the one actually providing the funding for this undertaking.

On August 2, while still in Chicago, Lyons fired off a postcard to Schlegel which read:

Hello Ed,

Talked to both Mr. Grange and Mr. Coolley. Both on board so get the ball rolling as soon as possible! Only C.C. can mess this up. I will talk to you Tuesday, have meetings today.

Leo V.[38]

The C.C. referred to in Lyons' postcard was none other than Charles C. Pyle, the Champaign-Urbana, Illinois, theater owner who had famously taken over management of Grange's affairs back in March. Although Coolley was still involved as part of Grange's management team, Pyle was now the figure in charge. Just how much influence Coolley or Mr. Grange had over Red's career from that point on is questionable and most likely negligible.[39] Nevertheless, Lyons left Chicago believing he had an inside track on signing the Galloping Ghost to play for Rochester.

Lyons maintained contact with Coolley until a few days before Grange's final college game, scheduled for November 21, 1924, versus Ohio State. He was instructed by Coolley to "have the money in a hotel room in Chicago [the Morrison Hotel] at a certain time [the morning of November 22] and Red would sign."[40]

The check in the amount of $5,000 Leo Lyons had prepared to present to Red Grange. The uncashed check is dated November 20, 1925. Lyons' bank register shows a deposit in that amount from a reputed mobster.

Lyons' checkbook with the Union Trust bank in Rochester shows a $5,000 deposit made by A. Boscarino on November 19. A check in the same amount was made out to Harold E. Grange the following day. Later that same day, the Jeffersons boarded the New York Central bound for Detroit, where they were scheduled to play the Panthers the afternoon of the day Lyons was told to be in Chicago (Sunday the 22nd) to meet Grange. Lyons disembarked in Toledo and hopped on a separate train bound for Chicago. However, when Lyons arrived at the hotel at the agreed-upon time, he could not even get near Grange's suite.

"My last effort to stay with the pros occurred in nineteen twenty-five when I tried to sign Red Grange," Lyons recalled. "C.C. Pyle, his manager, brought him to the Morrison Hotel in Chicago. I had an associate bringing me a certified check for five thousand dollars that Grange was supposed to receive before each game, plus percentage privileges. The lobby was filled with the smoke of the reporters who had gathered from all over the country, but by the time he got to my room on the seventeenth floor, Grange and Pyle had already signed with the Bears for three thousand dollars."[41]

Lyons' figures were not entirely accurate, as Grange's deal amounted to $100,000 in return for playing 13 games for the Bears, which included their final two regular-season games and 11 more in a barnstorming tour across the United States.[42] Lyons' last-ditch

Hail Mary pass (long before the term had entered the football lexicon) to save his club had fallen short.

"I was lucky to get Red," said Halas. "I suspected many other owners had tried. Tim Mara had come to Chicago to sign him, and Tim telegraphed home he had been partially successful. Red and the Bears would play the Giants in New York. Leo Lyons, who had the Rochester team, wrote me twenty-four years after the event that he too was in the Morrison Hotel that day. Leo was so certain he would sign Red for $5,000 a game that his partner had come out with a certified check. While waiting in their hotel room, they heard of a lot of noise, looked out and saw Red telling the press he had signed with the Bears."[43]

Deeply disheartened, Lyons boarded the next train bound for Detroit, where his sad-sack Jeffersons were preparing to play the Panthers later that afternoon. Lyons knew he had missed his last chance at saving the Jeffs from extinction. "Try as I might, Grange is now a Chicago Bear," he jotted. "I wasted so much time, effort and cash on an impossible task. George warned me but I refused to listen. A wasted week ending at the Morrison Hotel with that snake in the grass Pyle. He and George were smiling from ear to ear and Red looked overwhelmed in the cigar smoke. My offer of $5,000 was not off the table but I could never sustain enough money to keep him like all the other greats that played on the Jeffs."

His mind raced as the train steamed toward the Motor City. "Red was my last resort to save my beloved team. Now it is the final nail in coffin. Unless I fall upon a bucket of gold, I have no chance. I do not want to make the call to Joe next year and say we are out. I am sure that Red Grange and crew will have plenty of gold buckets. I know my friend Tim Mara in NY is not a fan of CC Pyle either. There has to be someone out there that could help us financially for 1926 and beyond. Joe Carr said, 'You Mr. Lyons, were born and raised in the worst place.'"[44]

Lyons made it to Detroit in time for the snowy kickoff at Navin Field. The 6-1-2 Panthers needed a victory to keep their titular hopes alive as they trailed the Chicago Cardinals by a half game (7-1) and outpaced the Pottsville Maroons by yet another half game (6-2). The Jeffs, playing for little more than pride at this point, would do their best to knock the Motown 11 out of contention.

It was a rough game, with several players getting hurt, including Jimmy Conzelman of the Panthers and Cecil Grigg of the Jeffersons. "Conzelman tackled out of bounds," Lyons noted. "Broke thumb. Bone sticking out." Grigg received a nasty laceration to his leg that required deployment of Lyons' well-traveled first aid kit. "Johnson Johnson box—sew up Grigg gash on leg—hospital."[45]

Despite the brutality, the game was never in doubt as the Panthers seized the lead in the first quarter and never looked back. A pair of 15-yard runs by fullback Dutch Marion and a 48-yard scoring pass from quarterback Dick Vick to Conzelman (protruding bone notwithstanding!) gave the home team a comfortable 20-0 victory.

The Jeffs found themselves a week later back on the coast, where Lyons had his players scheduled to face the independent Atlantic City Blue Tornadoes. It was a close game, with the score knotted at 0-0 until midway through the third quarter when Butch Clark scored for the Jeffs. Lou Smyth's conversion attempt failed, and the Rochester advantage stood at 6-0. But the Tornadoes snatched victory from the jaws of defeat late in the fourth when backup quarterback Poss Miller scored from eight yards out to tie it up a six apiece. Fullback Les Asplundh then made good on the extra-point try, and the Tornadoes had all they needed for a 7-6 decision.

7. "We never played a game expecting to lose"

After returning to Rochester following the loss to the Tornadoes, the Jeffs were recalled to Atlantic City to fill in for the Tornadoes' originally scheduled opponent—the Pottsville Maroons—who were ordered by President Joe Carr to make haste to Chicago to face the Cardinals for the league championship.

"The Rochester club," wrote Atlantic City's *Daily Press*, "which will substitute for Pottsville, furnished the fans with the best football game seen at the Airport this season, and bids well to duplicate. In fact, the Jeffs went back home with the belief that the Tornadoes were lucky to win and promise to turn the tables."[46]

Tornadoes general manager Willard Shaner said, "With Pottsville cancelling on us, I did not know of any better attraction than the Jeffs. They gave the fans something which is usually read about in dime novels. We'll be out to beat them by more than one point despite their great forward passes."[47]

Included in the Jeffs' itinerary was a side trip to Philadelphia, where the Chicago Bears were scheduled to take on the Frankford Yellow Jackets Saturday afternoon at Shibe Park. Lyons had arranged with George Halas for the Jeffs to practice with the Bears in their morning workout before climbing into the stands to join the 36,000 paying customers to watch the game. Immediately following the contest, won 14–7 by the Bears behind a pair of touchdown runs by Grange, the Jeffs were off to Atlantic City for the rematch with the Tornadoes.

The exhausted Jeffersons did not put up much of a fight no matter what the final score suggests. The Tornadoes dominated throughout, rolling up 11 first downs to the Jeffs' 2. A lone touchdown in the third quarter by halfback Frank Chicknosky was all they needed to vanquish the visitors from New York.

When the train carrying the Jeffs back to Rochester pulled into the station, most of the players believed the season was finally, mercifully over. The team had traveled in excess of 8,900 road miles between late September and early December.[48] They were ready to return to their homes and to a sense of normalcy after two and a half months on the road. The cash-strapped Lyons, however, had other ideas. He had arranged one more game for his team. The players were no doubt relieved to learn the game was going to take place at Edgerton Park in Rochester, making it the only game the team would play in their home city all year. It would also be the Jeffs' last as members of the NFL.

The opponent for this game was an aggregation of All-Stars collected from three sandlot teams in the city—the Russers, the Greyhounds, and the reconstituted Oxfords. On Sunday, December 13, 1925, the Rochester Jeffersons gathered for the final time under Leo Lyons. Before a crowd of 2,000 local fans, the Jeffs defeated the Rochester All-Stars by a 19–0 count. Shag Sheard holds the honor of scoring the last touchdown in Jeffs history.

It had been another disastrous campaign for the Jeffs, who ended the year with a record of zero wins, six losses, and one tie. Their 3.7 points scored per game was an improvement over 1924 (1.0) as was their 15.9 points allowed (22.3), but the numbers still added up to a fourth straight winless campaign. It is quite surprising, then, that Ed Lynch was named to the end-of-the-season All-Pro team selected by the *Green Bay Press-Gazette*, giving him the distinction of being the last Rochester Jefferson so honored. Even more surprising is the fact that Lynch was selected to the First Team![49]

The season was rendered even more disastrous in Lyons' view by his inability to sign Red Grange. Although he was correct in seeing the Illinois halfback as a surefire superstar for the league, it is highly doubtful that his presence would have had the same impact had he played in Rochester. The city had a well-established indifference toward the pro game and lacked the mammoth media structure of the big metropolises of Chicago and New York. It is probable that interest in Grange would have swiftly run its course and Lyons would have lost everything he owned in the process. In short, Leo Lyons dodged a bullet when George Halas beat him to the punch in signing Red Grange.

8

"I already knew my part was caput"

(1926–1927)

The long ride to the league's winter meeting in Detroit, Michigan, must have seemed like an eternity to Leo Lyons after the difficult season he had just experienced. The dream was clearly over, but if he was planning to ask his fellow owners to suspend or discontinue his franchise, it was not mentioned in the meeting minutes as recorded by Secretary-Treasurer Storck. In fact, the Rochester honcho—accompanied on this trip by Ed Schlegel—was fairly active during the two-day session, seconding a number of motions made by the delegates. This was not a man giving the appearance of someone about to throw in the towel.

The meeting was held at the Statler Hotel on February 6–7, 1926, and in retrospect it can be viewed as one of the most consequential of the league's first decade. There were several matters requiring attention, starting with the handling of the controversy surrounding the 1925 championship. The Pottsville Maroons were claiming the title based on their 21–7 defeat of the Chicago Cardinals on December 6, which allowed the second-place Maroons (who improved to 10–2 as a result) to leapfrog over the first-place Cards (who dropped to 10–2–1). The league at that time awarded its championship to the team with the better record, so Maroons owner Doc Striegel felt justified in claiming the title. Despite this, both teams continued to schedule games. The Maroons played two more games, including one against a team of Notre Dame All-Stars at Shibe Park in Philadelphia on December 12. Since Philadelphia was within the Frankford Yellow Jackets' territory, President Joe Carr warned Striegel to cancel the game or face suspension. Striegel ultimately ignored the warning and the Maroons played anyway, winning by a 9–7 final in front of 8,000 spectators. Carr proved a man of his word and the Maroons were duly suspended.

Chicago Cardinals owner Chris O'Brien, meanwhile, scheduled games against the Hammond Pros and the Milwaukee Badgers. The Badgers, who had already disbanded for the season, filled their roster with four high school players—a clear violation of league rules. Both the Cards and the Badgers were censured by the league, but with Pottsville disqualified, the Cardinals were left with the best record and were awarded the championship. O'Brien, however, declined to accept the title, stating he did not want a championship that was not determined on the field of play. The Cards were nevertheless recognized as that season's champs, but it was not until 1933—after the team had come under the ownership of Charles Bidwill—that they proudly laid claim to the 1925 title.

Another serious matter the league moguls had to tackle involved Red Grange and his manager, C.C. Pyle. Grange's first year as a member of the Chicago Bears had been a grand success, and now the pair were seeking a franchise of their own to be based in New York City.

"In the end," wrote author Chris Willis in *Joe Carr: The Man Who Built the National Football League*, "Grange and the Bears played nineteen games in two months before over 469,000 fans. It is estimated that Grange and Pyle cleared about $250,000 on the second part of the tour (including endorsements). The Bears organization netted about $100,000, which George Halas described as 'the first financial cushion we'd managed to accumulate.' The bottom line for all the parties involved is that they all made money giving professional football a major boost in respectability."[1]

All things considered, the pair felt entitled to an even bigger payday.

"Pyle, accompanied by Grange," reported the Associated Press, "appeared before the league today to announce their plans for establishing a club in the Yankee stadium for which they hold a five-year lease becoming effective next October. Everybody seemed willing to permit a second club in New York territory but [New York Giants owner Tim] Mara's refusal was construed by Pyle to mean that the door would be closed to them."[2]

As owner of the league's only New York–based franchise, Mara held exclusive rights to the territory and was not about to allow Grange and the reviled Pyle to encroach on it. Shut out by the established NFL, the pair went to plan B. Within hours, Pyle was meeting with reporters, declaring his intention of putting together a circuit to rival the NFL with a Grange-led team playing in Yankee Stadium as its flagship franchise. They invited any other disgruntled owners to join them in the venture.

"The entire dynamic of professional football was about to change," Willis observed, "and Carr's NFL was about to face a war against what historians have called the 'Grange League.'"[3]

The only established NFL team to leave and join the Grange League, however, was the Rock Island Independents. As a result, the Independents became the only franchise to be charter members of two different leagues. The American Football League (the first of four eventual rival leagues to use that name) began play in September 1926 with nine teams. Only the New York and Philadelphia teams enjoyed box office success while the other seven clubs floundered, resulting in the league's dissolution after just a single season.

In other matters, the owners reasserted their commitment to honoring the integrity of college football by declaring their opposition to signing players still enrolled at institutions of higher learning. The league approved raising the guarantee for visiting teams from $1,000 to $1,500 and the franchise application fee from $500 to $2,500. Not surprisingly, President Carr, Vice President John Dunn, and Treasurer Carl Storck were all reelected to their respective offices.[4]

Meanwhile, Lyons never relented in his quest to bring pro football trading cards to market. Proposals continued throughout 1925 and 1926 with Lyons approaching Rochester-based Stecher Lithographic Company and several candymakers including the Goudey Gum Company, Rueckheim Bros. (makers of Cracker Jack), and William Wrigley, Jr. Although some of the responses received seemed promising, league president Joe Carr refused to give consent to move forward with production.

"Mr. Carr will not approve deal," Lyons scratched on the back of his copy of the proposal to Rueckheim Bros. "No $ for this," to which he added, "Missed opportunity."[5]

Like nearly all of Lyons' brainchildren, it was a simple matter of poor timing. Lyons once again just happened to be a step ahead of his contemporaries. The concept of football cards was not completely extinguished, however. It merely lay dormant until 1935, when the first official set of NFL trading cards was issued by the National Chicle Gum Company of Cambridge, Massachusetts.[6]

The league owners held their summer meeting in Philadelphia on July 10–11, but Ed Schlegel attended in Lyons' place. Whether Lyons had spoken with George Halas prior to this meeting or Schlegel had had the opportunity to confer with Halas earlier that day is not known. When Halas rose to speak late in the evening of Saturday the 10th, however, it was clear that Lyons and Schlegel had entrusted the fate of their team to Papa Bear. Sometime after 11:20 p.m., Halas took the floor to make a motion on behalf of the Rochester owners. As recorded by Secretary Storck, "Moved by Mr. Halas and seconded by Mr. O'Rourke that the Rochester Franchise be suspended for one year, at their request, with the understanding that the League dues be paid. Carried."

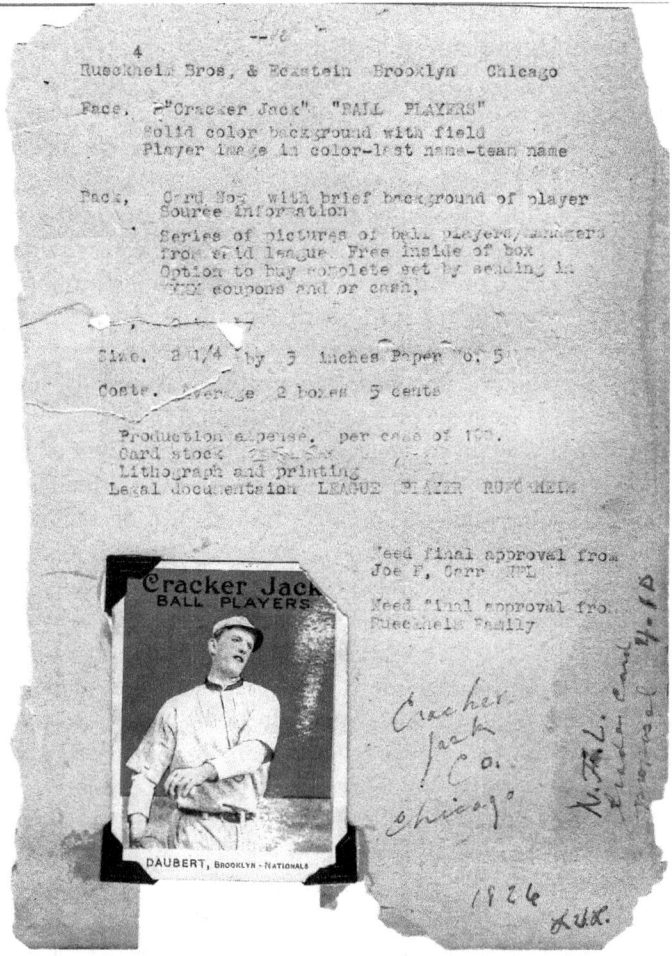

Leo Lyons' proposal for football trading cards, 1926. Lyons's design was larger than the typical tobacco card of the day. He believed companies like Cracker Jack and Wrigley provided greater allure to kids than the ones connected with tobacco.

By making this request, Lyons and Schlegel were buying time in hopes that another year might present an improved financial situation for their team. It was a move that, even at that time, could be viewed as little more than a pipe dream.

This was the only mention of the Jeffersons in the meeting minutes. Storck's notes indicate no meaningful activity on Schlegel's part, other than being listed as present both days.[7]

Lyons was alone when he returned for the winter meeting held at the Astor Hotel in New York City on February 5–6, 1927. He was still giving no indication that he was ready to call it quits or that this was indeed going to be his last meeting as a member of the ownership group he helped create that fateful day back in September 1920. In fact, in contrast to Schlegel's hushed presence at the previous convention, Lyons was an active participant. He was particularly involved in a deliberation that, perhaps unwittingly, hastened the impending end to the Rochester Jeffersons' tenure in the NFL. Midway through day 1 of the meeting (February 5), Dr. Harry March of the New York Giants made a motion—seconded by Halas—that a committee be formed to devise a way to reorganize the league. The prevailing sentiment was that the league had become "rather unwieldy at the present time" due to the growing number of franchises, which by this time had bloomed to 25 prospective members.

The nine-man committee met briefly before coming back to the group to declare it could not produce an appropriate means of accomplishing its goal. After further deliberation, which carried over to day 2, Dr. March made a formal motion that—as had been discussed earlier by the delegates—the league be divided into groupings to be known as class A and class B. Lyons seconded the motion, which was then carried unanimously. Another committee was created, tasked with determining to which class each team would be assigned. When the committee returned, it reported the teams be disbursed thus: class A to include Brooklyn, Buffalo, Chicago Bears, Chicago Cardinals, Cleveland, Detroit, Duluth, Frankford, Green Bay, Kansas City, Milwaukee, New York, Providence, Philadelphia, and Pottsville; class B to include Akron, Canton, Columbus, Dayton, Hammond, Hartford, Louisville, Minneapolis, Racine, and predictably, Rochester.

Three-man subcommittees representing the teams of each grouping were then instructed to discuss "ways and means of formulating the proposed division." Jerry Corcoran of Columbus, representing class B, reported that his group had decided "the only terms they would be willing to accept were the sale of their franchises back to the League at the present application fee of $2,500." After another lengthy debate, it was decided that a cash payment was not practical. At an impasse, Carr was asked to "propose a suitable plan for the re-organization of the League ... to be considered at an adjourned meeting of the present one ... no later than April 15th."[8]

When the owners reconvened in Cleveland on April 23, most of the teams lumped in the B division—including the Rochester Jeffersons—did not attend. If the owners of the more successful franchises were hoping for a voluntary exit of the weaker teams rather than a forced exit that would have resulted in a steep financial settlement, they seemed to be getting what they wanted.

President Carr laid out his six-part plan for reorganizing the league. The main points of the plan included offering the weaker franchises a "pro rata share of any money in the League treasury at the time said certificate is surrendered." This meant that teams desiring to accept the financial buyout would be entitled to a few hundred dollars each. If the owners of the A clubs had agreed to pay the B clubs the $2,500 as they had originally asked, the league itself would have been bankrupted.

Teams were given the option of suspending operations for 1927 while retaining their membership in the league. This would have allowed them to hold out for a year while deciding whether the risks outweighed the uncertain rewards awaiting them in 1928. B-club owners were also given the option of selling off their players' contracts to other clubs. Although this would not have generated a significant windfall, it allowed the cash-strapped teams the opportunity to recoup at least some of their losses from the previous season.

Carr's plan was adopted by a unanimous vote of those present. Then, as if to drive the point home, the owners set the guarantee fee at $2,500, knowing this sum was well out of reach for the weaker clubs.[9]

The end for the Jeffersons, along with several other underperforming franchises, finally came at the next league meeting, held in Green Bay on July 16–17, 1927. Again, most of the B teams had decided not to attend. When the roll of the clubs was called, asking each to state whether it planned to operate during the upcoming season, there was, of course, no response from the unrepresented Jeffersons. While all of the other folding franchises had already notified the league of their intentions, Leo Lyons seemed to be taking a recalcitrant stance. Next to ten franchises (Akron, Brooklyn, Columbus, Detroit, Hammond, Kansas City, Los Angeles, Louisville, Minneapolis, Milwaukee) listed in Secretary Storck's minutes appears the word "withdrew." Next to the Jeffersons' name, however, was written, "Not being present and not posting guarantee was assumed to have withdrawn."[10] Thus, the owners voted to move forward with a scaled-back roster of 11 teams in 1927. Irrespective of Lyons' intentions, the NFL was moving on without the Rochester Jeffersons.

"I already knew my part was caput," Lyons recounted several years later. "I promised my family I was done with the Jeffs. By '27 it was no more NFL for me. I turned the keys over to Ed [Schlegel] and he would run the Jeffs like they were long before, a local amateur sandlot unit. They kept the name and uniforms the same. Even some of the local boys who played for me way back, were on the field again for the Jeffs."[11]

The Jeffersons retreated to the sandlots of Rochester, joining the long list of failed franchises from the NFL's turbulent first decade. That list included championship teams such as the Akron Pros (1920), Canton/Cleveland Bulldogs (1922–1924), Frankford Yellow Jackets (1926), and Providence Steam Roller (1928). Their six-season stay was commendable when compared to the brief stints of some of the other original teams like the Cleveland Tigers (two seasons), Detroit Heralds/Tigers (two seasons), Chicago Tigers (one season), and Muncie Flyers (three games). The Redshirts compiled an overall record of 18–35–4, with a mark of 2–25–2 against league competition.

Leo Lyons' dream of bringing professionalized football to the fans of Rochester was over. He had done everything he could to make it work, literally going broke in the process. But it turned out that fans in Rochester did not share Lyons' passion for a big-league team. They were more interested in seeing local luminaries competing against one another than they were in the dazzling exploits of college All-Americans. Benny Boynton, Elmer Oliphant, Howard Berry, Joe Alexander? No thanks.

"Rochester fans remained unimpressed," wrote historian Bob Carroll. "The more outside stars Lyons packed into his lineup, the fewer fans turned out for his games. At the same time, crowds for the local sandlot teams increased. Clearly, Rochester wanted to cheer for its own. In his heart of hearts, Lyons felt the same. As much as he loved stars with big college reputations, his favorite player was an area lineman who never got past fourth grade. Blond Hank Smith could play tackle, guard, or center as well as any star with All-American credentials."[12]

Ironically, the downgraded Jeffs received diminishing coverage from the local press over the next few seasons. By the time the team finally ceased operations in 1929, one would have been hard-pressed to know the Jeffs had been playing at all. It was a sad ending for one of the proud founding franchises of the NFL.

9

"I miss my team badly"

After suspending his beloved team's franchise following the 1925 season, Leo Lyons focused his attention on the career in which he first embarked two years earlier when George Halas recommended him for a representative position with the Hockaday Paint Company. He had begun by taking classes to learn the company's ropes in January 1923 and, a year later, took a sales position with the F.P. Van Hoesen Company on St. Paul Street in Rochester. Within four years, he was managing the store. Eight years later, he was ready to branch off on his own. In this endeavor, he received another assist from Halas.

"I opened my store, thanks to the nicest guy I ever met," Lyons wrote in 1936. "I never like to mention to others what amount was scratched onto his check. I will pay him back no matter what, the total amount. [Halas] did mention later to never tell anyone other than my wife. He didn't want people coming out of the woodwork wanting help. In 1935, the Leo V. Lyons, Inc., paint store debuted on St. Paul St. Pratt & Lambert '61' and Hockaday paints were huge successes. The store was featured in newspaper articles around the country. One can find any paint supplies here in 1 stop shopping. I want this to succeed and make my patient and one of a kind wife proud of me because football nearly destroyed our special life together."[1]

Work and family became the priority as Leo settled into middle age. He and Catharine watched proudly as daughters Zelda and Sabina graduated from Nazareth Academy high school in Rochester before heading off to Nazareth College. Yet, no matter how much he tried to make up for lost time with Catharine and the girls, there is no evidence that he ever tried to reconcile with his father. The two had had a falling out in the early 1920s, and Edward's presence in Leo's life all but evaporated. Leo left no notes mentioning his father's name—nor his mother's, for that matter. No one seemed to recall hearing Leo even talk about his father and would turn sullen and agitated if someone else brought him up. It was as though Edward Lyons had been airbrushed from his son's life. Leo managed to emerge from his own disreputable dabblings unscathed, fortunate to have lived in a time when there was no social media, 24-hour sports programming, or internet to constantly remind him of his or his family's past. Most important, Leo became the loving, supportive father for his daughters that his own father never was for him.

The competitive outlet he found on the football field was replaced by bowling, a sport he enjoyed as both a player and organizer of teams and leagues for much of the rest of his life. And just like he had with the Jeffersons, Lyons organized competitions with teams and leagues from other cities, primarily the city of Buffalo, whose All-Americans (and later Bisons) once stood as the Jeffs' chief rival outside of Rochester.

Still, even as his paint store flourished and he involved himself in various civic and recreational activities in and around Rochester, the smell of old leather and moldy moleskins continued to haunt him. He followed the pro game as a fan and kept tabs on league activities, longing to be a part of the old fraternity.

"I miss my team badly, but not like before," he wrote. "I need to make up for lost time. Catharine and the girls will be going on a much-needed vacation to Florida. George [Halas] and Joe [Carr] both offered me jobs with the Bears and the league but respectfully declined. I still want to be involved with the NFL."[2]

If his pride would not allow him to be a mere employee of the league he helped start, Lyons managed to stay connected in a unique and somewhat innovative way. Long before the collecting of sports memorabilia exploded into a national pastime, Leo Lyons was one of the hobby's seminal figures. From the earliest days of his playing career, Lyons collected seemingly everything related to his team and the game of football. He maintained a journal and saved scraps of paper on which he had scratched out everything from addresses and important dates to rosters and offensive formations. He carried this obsession through the Jeffersons' pre- and NFL eras, constantly adding to his vast collection of artifacts and ephemera from pro football's formative years. He continued collecting historical items even after leaving the owners fraternity. As early as 1931, he was reaching out to representatives from the various franchises seeking photos, documents, or artifacts from their respective pasts in his quest to preserve the remnants of the league's history.

GREEN BAY, WISCONSIN

March 19, 1931

Leo Lyons
Rochester, New York

Dear Mr. Lyons,

I was pleasantly surprised to receive your kind letter last week, very happy you are doing well. Those early years were tough on the wallet and no one had it easy. Have you spoken to league members about serving their teams in some way or a job with the N.F.L.?

You mentioned that you are collecting league mementos like pictures, documents and pieces from the start of the league to now. We certainly can put together some pieces to send you, not sure how good or important they are.

Coach Lambeau was jesting that you already have some Packers items he gave you a while back. Coach and I wish you well,

Yours truly,
L.H. Joannes [signed][3]

Lyons experienced an epiphany in the mid–1930s when he heard of the impending construction of the National Baseball Hall of Fame in Cooperstown, New York, and other planned sports museums. He now knew why he had been saving these relics all of his adult life. Such a shrine dedicated to pro football would be the perfect repository for the collection. His outgoing letters to friends among the ownership group have been lost to history, but a good number of their responses have survived. Readers can see the high regard Lyons' one-time colleagues and owners still held for him and the seriousness with which they took his idea.

COLUMBUS, OHIO

September 4, 1936

Mr. Leo V. Lyons
604 Beach Avenue
Rochester New York

Dear Leo,

It is always good to hear from you, how is everything in Rochester? I am aware of the talk about a possible football hall of fame around Rutgers U. in New Brunswick, N.J., as well as the folks in Cooperstown, New York, proposing a construct of a Pro Baseball HOF. I am also very aware of the funds necessary to build such a building, something the National Football League is experiencing, lack of extra funds for such projects as a Pro Football museum.

I thank you for your passion to preserve our leagues short history as of now, and appreciate you holding on and not donating some of said items you have to men like Mr. Schroeder and Mr. Helms. Hopefully in the near future, we can have a N.F.L. museum and Hall to honor and preserve the years gone by and the men who made it happen. Mr. Halas told me about some of the items you have in your collection. I only shake my head and hope to God that the league we started in 1920 is still thriving and growing long after we have passed away.

Deciding on a location for a museum would be most daunting, as you mentioned, Latrobe, Canton and L.A.

Very truly yours,
Joe F. Carr [signed][4]

Tragically, less than three years later, the man who had served as league president since 1921 died of a heart attack at the age of 59. Lyons had maintained a cordial friendship with the former Columbus head man, but fearing that hall of fame talks would end with Carr's passing, Lyons redirected his pleas toward Carl Storck. The former secretary/treasurer of the league assumed the role of acting president upon Carr's death in May 1939 before being elected to the office in his own right the following April.[5]

In March 1940, Lyons sat down and typed up a complete list of items he had accumulated over the years. It is not known whether he shared the list with Storck, but the timing of his letter and the new president's references to specific items in it indicate he was aware of the contents of Lyons' burgeoning collection.

March 4, 1940

OVER 75 PLAYER CONTRACTS 1910 to 1925
OVER 100 PLAYER AND TEAM PICTURES 1906 to 1925
NEW YORK STATE FOOTBALL TROPHY 1916
STOPWATCH FROM THORPE 1917
HENRY MCDONALDS FOOTBALL SHOES 1917 season
TRAIN STUBS AND MAPS 1922 to 1926
[?] BOOKS, TEAM LINEUPS OPPONENTS 1922 to 1926
JOHNSON AND JOHNSON FIRST AID BOX 1920 gift from Geo. Eastman
CANCELED AND UNCASHED BANK CHECKS (THORPE, HALAS, RAMMACKER, GRANGE, LEAGUE)
WOODEN MONEY BOX FROM C. LAMBEAU FOR PACKER TEAM 1925
Joe Alexander coaching whistle and game plays designed
JOE BERRYS HELMET, PANTS AND SHOES USED 1921 JEFFS V. STALEYS
MY OFFICE PHONE many important football calls
SPAULDING FOOTBALL USED IN 1920 JEFFS V. BUFFALO
WILSON FOOTBALL USED IN 1921 JEFFS V. STALEYS
SPAULDING FOOTBALL USED 1925 JEFFS V. GIANTS

9. "I miss my team badly"

BOX OF POSTCARDS FOOTBALL RELATED 1916 to 1925
NFL FRANCHISE CERTIFICATES 1922, 1923, 1924
9 EXPERIMENTAL FOOTBALL TRADE CARDS FROM CRACKER JACK AND AM. CHICLE
JEFFERSONS PENNANT 1925
Art's tape measure from 1933 FORBES FIELD PITTS. FOOTBALL PIRATES
CORRESPONDENCE LETTERS FROM PLAYERS, TEAMS, APFA AND NFL, BUSINESS AFFAIRS
28 JEFFERSON PROGRAMS 1916 to 1925
MEGAPHONE, CHALKBOARD, NOISE MAKERS ("HUB UBS") JEFFS EARLY SEASONS
FIELD MARKERS FROM 1925 SEASON
MY ROCH JEFFS UNIFORM FROM 1916 SEASON
VARIOUS GAME DAY PLAYS JEFFS 1917 to 1925 IN LARGE BINDER
VARIOUS NOTES SCRIBBLED ON MY SAT. EVENING POSTS
OTHER NFL TEAMS SENDING PHOTOS AND [?] TO ADD TO MY COLLECTION

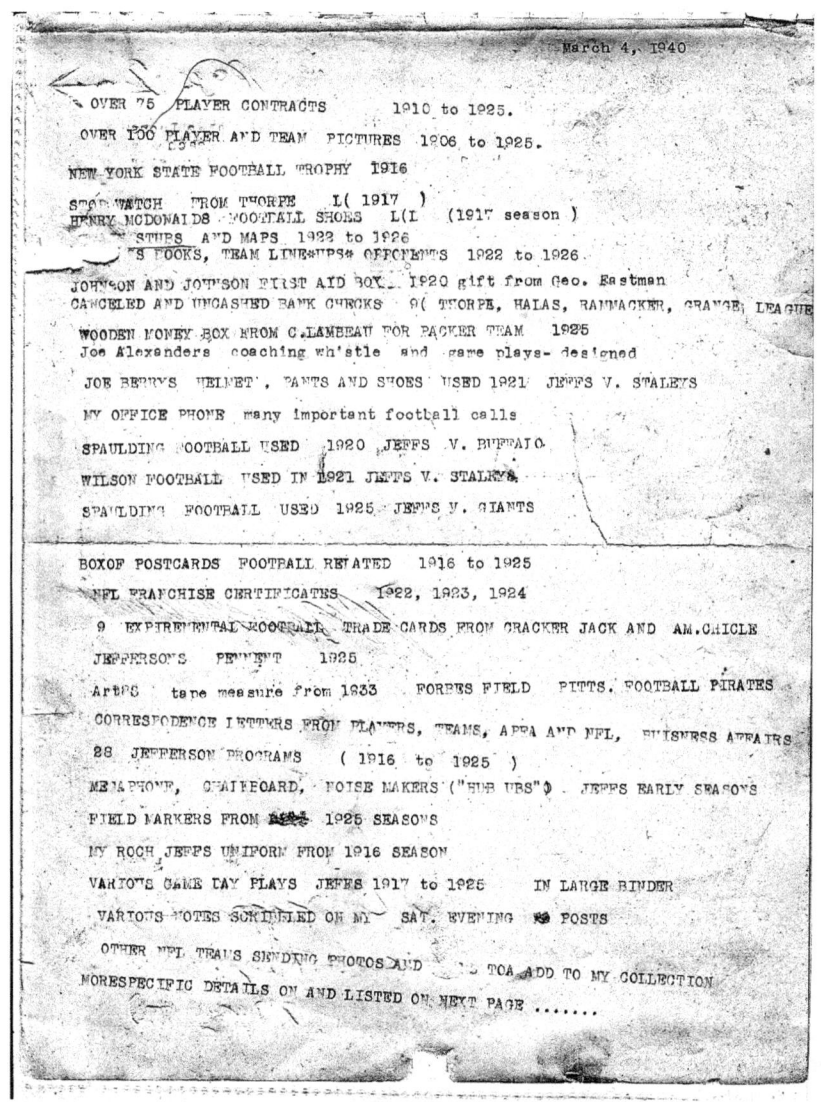

Inventory listing the items in Leo Lyons's ever-growing collection of football relics. Compiled by Lyons, March 4, 1940.

1928 football from Prov. Steam Rollers vs. Yellow Jackets
1929 [?] papers from Chic Bears
1930 Various notes—plays from Jimmy Conzelman
1935 Photos from team photogs Giants [?] Eagles
1937 Copies of player contracts 1922 to 1929
    courtesy of Joe F. Carr and George Halas
74 contracts not counting 4 Roch
1938 Individual team players photos 1929 to 1938
133 photos from teams courtesy of Halas

[The following items were written in Lyons' hand]

1919	Thorpe uniform (Canton)	
1929	Red Grange uniform	29 season
1935	Bears uniform top	
	Cardinals	"
	Pirates	"
	Packers	"
1935	Box of [?][6]	

While Storck's reply clearly acknowledges Lyons' hall of fame idea, it also offers the same worn-out advice on the subject he had received from Mr. Carr.

DAYTON, OHIO

August 1, 1940

Mr. Leo Lyons
604 Beach Avenue
Rochester, New York

Dear Leo:

    I received your letter last week from Rochester, thank you for staying in contact. It definitely feels odd without Joe at the helm. Mr. Halas mentioned he learned of your football collection and would like to browse the photos, letters and items, many from before the N.F.L. A pro football hall of fame/museum would be a great idea, of course it would have to be located in Ohio, just my humble opinion of course. I do hear wonderful things about the baseball HOF in Cooperstown, New York.

    All I can advise you to do is be patient and soon we will talk about the hows and means of such an endeavor, but right now is not the time. The league appreciates your dedication to it, when a pro football museum is on the docket, we know who to reach out to. I do also agree with you that Jim Thorpe should be a part of it as well.

    I also hear that your new paint business is doing quite well. I wish you much success. Rest assured, we will find a good home for your collection, just do not give it to another state or local museum.

    Sincerely yours,
    Carl Storck, President [signed][7]

Having learned from the football trading card nonstarter what the owners meant when they told him to "be patient," Lyons continued to harangue them for the establishment of the pro football museum. When Bert Bell took over as commissioner of the league in 1941, replacing Storck and the retired title of president, he subsequently became the target of Lyons' missives.

November 7, 1953

Mr. Leo Lyons
604 Beach Ave.
Rochester, New York

Dear Mr. Lyons,

I want to thank you for your interest in the National Football League, and the items you have collected over the years. I am aware of the baseball museum in Cooperstown, New York. I will speak with Art soon on your ideas on a museum of some kind, so do not part with your collection please.

Again, thank you Leo for your strong dedication to the National Football League. I am

Very sincerely
Bert Bell, Commissioner [signed][8]

Indeed, Lyons' "dedication to the National Football League" never waned as he waited for the powers-that-be to act. Nor did his friendships with many longtime owners, including George Halas and Tim Mara's son, Jack. His faith and patience were finally rewarded at the league's annual meeting in March 1960 when Halas took the floor to introduce a motion to make "Mr. Leo V. Lyons of Rochester, New York, a charter member of the National Football League, an honorary historian without salary or travel expenses." The motion was seconded by Mara and approved by unanimous consent.[9]

It was a validation of his commitment to preserving the league's history and the first real step toward the realization of his dream of a hall of fame dedicated to professional football. One year later, at the league meeting held on April 27–28 in San Francisco, California, the owners approved the construction of a hall of fame building in Canton, Ohio. The city of Canton might seem like an obvious choice to the modern reader, but competitive bids for the placement of the museum were also received from Detroit, Green Bay, Los Angeles, and Latrobe, Pennsylvania, considered at that time to be the birthplace of the paid variety of the sport.[10] A coalition of Canton entities including political, business, and private interests came together to raise north of $350,000 in seed money for the construction project. The new build was proposed to sit on a 14-acre lot across the street from Fawcett Stadium, itself the largest football facility in the country when it was built in the late 1930s. The owners planned for an exhibition game to be played in the stadium as part of the groundbreaking ceremony in August 1962, and yearly thereafter as part of the hall's annual enshrinement celebrations.[11]

Now that the league was going to have a building in which to store and display its historical documents and artifacts, it needed someone not only to provide much of that material but also to assist in overseeing its appropriate placement and conservation. Who better than the man who had pioneered the craft of collecting football memorabilia some five decades earlier?

From the desk of Pete Rozelle, who had taken over as commissioner of the league in January 1960 after Bert Bell's death, came the news Lyons had been waiting for most of his adult life.

Dear Leo:

As you may have heard, the league at its meeting in San Francisco selected Canton, Ohio, as the site for its Professional Football Hall of Fame.

As you are the league's historian, I am writing to advise that we would all appreciate it if you would take an active part in the establishment of this project.

I know that all of the members would benefit from you counsel and any suggestions you might have regarding the establishment and operation of the Hall of Fame.

We are all concerned that proper planning in regard to the selection of members to the Hall of Fame, and other facets of its operation, be made to avoid any possible major mistakes.

We are in the process of securing similar information from other members of the league and after we have all the information compiled will go ahead with the final plan.

Incidentally, after the Hall of Fame is in operation we all feel that you should play a strong part in its many important functions.

As I did in the case of the San Francisco and Miami meetings I will advise you of the site for our next meeting.

> Sincerely,
> Pete Rozelle
> Commissioner[12]

Lyons' involvement in the venture, however, was not going to be as in-depth as he had hoped. Rozelle and the Hall of Fame committee were looking for an insider who possessed proven administrative skills to oversee the project, and Lyons was not that man. To Lyons' dismay, just two months after receiving the above letter from the commissioner, the committee announced that Richard P. McCann, veteran general manager of the Washington Redskins, had been selected as the hall's first executive director.

"On April 4, 1962," wrote historian Chris Willis, "the Hall of Fame made another brilliant move by hiring Dick McCann. It was his responsibility to collect the football memorabilia that would help trace the history of the game. It was his innovation, foresight, and endless dedication that made the Hall of Fame a success from the very beginning."[13]

With all functions of the hall falling under McCann's purview, Rozelle gladly relinquished any responsibility he once had in the project. When Lyons subsequently approached the commissioner with questions or concerns regarding the hall or his own role in it, he was advised to speak to McCann. McCann, however, appears to have been dismissive of Lyons' history with the league and his vast collection. After Lyons experienced what he felt was "coolness" from McCann when the two first met, he refused to have any further dealings with him.[14] McCann, for his part, chose to disregard Lyons' lifework and unilaterally initiated what United Press International described as "the world's greatest scavenger hunt" to find relics of the game's past.[15] Understandably hurt and angered, Lyons returned the favor by pretending McCann did not exist and continued sending letters directly to Rozelle. When Rozelle advised Lyons that his office had no authority and that he should direct his concerns to McCann, Lyons complained about both men to his friends among the ownership group.[16]

Despite the acrimony resulting from this whole episode, Lyons still provided many of the items that were included in the hall's initial exhibits and collection of historical documents, though exactly which and how many pieces he gifted was not properly recorded.[17] It was quite possible, however, that a good number of those relics would not have made it to their final resting place had fate not intervened in a near-catastrophic scene occurring at Lyons' Rochester home back in 1954. On the afternoon of October 18, the Lyonses' two-and-a-half-story dwelling at 604 Beach Avenue in the Charlotte section of the city caught fire, with the attic and much of the second floor sustaining the brunt of the damage. Catharine was the only one home at the time the fire was discovered and was able to evacuate unharmed. Lyons was known to keep the lion's share of his collection locked in the vault of his paint store while storing some items at home as well. There is no record, however, of how many items Lyons had stored at home at the time, so it is impossible now to quantify the number of pieces damaged or destroyed by the blaze.[18]

The groundbreaking for the Hall of Fame building was held on August 11, 1962. Thirteen months later, September 7, 1963, it was open to the public. As the league's honorary historian, Lyons was of course invited to take part in the hall's dedication ceremonies. He was among an estimated 6,000 revelers taking in the dedication celebration that day. This included a 93-car parade of honored guests and speeches by NFL Commissioner Pete Rozelle, U.S. Senator Frank J. Lausche of Ohio, and Supreme Court Justice Byron R. "Whizzer" White, himself a former star player with the Pittsburgh Steelers and Detroit Lions.

The inaugural class of the Pro Football Hall of Fame comprised 17 men, many of whom were active during that same six-year period when the Rochester Jeffersons played. The list included Sammy Baugh, Bert Bell, Joe Carr, Dutch Clark, Red Grange, George Halas, Mel Hein, Pete Henry, Cal Hubbard, Don Hutson, Curly Lambeau, Tim Mara, George Preston Marshall, Johnny McNally, Bronko Nagurski, Ernie Nevers, and Jim Thorpe. Pete Henry and Lyons' old friends Thorpe and Carr were being enshrined posthumously, leaving Halas as the only honoree surviving from the league's debut season. Halas' acceptance speech was relatively brief, especially when measured against some presented by more recent enshrinees. Lyons looked on as Halas waxed nostalgic about the league's organizational meeting held some 43 years earlier at a small automobile showroom in the Hall of Fame's host city. He watched proudly as Halas mentioned the names of a handful of people he felt were essential in the establishment and development of the league that was now on the verge of surpassing Major League Baseball as America's favorite professional sport. One of those people just happened to be the league's recently named honorary historian from Rochester.

> Ladies and gentlemen. A few weeks ago a few of our grandchildren visited the Bears training camp and I was talking to them about this trip to Canton to participate in the dedication of Pro Football's Hall of Fame. Somehow the conversation got around to an earlier trip that I made to Canton some 43 years ago when we met in Ralph Hay's automobile showroom and founded the National Football League. I told them some of the informal aspects of that meeting and among them being that there was a lack of chairs and also that we had to sit on the running board of the car. That prompted my nine-year-old grandson to say what is a running board Grandpa? I would say the problem of answering that difficult question when my fourteen-year-old grandson said running boards are those things that you see on those funny old cars in that television series known as the "Untouchables."
>
> That little incident demonstrated to me how things can change or disappear until a chance remark or a question—a child's question—stirs your memory. On my trip down here my memory was stirred back quite a few years when I think of the wonderful men who did so much to develop football in this area and through the country. Such fellas like the Nesser Brothers, Ralph Hay, Frank McNeil, Leo Lyons, Joe Carr of the Columbus Panhandles, who was president of the National Football League from 1921 to 1939 some 18 years and you may be sure that some of those years were pretty tough. They were the pioneers and this is the land where football set down its roots and here is the Hall of Fame where its history and traditions will be preserved and remembered. To all of you who have contributed so much to the realization of this Hall of Fame you people of Canton, Mr. Umstattd, and all the rest of you, let me say for all the Chicago Bears right from the original Staley's in 1920 down to the 1963, just two heart-felt words. Thank you.[19]

Just a few months later when the owners met in Miami, Florida, in January 1964, rumors were circulating that Lyons himself was receiving a groundswell of support for induction into the hall. Several owners with whom he had remained close over the years were looking to honor the man from Rochester for his dedication and hard work on behalf of the league. United Press International correspondent Oscar Fraley reported the league "may get behind long overdue recognition for Leo V. Lyons of Rochester, N.Y., one of the original founders with the Rochester Jeffs. Word has it that the Bear's George Halas, Giants' Jack Mara and Steelers Art Rooney will join to propose him for the pro football hall of fame."[20]

Unfortunately, there is no mention of Leo Lyons in the minutes from that meeting. Whether Halas, Rooney, or Mara ever presented Lyons' name for consideration for enshrinement is a question that most likely will never be answered.

Lyons was accorded a place of honor at the hall's second enshrinement celebration which took place the first weekend in September 1964. He was included in another parade through downtown Canton that featured a 70-car motorcade carrying a mishmash of dignitaries and football legends. The list of distinguished gentlemen included Ohio Governor James A. Rhodes and such NFL greats as Bobby Layne, Art Donovan, Buddy Young, Johnny McNally, and Ernie Nevers, along with Harry Stuhldreher and Don Miller of Notre Dame's famed Four Horsemen. Also honored was hometown hero Cecil Grigg, a member of two championship teams with the Canton Bulldogs (1922 and 1923) and player-coach of the 1925 Rochester Jeffersons.

Leo Lyons enjoys a ride in the Pro Football Hall of Fame parade, August 3, 1968. Standing alongside the automobile is Chicago Bears Hall of Famer Bronko Nagurski.

The next day, Lyons attended the third annual Hall of Fame game at Fawcett Stadium, which featured the Baltimore Colts facing off against the Pittsburgh Steelers. Prior to kickoff, Lyons was escorted to midfield to present a specially minted coin to Governor Rhodes, who executed the pregame coin flip.[21]

Lyons continued to attend Hall of Fame events throughout the 1960s and into the early '70s. His displays of artifacts, photos, and documents became must-see viewing for those in attendance. He loved nothing better than hobnobbing about the glory days with old friends or telling younger fans how much better the players were back in his day. Lyons also attended the league's annual winter meetings through the beginning of 1965 when Rozelle wrote to advise him that although he was still welcome at the annual Hall of Fame game, his presence was no longer required at the league meetings.[22] Lyons, of course, saw this as another slap in the face from the brash young commissioner who did not fully appreciate his role in the league's history. Their already strained relationship began to take on an adversarial tone as Lyons pestered Rozelle to include him in all league and hall functions and squabbled with him over reimbursement checks he felt were insufficient in covering expenses incurred during these events. It eventually devolved into a vicious circle with Lyons complaining to anyone who would listen (Halas, Rooney, etc.) about his ever-diminishing role and perceived lack of respect from Rozelle.

Lyons' pleadings, however, fell on deaf ears. Rozelle was bringing a sense of modernity to the NFL, along with unprecedented revenue. He began by convincing the owners to adopt a league-first philosophy rather than relying on the every-team-for-itself approach of the past.

"Rozelle convinced the individual owners that by pooling their resources and sharing their profits, they would be able to provide a product that, as a whole, was much more valuable than the sum of its parts," wrote Clay Moorhead in the *Vanderbilt Journal of Entertainment & Technology Law*. "The idea took off in 1961 when Rozelle successfully persuaded the individual owners to give up their local television broadcasting rights and instead sell all broadcasting rights together as a national package; the proceeds were then split evenly among each NFL team."[23]

The commissioner then negotiated a contract with the Columbia Broadcasting System (CBS) worth $9.3 million, bringing the average broadcasting revenue of each team from $198,000 per season to $332,000. Three years later, CBS upped the ante to $14.1 million, bringing each team's average broadcast revenue to over $1 million per year. The sharing of profits from gate receipts and television played a major role in stabilizing the league and ensuring success for smaller-market teams.[24] While Lyons enjoyed special bonds with senior owners like Halas, Mara, and Rooney, Rozelle was making them wealthier than they had ever imagined. Sadly, the catch-as-catch-can days of Lyons' wistful memory had been reduced to a couple of bulletin boards of grainy black-and-whites and a few moments of reminiscing with old cronies as they passed by on the way to meetings to discuss their latest multimillion-dollar deals. This was no longer, by any stretch of the imagination, Leo Lyons' NFL.[25]

"When I think of what the pro game has become," he reflected, "the teams with all that TV money and compare it with what it was, I simply have to marvel. We used to play under conditions that would be smiled at by the players of today and pay they would laugh out loud at. I often wondered whether, if I had landed [Red] Grange, the Rochester Jeffs would be a member of the National Football League today and cashing in on all that wonderful TV money."[26]

Despite it all, Lyons remained fiercely loyal to the league he helped start. He never stopped chronicling the NFL's history and never commented publicly about his feelings toward Rozelle. He was a go-to guy for journalists seeking quotes about the glory days and every once in a while popped up in the local paper or a television show talking about the Jeffs, the league, or one of its seminal figures. He relished his role as one of the NFL's founding fathers and even contributed stories and photographs for several books on football history.

One writer who found Lyons' input invaluable was Robert W. Wheeler, a 23-year-old graduate student who had the opportunity to confer with the sage of Rochester in the summer of 1967 when he was working on a project telling the life story of Jim Thorpe.

Leo Lyons (left) and George Halas share a laugh over some old photographs Lyons had displayed at the first meeting of the Professional Football Writers Association, held at the Waldorf-Astoria Hotel in New York City, February 19, 1968.

I was working on my Master's Thesis at Syracuse University and wanted to write it about Jim Thorpe. I believed Thorpe's life deserved an honest treatment. There was a lot of opposition because my thesis was about sports. My mentors wanted me to write about the Erie Canal. They didn't consider sports to be history even if it was about Jim Thorpe. I said, "There are 46 books on the Erie Canal!" I did not feel we needed another. My journey to tell Jim's story necessitated hitchhiking over ten-thousand miles through twenty-three states, with my reel-to-reel tape recorder in hand.

I was 23 when I visited Leo at his 57 Oak Manor Lane home on July 1, 1967. It was one of the pivotal events in my life. The person who provided me with Leo's contact information was my beloved uncle, Lou Dwyer. Lou and his family were fellow residents of Leo's in Pittsford. As a sports aficionado, Lou was well aware of and grateful for Leo's role in the founding of the NFL. I contacted Leo and he invited me to his home in Pittsford. He had a big smile on his face when he saw me carrying a thirty-pound reel-to-reel tape recorder up the sidewalk. I didn't know how to write, but I knew how to push a record button! We talked and I recorded everything.

His den housed treasures that defined the earliest days of the NFL and his role as a player, coach, and owner of one of the original teams. His countless files not only contained scorecards, stat sheets, and newspaper accounts of the games but his personal handwritten letters and those of the pioneers of the league that revealed the heartbreak, euphoria and exhaustion as a result of the endless hours of practice, game strategizing, field securance and preparation, player contract negotiations, and extensive train travel. The side walls surrounding his file cabinets were filled with game programs, a Rochester Jeffersons jersey, photos of players, an oil painting of Jim Thorpe wearing his Carlisle Indian School football uniform, and shelves filled with footballs, one signed by Jim, handmade cleated shoes, leather helmets, and trophies, including one awarded to the Jeffersons commemorating their 1916 season as champions of New York State.

The piece of furniture I will remember the rest of my life was a large oak rectangular table in the middle of the room. It was here that Leo invited me to sit with him as he placed a blank sheet of paper on it and hand drew an outline of a map of the US. He drew stars for landmarks at various points on the map, and the first place he pointed to was Chicago, for George Halas. He then wrote down the contact information for several important people—Joe Alexander, George Trafton, Jimmy Woods, Ernie Nevers. He proceeded to pencil in the names, addresses and telephone numbers of more than 50 of his and Jim's contemporaries. Can you imagine doing that for some kid? But that was Leo. All I had to say was "Leo gave me your number." Their respect for Leo was so strong they welcomed me every time I called on them. Leo set all that up for me and without that it never would have happened. Thanks to Leo's itinerary, one of my first interviews was with Dick McCann at the Hall of Fame. He not only gave me the names of additional pro football pioneers to interview but also offered me a job, then and there, with the Hall of Fame and told me I could start immediately. He said he was impressed with my dedication and commitment to preserve the legacy of Jim Thorpe and the history of professional football.

Leo had so many stories that shed light on Jim Thorpe. Never about himself. He told me about accompanying Jim when he'd speak at the Rotary Club or a local school and how the kids were in awe the whole time Jim spoke. I have never experienced a home that more resembled a museum and Leo's warmth, detailed expertise in the history of pro football, and eager willingness to not only facilitate my research on the life of Jim Thorpe, but set up scores of interviews for me surpassed any curator on the planet.[27]

Wheeler's seven-year odyssey in search of Thorpe's true story was published in 1975 as *Pathway to Glory*. This work is still considered essential reading for anyone researching Thorpe or the myriad issues surrounding his life.

* * *

Leo and Catharine had moved to 604 Beach Avenue in Rochester's Charlotte section along Lake Ontario in 1936. After the fire in 1954 that destroyed most of the upstairs of the dwelling, the couple had the house repaired and lived there another 13 years. By 1967, however, they were finding taking care of the large house too much and decided to downsize. They moved to 57 Oak Manor Lane in Pittsford, where they lived out their remaining years.

Eldest daughter Zelda passed away on July 21, 1957, at the age of 42 after losing a brave battle with leukemia. She never married and had no children. After graduating from Nazareth College, Zelda had spent much of her adult life at St. John Fisher College in Pittsford, New York, where she was serving as school registrar at the time of her death. The Very Reverend John F. Murphy, president of St. John Fisher, said of her, "I regret the passing of one of the outstanding Catholic women in the Rochester Area. She must be listed and remembered as one of the founders of St. John Fisher College."[28]

Sabina married U.S. Army Lieutenant John A. Bosner in November 1942. They lived for a short time in San Antonio, Texas, where he was stationed due to military service. They returned to Rochester in 1943 to raise their family. Sabina worked as a secretary at Nazareth College while John later found employment with Allied Industrial Laundry, eventually rising to the position of company president. The couple raised five children (John, Sabina, Leo, Kevin, and Maureen).

The Leo V. Lyons Paint Company moved from its original location at 29 St. Paul Street to 142 Andrews Street in 1943. Ten years later, it was removed to 177 St. Paul Street, where it remained until closing shortly after Leo's passing in 1976. Leo claimed at one point to have created a special type of paint that could have made him as wealthy as he would have being an NFL owner. "I invented a paint for lining highways in the early 1920s," he lamented, "but was so busy hopping around lining up players and opponents that I never got around to getting a patent. Someone else did and made millions."[29]

Lyons never lost his yearning to be involved in the NFL, but the league clearly wanted nothing to do with the city of Rochester. An opportunity to be a part of a new franchise in a new league came his way in 1936 when a second American Football League was formed. The team originated in Brooklyn as the Tigers but moved to the Flower City midway through the inaugural season and was rechristened the Rochester Tigers. They played their first game at Red Wing Stadium on Norton Street on November 19, 1936. Co-owners Harry Newman and Mike Palm had turned to Lyons for help with promoting the team when it moved to Rochester. Despite countless hours of meetings and negotiations between Lyons, the team, and city officials between 1936 and 1937, it became clear fans were no more interested in this new venture than they were in the old Jeffersons. The league and the team never gained traction, and by the second season, money was already running out. The team played its last game in Rochester on October 24, 1937, and folded with the rest of the league at season's end.[30]

Devotion to his home city led Lyons to involve himself in numerous community and fraternal organizations, often rising to leadership roles within each. At one time or another, he was a member of the Rochester Ad Club, the Rochester Area Chamber of Commerce, the Lake Shore Country Club, the Knights of Columbus, and the Rotary Club.

It was in his role as a Rotarian that Lyons was able to persuade old friend Jim Thorpe to add Rochester to the itinerary of his national lecture tour in November 1940. Thorpe spent a busy day in the city on November 26, speaking at a Rotary Club luncheon at the Powers Hotel after a morning assembly at Monroe High School.

"An auditorium in a high school with maybe 1,500 or 2,000 youngsters is ordinarily like a beehive," Lyons told Thorpe biographer Robert Wheeler, "but when Jim stood up on the stage, just at a bare desk, with no microphone, you could have heard a pin drop. The kids probably didn't know Thorpe, but their fathers and grandfathers did. Jim looked out and began: 'I think the best way to talk to you boys and girls is to give you the story of my life.' They loved every minute of it."[31]

Thorpe later visited the Kodak plant before stopping by the River Campus of the University of Rochester to reminisce with Lyons and head football coach Dud DeGroot.[32]

As a longtime high-ranking member of the Rochester Council of the Knights of Columbus, Lyons was asked to perform many important civic and charitable functions. Among these was taking the lead in organizing and promoting two NFL charity exhibition games in the city in the early 1950s. Lyons was able to use his influence with Pittsburgh Steelers owner Art Rooney and league commissioner Bert Bell to convince them to stage a game at Rochester's Aquinas Memorial Stadium. On August 26, 1953, the Art Donovan–led Baltimore Colts faced off against Jack Butler's Pittsburgh Steelers in front of a reported 15,000 paying customers. Lyons sat with Steelers owner Art Rooney and his brother, the Reverend Silas Rooney (athletic director at St. Bonaventure University in Olean, New York, where the Steelers held their training camps at the time) as the Colts defeated the Steelers, 13–6.

A year later, the Steelers met the Philadelphia Eagles—featuring future Hall of Famers Chuck Bednarik and Pete Pihos—before 13,000 fans at Aquinas Stadium. The Eagles prevailed in a brawl-marred shootout, 24–14.[33]

As years passed, awareness of the Rochester Jeffersons tumbled further and further into the crevices of history. By the early 1970s, nearly a half century had come and gone since the Jeffs scarred up NFL gridirons. Meanwhile, professional football had seen a meteoric rise in popularity, especially so during the 1960s as television brought the game into tens of millions of homes. At the same time, a new American Football League—the fourth league to use that name and the first successfully—created a whole new legion of fans in cities previously unrepresented by NFL teams. Many young fans would have been surprised and amused to see old photos of Jim Thorpe, Fritz Pollard, or Ernie Nevers wearing leather helmets with no face masks, playing for teams with names like Oorang Indians, Akron Pros, or Duluth Eskimos. And if this generation of fans did not know of these early players and teams, they undoubtedly had no idea who Leo Lyons was.

One such fan was 12-year-old Joe Bock. In 1971, Bock was a fan of the NFL Cleveland Browns and enjoying his first year of Pop Warner football. That was also the year he began delivering the *Rochester Democrat & Chronicle* and *Times-Union* papers around his Sherwood neighborhood. As expected, young Bock had dozens of stops on his route, including 57 Oak Manor Lane. Little did he know that the gentleman residing at that address was partially responsible for creating the league in which Bock dreamed of playing. And although he might not have been aware of Lyons' identity, he still remembers the day he found out.

> Leo lived on Oak Manor Lane in Pittsford and my family lived nearby on Charmwood Road. I began delivering newspapers when I was in the seventh grade, around 1971. I had been only doing it for a day or two when I noticed the NFL-1 license plates on his car. My attention to detail and the fact that I was a football fan made me take notice pretty quickly. I remember thinking, "Who does this guy think he is driving around with NFL-1 on his plates?" Well, maybe two or three weeks later I finally saw him outside. He stopped me and asked if I like football. I told him I did and it was my first year playing little league ball. He said, "Would you like to come into the basement and see my football stuff?" I didn't know who he was, but I figured he was old and weak and I could probably take him if he tried to kidnap me, so I said yes. I remember the basement was huge with a U-shaped bar. There was football stuff everywhere—plaques, pictures, trophies, certificates. He pointed out some things on the wall, showed me a players' contract from 1921, a scrap book which was pretty cool. I was only there for about half an hour or forty-five minutes, but it was amazing! When I left, I thought, "Yeah, he can drive that car with those plates!"

Bock went on to star at local East Rochester High School before shining as a defensive lineman at the University of Virginia. Along the way, his loyalty migrated from the Browns to the Buffalo Bills, and he vowed that one day he was going to play for them. After going unpicked in the 1981 college draft, Bock realized his goal by signing a free agent contract with the Bills. He enjoyed a long stay in professional football, including stints with the St. Louis Cardinals, the Birmingham Stallions, and Houston Gamblers in the United States Football League, the Chicago Bruisers in the Arena Football

League, and the Rochester Raiders and New York/New Jersey Revolution of the Great Lakes Indoor Football League. Bock played his last pro game with New York/New Jersey in 2006 at the age of 46! Despite a long and colorful career, the memory of that fateful day in 1971 never left him.

> Ten years later when I signed to play for the Buffalo Bills, I noticed the contract I was signing had almost exactly the same wording as the one Leo had hanging in his basement from 1921. It also got me thinking. He was a cofounder of the NFL and, who knows, maybe Rochester had a fifty-fifty chance of being the home of the Hall of Fame if he had kept that team going.[34]

Lyons' eminence in the city's athletic community was honored on November 21, 1974, when he was enshrined in the Rochester–Monroe County High School Athlete's Hall of Fame. Since Lyons did not attend school past the ninth grade, he was inducted in a "Special Award Category" as the "Father of Professional Football in the United States" and for his role as "an active participant in sports and community affairs to this day." Joining Lyons in his enshrinement class was his old friend and one-time teammate Henry McDonald.[35]

Sadly, this event was one of the last times Lyons ventured out of the house for anything other than medical appointments or emergencies. His physical condition declined sharply and he experienced frequent falls as he became unsteady on his feet.

"According to my mom," said Lyons' great-grandson John Steffenhagen, "Leo had been in and out of Rochester General Hospital constantly for weeks before he died. She was at Leo's the day he died. He fell again and an ambulance was called. Leo whispered something to Catharine and then they grinned at each other in tears and he said, 'I will be waiting for you.' They all knew it would be the last time. Leo passed away as he got to the hospital. He was always falling towards the end. He had multiple problems that were getting worse. I think Leo knew his time had run out."

Lyons showing off his NFL-1 license plates, 1974. The plates were a gift from NFL commissioner Pete Rozelle and New York State governor Nelson A. Rockefeller.

Lyons died at Rochester General Hospital on May 18, 1976. He was 84 years of age. A devout Catholic, Lyons was interred at Holy Sepulchre Cemetery in Rochester. Tributes poured in from all corners of the football world, including from some of his oldest friends.

"I have always regarded Leo as a friend," George Halas told the *Rochester Democrat & Chronicle*. "I've known him for more than 50 years and in all those years he always did what was best for the league. His loyalty to the NFL never wavered, even after his team left the league."

Art Rooney added, "Leo was really a fine gentleman and I have considered him a close friend for years. He was as dedicated to the National Football League as any man. We became friends during those early years and he was always very proud of the accomplishments of his team. He has been our historian for these many years and furnished the league with much of the material which chronicles the NFL's beginnings."

"If anyone had the Hall of Fame at heart," said retired Hall of Fame Executive Director Dick Gallagher, "it was Leo Lyons. He was just so dedicated and enthusiastic. He never missed an induction weekend since the Hall of Fame was formed. It's really too bad that Leo has not been recognized more for his many contributions to the NFL. He has many qualifications for being a member of the Hall of Fame, but so much of the early years of the league is lost now."[36]

Catharine outlived her husband by little more than a year, passing away on July 3, 1977. She was laid to rest next to Leo at Holy Sepulchre Cemetery. Youngest daughter Sabina passed away on April 7, 2003. She was predeceased by her husband John Bosner, Sr., and survived by their five children and seven grandchildren.[37]

* * *

Coauthor John Steffenhagen is the son of Sabina's daughter and namesake, Sabina Bosner Steffenhagen, and thus a great-grandson of Leo Lyons. He has vivid memories of spending time at his great-grandparents' home when he was very young. "I had been going to his house on Oak Manor since I was born," he recalled. "They lived in Pittsford and my family lived in Rochester and

Catharine Lyons holds great-grandson John Steffenhagen at his baptism as Leo looks on, 1967.

then nearby Fairport, New York. I was nine when he passed away but keenly remember his office downstairs because Leo would show me all the things he collected. However, I liked auto racing and had no interest in football. According to my mother, as a baby he showed me the shiny football trophy for the 1916 Jeffs state title that sat on top of the television. The trophy that I still possess thanks to my uncle Leo, who is known to family and friends as 'Vinnie.'"

John remembers that trips to Leo and Catharine's house were sometimes punctuated by visits from strange elderly gentlemen in fedoras. "One day at Leo's when I was six or seven years old, I was playing with my Hot Wheel cars, my mother said to hush down because Leo had company. She told me years later those 'two old guys with hats,' as I called them, were in fact George Halas and Art Rooney visiting during the spring."

All the while, Leo was sitting on a collection of items no one in the family was prepared to store or qualified to appraise. At some point, however, whether as a safekeeping measure or simply a gift-giving gesture, Leo felt it necessary to distribute the collection among his four adult-aged grandchildren.

"Before Leo passed away," Steffenhagen continued, "he had given his grandchildren Sabina, Kevin, John, and Vinnie some items from his collection [the fifth grandchild, Maureen, was only 15 at the time]. It was not known what the items were at that point, but Leo told them to 'hold on to them.' This took place around 1975. Leo had things at home and his paint store. After he passed away, I remember playing pool with my sister Joann on Leo's pool table. Never dared doing that when he was around! I remember endless photos, documents, and 'stuff' all around the large downstairs area, the office. Unfortunately, the family was not aware of what exactly was there."

There were, however, people at the Pro Football Hall of Fame who were well aware of the significance of Leo's collection. On August 25, three months after Leo's passing, Jim Campbell from the Hall of Fame sent Catharine a letter inquiring as to her plans for the "Lyons Collection."[38]

"My business card actually said Librarian/Researcher/Curator," Campbell recalled. "I found it easier to just say 'historian.' I recall meeting Leo when I first started working at the hall in 1972 or '73. I was in a group and Leo was giving a talk about Henry McDonald. I remember him riding in the parade in the back of the car with a banner saying 'Leo Lyons, NFL Historian' on the side. We knew he had things, but we didn't know how extensive his collection was."[39]

Campbell left the Hall of Fame in April 1977 to work for NFL Properties in Los Angeles. The family heard nothing further for several months.

"For another year, it mostly sat untouched," said Steffenhagen. "Catharine died in July of 1977. A month later, a large moving truck from the Hall of Fame arrived at her house, along with a young Joe Horrigan, who later became the hall's executive director. Pictures appeared in the *Rochester Democrat & Chronicle* of boxes being packed up. My uncle said that they took nearly everything. Leo's daughter Sabina and son-in-law had donated it all unbeknownst to other family members. A month after that, Sabina received a certificate from the Hall of Fame, signed by Hall of Fame President Earl Schreiber, thanking her for the donation."

It turned out that those items Lyons had distributed among his grandchildren before his death were not included in Horrigan's haul. Those items were scattered over four separate homes in various spaces with no record of who had what. In fact, the items were, in some cases, packed away and forgotten for decades.

9. "I miss my team badly"

Steffenhagen's interest in his great-grandfather's collection began in his early 20s, when his mother presented him with some boxes containing items Leo had given directly to her.

> Around 1980, my mother gave me several boxes of Leo's football things from his house. I was 13 and had no interest in football whatsoever. My father was a race car driver, so I loved everything racing. I knew who Richard Petty was but never heard of Red Grange. The boxes sat in my bedroom closet for decades. I would occasionally take a gander at them but with no Google to help me back then, they just looked like old pictures and antiques. My mother told me to never throw them away no matter how unimportant they looked. She too did not know exactly what was in those boxes other than things from Leo's past. There was no way of knowing what the items were since they were haphazardly thrown in those boxes with no labels or reference.
>
> Around the year 2000, I dug into things inside the boxes and used the internet to help research. I visited the Hall of Fame, wrote to Dan Rooney and the NFL and the PFRA and contacted historians Jeffrey Miller and Ken Crippen. With their help, I was able to ascertain much about Leo and the Jeffersons team.
>
> Over the next few decades, I would do some research here and there, still holding on to everything. In 2020, I moved into a new house and the old "Leo boxes" were falling apart. I was transferring things into new bins when something fell out of an old Hall of Fame program from 1966. I discovered two leafs of paper folded together—one a copy of an NFL memo from Pete Rozelle dated 1966 asking Leo for an inventory list of his collection and the other an actual list of items in his collection. I was shocked to see many items that were in the boxes listed on Leo's inventory. After that day, I was obsessed with learning all I could about Leo and his involvement with the NFL. More of Leo's collection was discovered by other family members after I pestered them to go through their attics and basements. Fortunately, they were all cooperative and sent or gave me what they found or already had unknowingly, like the Jeffersons New York State championship trophy from my uncle Vinnie, the franchise certificate from Uncle John Bosner and countless documents from my uncle Kevin Bosner. My mother unknowingly stored her needles and threads in an old antique wooden box that use to adorn Leo's mantel. With a metal tag stamped "G.B.P." on top, she figured they weren't Leo's initials so can't be that important. Until that newfound inventory list, which included a wooden box with the letters G.B.P. on top. It was an acronym for "Green Bay Packers!" The item was the money box Packers player and manager Curly Lambeau gave to Leo in 1925 after their teams played one another. It had a sticky latch—still does—and Curly was going to throw it out. Leo decided he could fix and use the waterproof, specially designed box to keep money in from cash at the gate for his team.
>
> Many of the things I believed to be Leo's personal items were later discovered to be someone else's, based on Leo's inventory. Football pants and a leather helmet were Howard Berry's from the 1921 game against the Staleys at Cubs Park, both with hardly legible initials carved in them. The crude football cleats belonged to Henry McDonald, not Leo as originally thought. People at the Smithsonian helped me discover his initials deep inside one of the shoes, which was only visible with a blue light turned at a certain angle. A Johnson & Johnson first aid kit No. 1 that I thought was just an antique, sat on a shelf in my garage for years, only to discover it was from George Eastman, given to Leo for his first season in 1920, the league's first season. Eastman took it from his Kodak factory, at the time the kit was revolutionary. It was used during the league's first six seasons. Two NFL-1 license plates, one from 1967, the other 1973, were New York State–issued and used on Leo's cars during that time frame. According to Leo's inventory, Pete Rozelle and New York Governor Nelson Rockefeller honored Leo with those plates. The countless letters, pictures, and correspondence that I originally had were easier to identify through research. Sometime in 2021, my mother realized an old watch in her jewelry box was in fact Leo's, given to him by Jim Thorpe sometime between 1917 and 1925.

Even old objects in boxes that relatives thought were nothing special turned out to be priceless pieces of the collection. A small stack of what looked like scrap papers at my aunt and uncle's house in Florida turned out to be Leo's personal journal from 1908 to the late 1920s. In them, details of the founding of the NFL at which he was present in 1920, game day accounts during the first six seasons, and more. There were old copies of the *Saturday Evening Post* on which Leo wrote down historical football events as they happened. An old Lufkin tape measure sitting at the bottom of another box was Art Rooney, Sr.'s from 1933. Through research and Leo's notes, it was revealed the tape measure had sat in Art's office desk for decades. It was used by the field crew at Forbes Field in 1933 to mark off the baseball field into a football field, the Steelers' (then known as the Pirates) first NFL game. Leo, as league historian, pestered his good friend for the tape for years to add to the collection. An old Pennsylvania Railroad whistle was found by another uncle which turned out to be Frank Nesser's work whistle which was used by the referee in the first NFL game at Triangle Park in 1920. Among the hundreds of tattered pieces from Leo's boxes, there was a piece of a letter stating Frank's brother Al gave it to Leo in 1965.

Among old stuck-together pieces of paper in the boxes was a bank check from 1925. After many hours of tedious work, steaming and picking apart layers with tweezers and dental picks and time in and out of the freezer, I was able to separate several checks with Leo's name

Lyons pictured in 1970 holding the New York State championship trophy from 1916, and the football used in the game between the Jeffersons and the Chicago Staleys at Cubs Park, Chicago, October 16, 1921.

on them. One was of particular interest, made out to Harold Grange for $5,000 and included the checkbook register pages! An old football that looked smallish and torn was at the bottom of another box. My uncle John from Florida had sent it to me sometime around 2001. I figured it was an old Jeffersons football from some random time, but Leo's inventory listed it as an original Thomas E. Wilson football used in the Jeffs-Staleys game at Cubs Park in 1921. Research found a 1934 newspaper photo of Leo holding the ball and saying it was from that 1921 game. The hardly visible Wilson logo on the ball piqued my interest and I contacted Wilson Sporting Goods' main office. The company president asked for photos of the ball and how I had it. He said it was an early collegiate football from 1919–1921 and found the company no longer had records from that time period. He agreed that it was authentic. The ball had been stuffed for nearly 100 years—though insufficiently—which resulted in terrible shrinkage.

Indeed, the collection of items in Steffenhagen's possession could fill a small museum on its own. He is fully aware of the historical, cultural, and monetary significance of the collection but remains uncertain about its fate.

I am still pondering the future of the collection. I have had many offers, from the Pro Football Hall of Fame to top memorabilia dealers in the world. So far, I have declined those offers, but future options are still being considered. It is a fine line between preserving and displaying, especially with century-old pieces. I do know I do not want these artifacts stored away in a vault or closet at some museum where they might never see the light of day. The perfect scenario would be to have the items on permanent display for football fans to see and enjoy. I am hopeful that is what will happen.

10

"His loyalty to the NFL never wavered"

Sadly, the average casual fan of today's NFL has little clue who Leo Lyons was or how he helped shape the pro game. Whereas most can cite George Halas and Jim Thorpe among the league's founders—and perhaps a few more hardcore followers can add Joe Carr to the short list—scant few could come up with names like Lyons, Storck, Nied, or Hay, let alone say very much about them. And that is a shame. Carl Storck managed the Dayton Triangles from 1918 to 1926 and served in various league offices before taking over as president in 1939 following Joe Carr's passing. Frank Nied, as a co-owner of the Akron Pros, hired the first African American head coach when Fritz Pollard was named to the post in 1921. Ralph Hay owned the Canton Bulldogs and hosted the league's organizational meeting at his Hupmobile dealership in Canton, Ohio, on September 17, 1920.

Leo Lyons was among those present at that late-summer meeting in Hay's showroom, a 28-year-old visionary convinced pro football could one day eclipse major league baseball as America's pastime. And although Mr. Lyons' name might not ring as loudly as Halas or Thorpe or Carr or any of the other seminal figures of the game's first decade, his list of deeds and accomplishments warrants a reconsideration when historians list the league's essential characters.

He enjoyed a 16-year run as the owner of the Rochester Jeffersons, which at its peak reigned as one of the best-known pro teams in the northeastern United States. This was no accident. Immediately after taking ownership of the sandlot Jeffersons as an 18-year-old in 1910, Lyons plotted the course for making them a truly professional outfit. Under his leadership, the Jeffs stood out from the other squads in the city for their coordinated uniforms, practice regimen, log of designed plays, and better pay.

He was committed to recruiting the best players in the Rochester area to build a strong roster. In doing so, he became a pioneer in the integration of the game by hiring the fourth-known Black professional player in 1912 when he lured Henry McDonald away from the crosstown rival Oxfords.[1] McDonald went on to a long sandlot career, playing on and off with the Jeffersons and other teams throughout the remainder of the decade.

In 1915, Lyons introduced the first actual logo used in pro football when he had the team name embroidered in script font on the front of the jerseys. Although the logo was used only between 1915 and 1919, it remains a symbol recognized by legions of football fans to this very day. Jerseys and other apparel bearing the classic Jeffs script logo have been a hot seller via online retailers.[2]

In 1916, borrowing from the model established by Major League Baseball, Lyons conceived the idea of creating a set of football trading cards to promote the gridiron game. This was nearly two decades before the first official set of football cards was produced by the National Chicle Gum Company of Cambridge, Massachusetts, in 1935. Throughout his tenure as an owner, Lyons continued to pester his cohorts to invest in the production of football cards as a means of promoting their young league but to no avail. If only he had patented the idea!

That same year, while still performing double duty as a player on the field and manager off it, Lyons guided the Jeffs to the championship of New York State. The team remained a statewide power for the remainder of the decade. Following the lead of nationally recognized football Goliaths like the Canton Bulldogs, the Jeffs began traveling outside western New York to face teams from across the state and, in 1917, crossed state lines for the first time, taking on Thorpe's Bulldogs. Although they were crushed that day, Lyons had an opportunity to chat briefly with the Olympian and discuss his idea of a nationalized professional football league, only to find out the teams in Ohio had been discussing the same concept for some time. This encounter can be seen as the seed that eventually led to the formation of the league that now dominates the American sports landscape.

Three years later, Lyons was present in Ralph Hay's automobile showroom to help organize the first pro circuit, making the Rochester Jeffersons one of only ten teams recognized as charter members of the NFL. In the six years the Jeffs played in the league, Lyons was one of its most dynamic owners. His notes indicate that he either conceived or at least took an active part in several important deliberations, including splitting the league into eastern and western divisions, a year-end playoff to determine a league champion, and the renaming the APFA to the NFL. Lyons even sketched some of the earliest mockups of a new logo for the league in his journal, including at least two in the shape of a shield based on the emblem Jim Thorpe had worn on his track shirt in the 1912 Olympics, which very closely resemble the current NFL logo.

He took an active role in efforts to redesign the football being used at the time. Lyons' notes show his observations that the ball's shape was hindering offensive play. His collaborations with Halas and representatives from the Wilson Sporting Goods Company laid the groundwork for the transformation of the ball into the one fans recognize today.

But perhaps Lyons' most important contribution was that of his pioneering role as a collector of sports memorabilia. Decades before the hobby bloomed into a multimillion-dollar industry, Lyons was saving football artifacts for their historical significance. His passion for collecting became an obsession as Lyons began gathering items from other teams as well as anything related to the league itself. He might not have realized early on that this passion was providing the foundation for what would eventually morph into the football shrine that sits majestically at 2121 George Halas Drive in Canton, Ohio.

After learning about halls of fame being established in the mid–1930s for some college sports teams and Major League Baseball, Lyons experienced an epiphany. The NFL needed a similar venue to store and display the bits and pieces of its history, and his collection would be the appropriate starting point. He campaigned exhaustively for the construction of a similar building for the league he so loved, and it became a reality when the Pro Football Hall of Fame opened its door in September 1963.

"Lyons was one of the old guard who could explain what happened when the league was just beginning," wrote historian Bob Carroll. "As George Halas said, 'His loyalty to the NFL never wavered.' As an historian, Lyons was understandably limited by his own participation in events. It could make for a one-sided view. One consequence is the Rochester Jeffersons loom much larger in many pro football histories than their record warrants. After all, in six years they managed only two league victories, those against poor Tonawanda and the bedraggled Columbus Panhandles in 1921. Yet, one popular history devotes five pages to the Jeffs, but barely mentions the Providence Steam Roller, the 1928 champions! And, although his memory was exceptional, it was not perfect."

According to Carroll, Lyons' reputation as a historian is blemished by his inexplicable claim that the league was organized a year earlier than it actually was. "Somehow, he 'remembered' the league starting at a meeting in Canton in 1919—a full year before the traditional date." This was problematic due to the fact several historians seeking his reflections on the game's founding quoted his incorrect date without seeking verification. As Carroll noted, "[Lyons] remembered it so completely that several respected historical works actually list 1919 as the NFL's first year. Dubious researchers have hunted in vain for any confirmation and have concluded that such a 1919 meeting did not happen. As a matter of fact, contemporary sources prove it COULD NOT have taken place. Lyons had simply—and quite humanly—confused some later meetings that he did actually attend."

Still, Lyons' role in chronicling the league's history should not be underestimated. "On balance," Carroll concluded, "Lyons served well as an historian, keeping alive memories of the league's formative years and aiding many researchers immeasurably. He was a tireless campaigner for the establishment of a Pro Football Hall of Fame and a regular visitor and contributor of memorabilia once the Hall opened. Both before and after his death in 1976, he was nominated for enshrinement in the Hall. If love of pro football, willingness to work, and courage in adversity were the only criteria, he would have been a charter member."[3]

Lyons' descendants, however, are not necessarily seeking his induction into the Pro Football Hall of Fame. What they hope for, says great-grandson John Steffenhagen, is football fans to know who Lyons was and the important role he played in the founding and early development of the NFL.

"My great-grandfather was an integral part of the league's early years and should be remembered alongside the likes of Halas, Thorpe, and the other founders," says Steffenhagen. "It is our hope he will be recognized for his role in NFL history. Just look at all he did! Leo dedicated his life to the game and the league. He deserves at least that much."

Appendix 1

Items from the Leo V. Lyons Collection

First aid kit presented by George Eastman to Leo Lyons, 1920. Used by the Rochester Jeffersons, 1920–25 (photograph by Steven D. Desmond).

Football cleats worn by Henry McDonald while with the Rochester Jeffersons in 1917. McDonald was the fourth known Black professional football player (photograph by Steven D. Desmond).

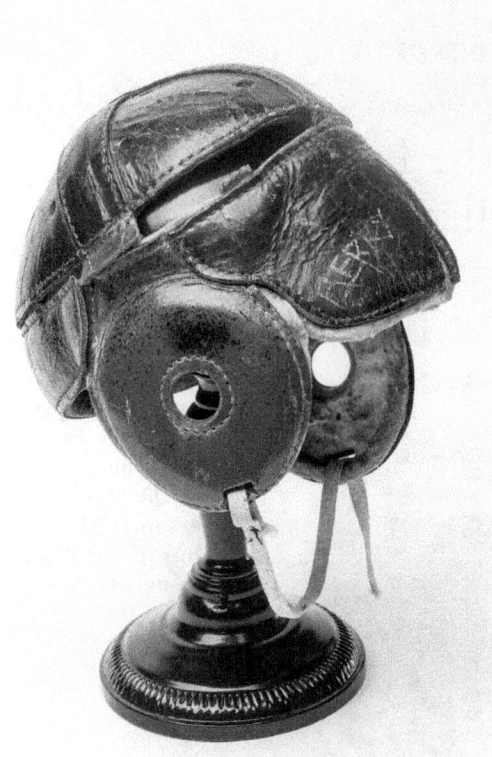

Game-worn helmet used by Howard Berry while with the Rochester Jeffersons, 1921 (photograph by Steven D. Desmond).

Football used in the game between the Rochester Jeffersons and the Chicago Staleys at Cubs Park, Chicago, October 16, 1921 (photograph by Steven D. Desmond).

Stopwatch belonging to Leo Lyons used to time Jeffersons games during the 1910s and '20s. Leo claimed to have used it to measure the hang time of Jim Thorpe's punts when the Jeffs faced off against the Canton Bulldogs, October 28, 1917. This watch is a Lawson "FOOT BALL TIMER" model, manufactured by New Haven Watch Co. between 1883 and 1887 (photograph by Steven D. Desmond).

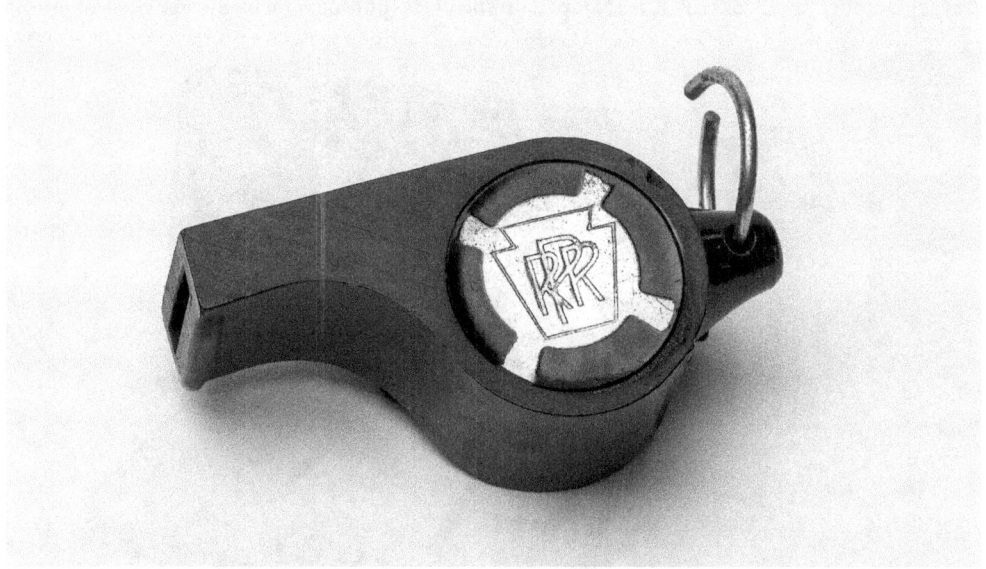

Whistle bearing the logo of the Pennsylvania Railroad, employer of the famous Nesser brothers of the Columbus Panhandle football team. This whistle was used by referee "McCoy" during the game played on October 3, 1920, between the Dayton Triangles and the Panhandles at Triangle Park in Dayton, Ohio, considered to be the first game played between two officially recognized APFA member teams. Given to Leo Lyons by Al Nesser in 1965. The whistle had belonged to Al's brother Frank prior to his death in 1953 (photograph by Steven D. Desmond).

Cashbox gifted to Leo Lyons by Curly Lambeau after the game played at City Stadium in Green Bay on October 25, 1925. G.B.P. is stamped on the plate (photograph by Steven D. Desmond).

NFL-1 New York State license plates gifted to Leo Lyons by NFL commissioner Pete Rozelle and New York State governor Nelson A. Rockefeller (photograph by Steven D. Desmond).

Tape measure used to mark the playing field for the Pittsburgh Pirates' inaugural game at Forbes Field, September 20, 1933. "That day the baseball Pirates had a game prior to the football Pirates," explained John Steffenhagen. "A relative of Art Rooney's was on the grounds crew that measured out and marked the field for football. After the game (a 23–2 loss to the New York Football Giants) the relative walked over to Art, handed him the tape measure and said, 'This is your consolation prize.' Art had it lying around in his desk in the early 1970s and gave it to Leo for his collection." A close inspection shows Rooney has scratched his initials and the team's inaugural year into the metal casing (photograph by Steven D. Desmond).

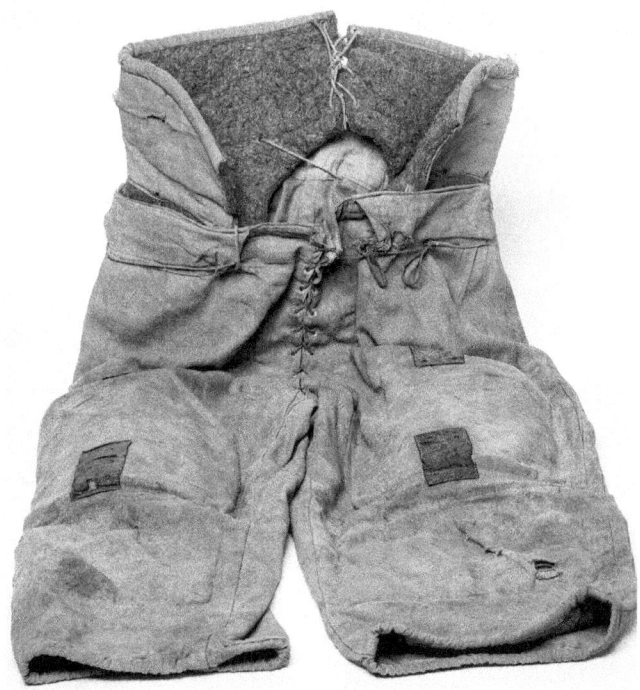

Game-worn pants used by Howard Berry while with the Rochester Jeffersons, 1921 (photograph by Steven D. Desmond).

Appendix 2

Season-by-Season Results

1. Rochester Jeffersons Pre-NFL Era

1908

Date	Opponent	Result	Site	Attendance
October 4	Rochester Scalpers	n/a	Genesee Valley Park, Rochester	n/a
October 11	Rochester Belmonts	W, 15–0	Sheehan's Field, Rochester	n/a
October 25	Rochester Columbias	W, 5–0	Reid's Field, Rochester	n/a
November 8	Rochester X-Rays	W, 6–0	Sheehan's Field, Rochester	n/a
November 22	Rochester Genesees	L, 11–6	Charlotte Field, Rochester	n/a
November 26	Churchville (NY)	W, 5–0	Turner's Field, Churchville, NY	n/a

1909

Date	Opponent	Result	Site	Attendance
October 31	Rochester Columbias	T, 0–0	West End Park, Rochester	2,000
November 7	Geneva (NY) Hogarths	W, 14–0	West End Park, Rochester	2,000
November 14	Rochester Oxfords	W, 16–0	West End Park, Rochester	n/a

1910

Date	Opponent	Result	Site	Attendance
October 23	Rochester Scalpers	W, 11–0	West End Park, Rochester	3,000
November 6	West High Independents	W, 5–0	West End Park, Rochester	2,500
November 13	Rochester Scalpers	T, 0–0	West End Park, Rochester	1,500
November 20	Rochester Oxfords	T, 0–0	West End Park, Rochester	400
November 27	Rochester Rox	T, 0–0	West End Park, Rochester	2,000

1911

Date	Opponent	Result	Site	Attendance
October 15	Rochester Oxfords	T, 5–5	Premier Park, Rochester	n/a
October 22	Rochester Dreadnaughts	T, 0–0	Kiefer's Park, Rochester	n/a

Date	Opponent	Result	Site	Attendance
October 29	Lockport (NY) North Ends	T, 0–0	Lockport Field, Lockport, NY	n/a
November 5	Rochester Oxfords	L, 5–0	Premier Park, Rochester	n/a

1912

Date	Opponent	Result	Site	Attendance
October 12	Fairport (NY) Athletic Club	W, 3–0	Fairport Field, Fairport, NY	n/a
October 20	Lockport (NY) North Ends	L, 12–0	Pioneer Hill Park, Lockport, NY	n/a
November 3	All-Rochester	W, 6–0	Sheehan's Field, Rochester	1,000
November 10	Lancaster (NY)	L, 23–6	Sheehan's Field, Rochester	1,000
November 17	Rochester Atlantics	W, 19–0	Sheehan's Field, Rochester	1,600
November 28	All-Syracuse	W, 18–0	Sheehan's Field, Rochester	1,000
December 1	Rochester Scalpers	T, 0–0	Sheehan's Field, Rochester	2,000
December 15	Rochester Scalpers	T, 0–0	Reid's Field, Rochester	n/a

1913

Date	Opponent	Result	Site	Attendance
October 5	Lancaster (NY)	L, 26–0	American Malleable Park, Lancaster, NY	1,000 (a)
October 12	Buffalo Cazenovias	L, 30–0	Columbia Park, Buffalo, NY	n/a
October 19	Rochester Pullmans	W, 12–0	Genesee Valley Park, Rochester	n/a
November 2	Tonawanda (NY) Irontons	W, 7–0	Sheehan's Field, Rochester	1,300
November 16	Brockport (NY)	W, 46–0	Sheehan's Field, Rochester	n/a
November 30	Rochester Scalpers	L, 7–0	Reid's Field, Rochester	4,000
December 7	Rochester East Ends	W, 32–0	Sheehan's Field, Rochester	1,200

1914

Date	Opponent	Result	Site	Attendance
October 4	All-Lockport (NY)	T, 0–0	Lockport Field, Lockport, NY	n/a
October 17	Rochester Atlantics	W, 26–6	Baseball Park, Rochester	2,700
November 22	Rochester Scalpers	L, 7–6	Reid's Field, Rochester	3,500
November 26	Rochester Pullmans	W, 22–0	Baseball Park, Rochester	1,400
December 6	All-Rochester	W, 39–6	Maple St. Grounds, Rochester	n/a

1915

Date	Opponent	Result	Site	Attendance
February 19	Rochester Scalpers	W, 18–0	NY State Armory, Rochester (indoors)	700
March 13	Lancaster (NY)	L, 12–6	NY State Armory, Rochester (indoors)	200
October 17	Syracuse Westcotts	T, 0–0	Sheehan's Field, Rochester	n/a
October 24	All-Buffalo	T, 0–0	Sheehan's Field, Rochester	5,000 (b)
October 31	Lancaster (NY)	T, 0–0	Sheehan's Field, Rochester	4,000 (a)
November 7	Geneva (NY) Glenwoods	W, 27–0	Sheehan's Field, Rochester	2,500
November 14	All-Buffalo	L, 34–0	Ryan's Park, Buffalo, NY	3,000 (c)
November 25	Rochester Scalpers	W, 13–3	Baseball Park, Rochester	3,000
November 28	Geneva (NY) Glenwoods	W, 18–0	Standard Optical Field, Geneva, NY	n/a

1916

Date	Opponent	Result	Site	Attendance
January 28	All-Rochester	DNF	NY State Armory, Rochester, NY (indoors)	100
October 15	Lancaster (NY)	T, 0–0	Sheehan's Field, Rochester	4,200 (a)
October 22	East Syracuse	W, 7–3	Sheehan's Field, Rochester	3,000
October 29	Onondaga (NY) Indians	W, 48–0	Sheehan's Field, Rochester	2,500
November 5	North Tonawanda (NY) Frontiers	T, 0–0	Sheehan's Field, Rochester	n/a
November 11	Syracuse University	L, 32–0	Baseball Park, Rochester	n/a
November 12	Rochester Crimsons	W, 26–6	Sheehan's Field, Rochester	n/a
November 19	Rogan & Johnson (Geneva, NY)	W, 13–0	Sheehan's Field, Rochester	n/a
November 26	Syracuse Westcotts	T, 6–6	Sheehan's Field, Rochester	n/a
November 30	Rochester Scalpers	W, 21–0	Sheehan's Field, Rochester	5,000
*December 3	All-Buffalo	W, 6–0	Ryan's Park, Buffalo, NY	n/a

*New York State Championship

1917

Date	Opponent	Result	Site	Attendance
September 29	All-Buffalo	L, 21–6	Baseball Park, Buffalo, NY	n/a
October 7	East Buffalo	T, 0–0	Sheehan's Field, Rochester	n/a
October 14	Tonawanda (NY) Groves	W, 32–3	Sheehan's Field, Rochester	n/a
October 21	East Buffalo	W, 20–0	Sheehan's Field, Rochester	n/a

Appendix 2. Season-by-Season Results

Date	Opponent	Result	Site	Attendance
October 28	Canton Bulldogs	L, 41–0	League Park, Canton, OH	3,000
November 11	Oneida (NY) Northside A.C.	W, 26–0	Sheehan's Field, Rochester	n/a
*November 29	All-Tonawanda (NY)	L, 9–7	Baseball Park, Rochester	n/a
December 2	Rochester Scalpers	W, 13–0	Sheehan's Field, Rochester	n/a

* New York State Championship

1918

Date	Opponent	Result	Site	Attendance
October 13	Detroit Heralds	L, 37–0	Navin Field, Detroit, MI	n/a
November 3	U.S. School of Air Photography	W, 6–0	Sheehan's Field, Rochester	n/a
November 10	Batavia (NY) Steel Products	W, 13–0	Baseball Park, Rochester	2,000
November 24	U.S. School of Air Photography	W, 19–0	Baseball Park, Rochester	n/a
November 28	Bausch & Lomb Senecas	W, 35–6	Baseball Park, Rochester	n/a

* No NY State Championship held on account of World War I.

1919

Date	Opponent	Result	Site	Attendance
October 5	Fort Niagara (NY)	W, 20–7	Baseball Park, Rochester	1,300
October 12	Flint (MI) Independents	L, 13–6	Athletic Park, Flint, MI	3,000
October 19	All-Syracuse	T, 6–6	Baseball Park, Rochester	n/a
October 26	Fort Ontario (Oswego, NY)	W, 32–0	Baseball Park, Rochester	n/a
November 2	All-Lancaster (NY)	W, 29–7	Baseball Park, Rochester	n/a
November 9	All-South Buffalo	W, 69–0	Baseball Park, Rochester	n/a
November 16	Bausch & Lomb Senecas	W, 27–6	Baseball Park, Rochester	n/a
November 23	Rochester Scalpers	W, 20–0	Baseball Park, Rochester	4,000
*November 27	Buffalo Prospects	T, 0–0	Baseball Park, Rochester	2,500
*November 30	Buffalo Prospects	L, 20–0	Baseball Park, Buffalo, NY	1,500 (c)

* New York State Championship

Attendance figures for pre–NFL-era games from Rochester Democrat & Chronicle, except (a) Buffalo Courier, (b) Buffalo Enquirer, and (c) Buffalo Times.

2. Rochester Jeffersons Pre-NFL Era

1920 (APFA)

Date	Opponent	Result	Site	Attendance
October 03	All-Buffalo*	W, 10–0	Baseball Park, Rochester, NY	2,000
October 10	Fort Porter*	W, 66–0	Baseball Park, Rochester, NY	n/a
October 17	Utica Knights of Columbus*	T, 0–0	Baseball Park, Rochester, NY	3,000 (a)
October 24	Syracuse YMHA Stars*	W, 21–7	Baseball Park, Rochester, NY	n/a
October 31	Buffalo All-Americans	L, 17–6	Canisius Villa, Buffalo, NY	7,500
November 7	Utica Knights of Columbus*	W, 27–7	Baseball Park, Rochester, NY	3,000 (a)
November 14	All-Tonawanda*	L, 6–0	Baseball Park, Rochester, NY	n/a
November 21	Rochester Scalpers*	W, 16–0	Baseball Park, Rochester, NY	4,000 (b)
November 25	All-Tonawanda*	L, 14–3	Baseball Park, Rochester, NY	2,500
November 28	Rochester Scalpers*	W, 7–6	Baseball Park, Rochester, NY	5,000 (c)
December 5	Rochester Scalpers*	T, 0–0	Exposition Park, Rochester, NY	n/a

1921 (APFA)

Date	Opponent	Result	Site	Attendance
October 09	All-Buffalo*	W, 41–0	Exposition Park, Rochester, NY	4,000 (d)
October 16	Chicago Staleys	L, 16–13	Cubs Park, Chicago, IL	8,000
October 23	Buffalo All-Americans	L, 28–0	Canisius Villa, Buffalo, NY	10,000
October 30	Akron Pros	L, 19–0	League Park, Akron, OH	4,000
November 6	Tonawanda Kardex	W, 45–0	Baseball Park, Rochester, NY	3,000
November 19	Philadelphia Quakers*	T, 3–3	Phillies Park, Philadelphia, PA	8,000 (e)
November 20	Columbus Panhandles	W, 27–13	Baseball Park, Rochester, NY	2,500
November 27	Syracuse Pros*	W, 12–0	Baseball Park, Rochester, NY	1,200 (f)
December 4	Washington Pros	DNP	American League Park, Washington, DC	400 (g)

1922 (NFL)

Date	Opponent	Result	Site	Attendance
October 01	All-Syracuse*	W, 13–0	Baseball Park, Rochester, NY	600 (h)
October 12	Akron Pros	T, 13–13	Elk's Field, Akron, OH	2,000
October 15	Chicago Bears	L, 7–0	Cubs Park, Chicago, IL	7,000 (i)

Date	Opponent	Result	Site	Attendance
October 22	Rock Island Independents	L, 26–0	Douglas Park, Rock Island, IL	3,000 (j)
October 29	Horlick-Racine Legion	L, 9–0	Horlick Athletic Field, Racine, WI	3,000 (k)
November 18	Conshohocken Ironworkers*	W, 6–0	Conshohocken Field, PA	3,000 (h)
November 19	Washington Football Club*	W, 7–6	American League Park, Washington, DC	n/a
November 25	Frankford Yellow Jackets*	L, 20–7	Brown's Field, Philadelphia, PA	10,000 (c)
November 30	Buffalo All-Americans	L, 21–0	Edgerton Park, Rochester, NY	2,500 (h)

1923 (NFL)

Date	Opponent	Result	Site	Attendance
September 30	Hornell Football Team*	W, 46–0	Baseball Park, Rochester, NY	680 (h)
October 7	Chicago Cardinals	L, 60–0	Normal Park, Chicago, IL	5,000 (i)
October 14	Rock Island Independents	L, 56–0	Douglas Park, Rock Island, IL	2,500
November 17	Frankford Yellow Jackets*	L, 33–0	Frankford Field, Frankford, PA	n/a
November 18	Wilkes-Barre Panthers*	L, 10–3	East End Park, Wilkes-Barre, PA	n/a
November 24	Toledo Maroons	L, 12–6	Edgerton Park, Rochester, NY	n/a
December 1	Buffalo All-Americans	L, 13–0	Edgerton Park, Rochester, NY	n/a

1924 (NFL)

Date	Opponent	Result	Site	Attendance
September 27	Frankford Yellow Jackets	L, 21–0	Frankford Field, Philadelphia, PA	7,000
October 05	Akron Pros	L, 3–0	Edgerton Park, Rochester, NY	1,200
October 12	Columbus Tigers	L, 15–7	Edgerton Park, Rochester, NY	2,000
October 19	Buffalo Bisons	L, 26–0	Bison Stadium, Buffalo, NY	3,500
October 26	Cleveland Bulldogs	L, 59–0	Dunn Field, Cleveland, OH	5,000 (l)
November 2	Utica Knights of Columbus*	W, 6–0	K. of C. Athletic Field, Utica, NY	500 (h)
November 9	Providence Steam Roller*	L, 3–0	Kinsley Park, Providence, RI	n/a
November 16	Columbus Tigers	L, 16–0	Neil Park, Columbus, OH	2,500

Date	Opponent	Result	Site	Attendance
November 22	Buffalo Bisons	L, 16–0	Edgerton Park, Rochester, NY	2,500
November 23	Atlantic City Roses*	W, 3–0	Airport Field, Atlantic City, NJ	1,500 (m)
November 30	Pottsville Maroons*	W, 10–7	Minersville Park, Pottsville, PA	500 (n)

1925 (NFL)

Date	Opponent	Result	Site	Attendance
September 27	Canton Bulldogs	L, 14–7	Lakeside Park, Canton, OH	2,500 (o)
October 4	Buffalo Bisons	T, 0–0	Bison Stadium, Buffalo, NY	5,000
October 18	Waterbury Blues*	L, 7–6	Brassco Park, Waterbury, CT	5,000 (h)
October 25	Green Bay Packers	L, 33–13	City Stadium, Green Bay, WI	2,700
November 1	Providence Steam Roller	L, 17–0	Cycledrome, Providence, RI	8,000 (h)
November 8	Hartford Blues*	L, 8–6	Eastern League Park, Hartford, CT	2,000 (p)
November 11	New York Giants	L, 13–0	Polo Grounds, New York, NY	10,000
November 15	Pottsville Maroons	L, 14–6	Minersville Park, Pottsville, PA	n/a
November 22	Detroit Panthers	L, 20–0	Navin Field, Detroit, MI	n/a
November 29	Atlantic City Blue Tornadoes*	L, 7–6	Airport Field, Atlantic City, NJ	n/a
December 6	Atlantic City Blue Tornadoes*	L, 6–0	Airport Field, Atlantic City, NJ	n/a
December 13	Rochester All-Stars*	W, 19–0	Edgerton Park, Rochester, NY	2,000 (h)

*Denotes nonleague opponent.

Attendance figures from Total Football II: The Official Encyclopedia of the National Football League, *except* (a) Utica Morning Telegram, (b) [Syracuse, NY] Post-Standard, (c) Pro Football Archive web page, (d) Buffalo Evening News, (e) Philadelphia Inquirer, (f) Syracuse Herald, (g) Washington [DC] Herald, (h) Rochester Democrat & Chronicle, (i) Chicago Tribune, (j) Davenport [IA] Democrat and Leader, (k) Racine [WI] Journal-News, (l) [New Philadelphia, OH] Daily Times, (m) Atlantic City Daily Press, (n) [Allentown, PA] Morning Call, (o) Pittsburgh Post-Gazette, *and* (p) Hartford Courant.

Appendix 3

Player Register

1. Rochester Jeffersons Pre-NFL/APFA Era

In compiling demographic information for the players who appeared in at least one game for the Rochester Jeffersons between 1908 and 1919, the authors conducted an exhaustive search of every conceivable potential source, including newspaper accounts, game programs, census reports, military records, college records, obituaries, and Leo Lyons' personal journal. In many cases, only a last name and position played was available. However, the authors believe this to be the most accurate and comprehensive listing of each player's vital statistics possible.

Elbert Angevine—T, E, G, B
R. Elbert Angevine
B: February 27, 1900, Rochester, NY
D: May 25, 1969, Rochester, NY
HS: West High (Rochester)
College: Colgate, Rochester, Syracuse
Ht: 5'9" Wt: 150
Seasons: 1916–19

Oliver Angevine—E, G
Oliver Laurence Angevine, Jr.
B: November 15, 1891, Rochester, NY
D: May 5, 1971, Orchard Park, NY
HS: West High (Rochester)
College: No
Ht: 5'8" Wt: 145
Seasons: 1916–19

Bob Argus—B
Robert Anthony Argus
B: January 21, 1894, Hammondsport, NY
D: December 8, 1945, Rochester, NY
HS: Corning Free Academy (NY), West High (Rochester)
College: No
Ht: 5'10" Wt: 193
Seasons: 1914–19

Chuck Ashton—T, C, E
Charles E. Ashton
B: December 8, 1893, Chicago, IL
D: December 23, 1939, Rochester, NY
HS: West High (Rochester)
College: No
Ht: 5'9" Wt: 174
Seasons: 1912–13

Ralph Avery—B
B: January 6, 1887, Waterloo, NY
D: December 6, 1959, Rochester, NY
HS: West High (Rochester)
College: No
Ht: 5'9" Wt: 160
Seasons: 1914

Joe Bachmaier—C, G, T
Joseph William Bachmaier
B: March 11, 1895, Rochester, NY
D: January 14, 1974, Rochester, NY
HS: West High (Rochester)
College: No

Ht: 5'9" Wt: 175
Seasons: 1915–17, '19

Ballicks—E
Seasons: 1910

Billy Bauer—B
William M. Bauer
B: October 22, 1892, Rochester, NY
D: December 6, 1982, Buffalo, NY
HS: No
College: No
Ht: 5'11" Wt: 180
Seasons: 1917

Beacham—E
Seasons: 1908

Eddie Benz—E
Edward Carl Benz
B: May 17, 1889, Rochester, NY
D: June 1, 1973, Rochester, NY
HS: Cathedral (Rochester)
College: No
Ht: 5'8" Wt: 153
Seasons: 1908

John Bergen—B
John H. Bergen
B: June 3, 1889, Rochester, NY
D: July 16, 1948, Rochester, NY
HS: No
College: No
Ht: 6' Wt: 180
Seasons: 1909

Robert F. Birecree—T
B: September 6, 1889, Fairport, NY
D: May 20, 1949, Rochester, NY
HS: West High (Rochester)
College: No
Ht: 5'11" Wt: 185
Seasons: 1910, '13

Britt—T
Seasons: 1915

Cliff Brothers—G
Clifford A. Brothers
B: August 22, 1892, Danby, VT
D: January 18, 1954, Rochester, NY
Ht: 5'8" Wt: 190
Seasons: 1915, '18

Chubby Brown—B
Alexander J. Brown
B: November 7, 1894
D: December 9, 1968
HS: Cathedral High (Rochester)
College: No
Ht: 5'9" Wt: 155
Seasons: 1917–19

Tom Burke—G
Thomas M. Burke
B: September 15, 1894, Rochester, NY
D: May 5, 1963, Port Ritchie, FL
HS: No
College: No
Ht: 6'0" Wt: 170
Seasons: 1912, '14

Denny (Dinny) Cahill—T, G
William Dennis Cahill
B: May 6, 1889, Rochester, NY
D: January 12, 1953, Rochester, NY
HS: Nichols School (Buffalo, NY)
College: No
Ht: 6' Wt: 225
Seasons: 1912–18

John Caler—G
John Owen Caler
B: January 24, 1889, Fairport, NY
D: April 18, 1955, Fairport, NY
HS: Fairport (NY)
College: No
Ht: 6'
Seasons: 1913

Cash—B
Seasons: 1910

Shorty Caske—B
William D. Caske
B: April 4, 1886
HS: No
College: No
Ht: 5'5" Wt: 123
Seasons: 1908–10, '15

Bill Caufield—G, C
William J. Caufield
B: June 12, 1889, Rochester, NY
D: June 25, 1965, Rochester, NY
HS: West High (Rochester)
College: No
Ht: 5'9" Wt: 155
Seasons: 1909, '12

Babe Clark—B
Harold K. Clark
B: January 14, 1891, Avon, NY
D: April 18, 1951, Rochester, NY
HS: East High (Rochester)
College: Cornell
Ht: 5'8" Wt: 170
Seasons: 1914–19

Butch Clark—E, B
Harold R. Clark
B: June 11, 1896, Rochester, NY
D: June 29, 1980, Rochester, NY
HS: Cathedral (Rochester)
College: No
Ht: 5'10" Wt: 195
Seasons: 1919

Bill Connell—B
William Joseph Connell
B: October 19, 1893, Rochester, NY
D: March 1, 1976, Canandaigua, NY
HS: West (Rochester)
College: No
Ht: 6' Wt: 181
Seasons: 1915–19

Ham Connors—E
Hamilton C. Connors
B: February 22, 1898, Pittsburgh, PA
D: February 27, 1967, East Rochester, NY
HS: East High (Rochester)
College: No
Ht: 5'10" Wt: 190
Seasons: 1915–16

Jack Corcoran—E
HS: West High (Rochester)
Seasons: 1908

H.T. Coy—B
Seasons: 1913, '15

Merwin Crandall—G
B: August 10, 1893, Rochester, NY
D: November 18, 1945, Webster, NY
HS: East High (Rochester)
College: Syracuse
Ht: 5'10" Wt: 180
Seasons: 1913

Doane (A, F, G, J)—G, T, E
(assumed names for Leo Lyons and others)
Seasons: 1908–10

Cam Doane—T, G, B
Donald Cameron Doane
B: August 2, 1889, Scottsville, NY
D: April 14, 1980, Springwater, NY
HS: Scottsville Union High (NY)
College: No
Ht: 6'0" Wt: 165
Seasons: 1908, '10

Bill Doane—B
William A. Doane
B: February 19, 1884, Scottsville, NY
D: February 28, 1974, Utica, NY
HS: Scottsville Union High (NY)
College: Mechanics Institute (Rochester, NY)
Ht: 6'0" Wt: 160
Seasons: 1908–9

John Dooley—E
John M. Dooley
B: September 29, 1897, Camillus, NY

D: October 31, 1991, Syracuse, NY
HS: Camillus (NY)
College: Syracuse, Bucknell
Ht: 6'2" Wt: 224
Seasons: 1918

Dutch Dow—T, G, B
Walter M. Dow
B: August 12, 1895, Rochester, NY
D: November 17, 1955, Rochester, NY
HS: No
College: No
Ht: 5'11" Wt: 165
Seasons: 1911, '14–15, '17–18

Harry Driscoll—T, G
Harold B. Driscoll
B: February 13, 1892, Rochester, NY
D: July 18, 1970, Rochester, NY
Seasons: 1911–12

Dick Emmett—T
Wt: 198
Seasons: 1919

Heinie Ester—T, G
George Henry Ester
B: April 17, 1901, Rochester, NY
D: September 10, 1975, Rochester, NY
HS: West High (Rochester), Mercersburg
   Academy (PA)
College: No
Ht: 5'11" Wt: 260
Seasons: 1915, '18

Ferris—T
Seasons: 1908

Ward H. Fleming—B, E
B: May 6, 1893, Cortland, NY
D: February 21, 1951, Hornell, NY
HS: Hornell (NY)
College: No
Ht: 5'10" Wt: 170
Seasons: 1916–17

Walter Fogerty—B
Walter T. Fogerty
B: December 23, 1888, Rochester, NY
D: July 3, 1961, Rochester, NY
HS: Cathedral (Rochester)
College: No
Ht: 5'10" Wt: 164
Seasons: 1908

Gene Frawley—B
Eugene H. Frawley
B: August 17, 1892, Chicago, IL
D: June 3, 1954, Cleveland, OH
HS: East High (Rochester)
College: No
Ht: 5'9" Wt: 160
Seasons: 1914

Walt Frickey—E
Walter Henry Frickey
B: August 8, 1895, Rochester, NY
D: March 12, 1972, Rochester, NY
HS: West High (Rochester)
College: No
Ht: 5'11" Wt: 220
Seasons: 1914–18

Graham—B
Seasons: 1910–11

Don Gray—B, T, E, G
Thomas Gray
B: May 6, 1887, Brooklyn, NY
D: 1968
HS: West High (Rochester)
College: No
Ht: 6' Wt: 165
Seasons: 1912–19

Avery Gretton—B
B: June 8, 1887, Brockport, NY
D: November 27, 1964, Rochester, NY
HS: No
College: No
Seasons: 1916

Ade Groot—G, E, B, T
Adrian W. Groot
B: March 28, 1892, Rochester, NY
D: June 27, 1969, Rochester, NY
HS: No
College: No
Seasons: 1909–13

Mike Hall—E
Seasons: 1914–15

Ed Hallet—C
Seasons: 1910

Pete Hardy—G
Seasons: 1913–14

Pete Heinlein—G, T
Edward A. Heinlein
B: June 22, 1890, Rochester, NY
D: March 30, 1957, Rochester, NY
HS: No
College: No
Ht: 5'11" Wt: 230
Seasons: 1912–18

Steamer Horning—T
Clarence Edward Horning
B: November 15, 1892, Phoenix, NY
D: January 24, 1982, Beverly Hills, MI
HS: Caledonia (NY)
College: Colgate
Ht: 6'1" Wt: 195
Seasons: 1917, '19

Alden Horth—T
Alden J. Horth
B: November 5, 1889, Rochester, NY
D: January 3, 1950, Rochester, NY
HS: No
College: No
Ht: 5'9" Wt: 186
Seasons: 1910, '13

Joe Hushard—B, G, E
Joseph S. Hushard
B: November 24, 1890, Rochester, NY
D: December 29, 1928, Rochester, NY
HS: No
College: No
Ht: 5'6" Wt: 158
Seasons: 1918–19

Dutch Irwin—B
Harry Stanton Irwin
B: August 11, 1899, Rochester, NY
D: June 6, 1967, Fairport, NY
HS: East High (Rochester)
College: Mercer
Ht: 5'7" Wt: 157
Seasons: 1913–19

Jackson—T, E
(see Leo Lyons)
Seasons: 1914

Johnson—G, T
Seasons: 1913–14

Earl Jones—B
Seasons: 1916

Jim Kane—T
Harold James Kane
B: November 28, 1896, Rochester, NY
D: April 10, 1976, Rochester, NY
HS: East High (Rochester)
College: No
Ht: 5'11" Wt: 200
Seasons: 1914–15, '19

Bill Kelley
(Appears in 1907 team photo but is not found in game summaries. No more information could be found)

Mike Kelly—B
Seasons: 1918–19

Hermie Klehr—B
Herman F. Klehr
B: April 1, 1888, Rochester, NY
D: May 29, 1947, Rochester, NY
HS: No

College: No
Ht: 5'6" Wt: 160
Seasons: 1910, '13

Joe Klehr—B
Joseph J. Klehr
B: October 14, 1889, Rochester, NY
D: January 1, 1959, Rochester, NY
HS: No
College: No
Ht: 5'6" Wt: 140
Seasons: 1910, '13

Parker Knapp—B
Parker Thomas Knapp
B: November 14, 1896
D: January 30, 1965
HS: North High (Syracuse, NY)
College: Syracuse
Seasons: 1919

Bill Kretchmer—B, E
William P. Kretchmer
B: January 17, 1887, Germany
D: July 3, 1963, Rochester, NY
HS: No
College: No
Ht: 5'4" Wt: 140
Seasons: 1909

Acton Langslow—E
H. Acton Langslow
B: December 21, 1884, Rochester, NY
D: November 12, 1956, Rochester, NY
HS: Rochester High (NY), East High (Rochester)
College: University of Rochester
Ht: 6'1" Wt: 180
Seasons: 1914

Nels Lengeman—G, C
Nelson E. Lengeman
B: November 29, 1894, Rochester, NY
D: July 16, 1961, Rochester, NY
HS: West High (Rochester)
College: No

Ht: 6'2" Wt: 168
Seasons: 1913–17, '19

Lines—E
(see Leo Lyons)
Seasons: 1914

Graydon Long—E, B
B: March 11, 1889, Rochester, NY
D: September 17, 1966, Rochester, NY
HS: West High (Rochester)
College: University of Rochester
Ht: 5'9" Wt: 148
Seasons: 1908, '13

John Loughlin—C
B: June 11, 1888, Rochester, NY
D: January 19, 1958, Rochester, NY
HS: East High (Rochester)
College: No
Ht: 5'10" Wt: 158
Seasons: 1908–10

Darby Lowery—E
Chester Lowery
B: January 30, 1894, Greenwich, OH
D: August 1982, Geneva, NY
HS: Greenwich High (OH)
College: Oberlin
Ht: 6' Wt: 213
Seasons: 1919

Leo Lyons—E, C, T, B
(also played as Doane, Lines, Jackson, and Man-Afraid-of-His-Wife)
Leo Vincent Lyons
B: March 11, 1892, Fairport, NY
D: May 18, 1976, Rochester, NY
HS: No
College: No
Ht: 5'11" Wt: 155
Seasons: 1908–19

Bill Lyons—G, T
(Willie)
William Timothy Lyons
B: April 2, 1895, Fairport, NY

D: May 1, 1970, Rochester, NY
HS: No
College: No
Ht: 5'9" Wt: 165
Seasons: 1913–15

Charlie MacLellan—G, T
Charles Blair MacLellan
B: July 15, 1892, Rochester, NY
D: August 23, 1961, Los Angeles, CA
HS: East High (Rochester)
College: No
Ht: 6'2" Wt: 220
Seasons: 1911–13, '15–17

Macrae—B
Seasons: 1913

Joe Maid—G, C
B: August 1, 1893, Rochester, NY
D: November 28, 1956, Fort Lauderdale, FL
HS: No
College: No
Ht: 5'8" Wt: 156
Seasons: 1917

Man-Afraid-of-His-Wife
(see Leo Lyons)
Seasons: 1915

Bill McCarty—B
William H. McCarty, Jr.
B: October 3, 1891, Brooklyn, NY
D: April 27, 1970, Grand Rapids, MI
HS: West High (Rochester)
College: No
Ht: 5'9" Wt: 155
Seasons: 1910–13

John McCrohan—G, T
B: April 19, 1884, Ireland
D: December 18, 1949, Farmingdale, NY
HS: Rogers High (Newport, RI)
College: Princeton
Ht: 6'1" Wt: 228
Seasons: 1916–19

Henry McDonald—B
Henry C. McDonald
B: August 31, 1890, Port-au-Prince, Haiti
D: June 12, 1976, Geneva, NY
HS: East High (Rochester)
College: No
Ht: 5'10" Wt: 153
Seasons: 1912–13, '15–19

Charlie McFadden—G, T
Charles J. McFadden
B: September 2, 1889, Rochester, NY
D: December 27, 1952, Hendersonville, NC
HS: East High (Rochester)
College: No
Ht: 6'2" Wt: 207
Seasons: 1912

George McIntosh—T
Seasons: 1916

Pete McKay—B
Robert Blaine McKay
B: June 14, 1890, Merino, CO
D: November 5, 1957, Rochester, NY
HS: Battle Creek High (MI)
College: Kalamazoo Western (MI)
Seasons: 1917

Dutch Mellody—B, E, G
Walter John Mellody
Born: February 17, 1893, Rochester, NY
Died: May 27, 1943, New York, NY
HS: No
College: No
Ht: 5'8" Wt: 188
Seasons: 1908–16, '19

Charles W. Morrison—E, T
B: April 11, 1889, Penn Yan, NY
D: March 6, 1959, Rochester, NY
HS: West High (Rochester)
College: No
Seasons: 1910–12, '14

Pop Morrison—T, G, B
Stewart E. Morrison

B: March 2, 1892, Penn Yan, NY
D: April 28, 1980, Rochester, NY
HS: West High (Rochester)
College: No
Ht: 6'3" Wt: 205
Seasons: 1910–16, '19

Pete Nicholson
(Appears in 1915 team photo but is not found in game summaries during that season)

Joe O'Brien—B
Joseph John O'Brien
B: October 9, 1896, Rochester NY
D: January 23, 1953, East Rochester, NY
HS: Cathedral (Rochester)
College: St. Jerome's College, Waterloo, Ontario, Canada
Seasons: 1915, '17, '19

Punk O'Brien—G, T, E
William A. O'Brien
B: March 8, 1890, Rochester, NY
D: May 2, 1919, Rochester, NY
College: No
Seasons: 1908–12

Bill Olin—T, B
William Olin
B: November 29, 1891, Rochester, NY
D: April 2, 1962, Pompano Beach, FL
HS: No
College: No
Ht: 6'2" Wt: 180
Seasons: 1909–11

Jimmy O'Toole
(Appears in 1913 team photo but is not found in game summaries during that season)

Mike Pfaudler—G, T
Howard Pfaudler
Seasons: 1909–13

Chief Poodry—E, B, C
Aaron Hawthorn Poodry
B: December 12, 1891, Tonawanda Reservation, NY
D: February 7, 1945, Rochester, NY
HS: Carlisle Indian (PA)
College: No
Ht: 6'
Seasons: 1912–13, '16

Powers—T
Seasons: 1916

Red Quigley—B
Gerald Quigley
B: December 18, 1895, Rochester, NY
D: September 21, 1966, Rochester, NY
HS: Cathedral (Rochester)
College: No
Ht: 5'9" Wt: 155
Seasons: 1916, '19

Ray Rice—G
(Yick)
Seasons: 1909–11

Rick—T
Seasons: 1915–16

Ed Roe—E
Joseph Edward Roe
B: January 24, 1885, New Mexico
D: February 18, 1967, Rochester, NY
HS: Cathedral (Rochester)
College: No
Ht: 5'8"
Seasons: 1910

Roth—B
Seasons: 1918

Walter Schaefer—G
Seasons: 1917

Walter Schiebel—E
Walter J.E. Schiebel
B: February 22, 1894, Buffalo, NY
D: April 21, 1978, Dallas, TX
HS: East High (Rochester)

College: University of Rochester
Ht: 6'1" Wt: 198
Seasons: 1916

George Schiller—B, T
George William Schiller
B: March 19, 1889, Stolberg, Germany
D: October 12, 1972, Rochester, NY
HS: Pittsburgh High (PA)
College: No
Ht: 5'8" Wt: 176
Seasons: 1918–19

Burritt Scrymgeour—B, E
Norman Burritt Scrymgeour
B: March 11, 1893, Rochester, NY
D: November 5, 1964, Rochester, NY
HS: West High (Rochester)
College: No
Ht: 6' Wt: 184
Seasons: 1913

Jack Slattery—G, T, E
John A. Slattery
B: December 9, 1888, Rochester, NY
D: January 13, 1964, Rochester, NY
HS: No
College: No
Ht: 5'9" Wt: 170
Seasons: 1908–12, '15

Slocum—E
Seasons: 1911

Charles Smith—B
Seasons: 1908, '10

Hank Smith—C
Henry A. Smith
(The Watertank)
B: July 23, 1893, Lancaster, NY
D: February 3, 1985, Buffalo, NY
HS: Lancaster High (NY)
College: No
Ht: 6'1" Wt: 189
Seasons: 1919

Ray Spiegel—E
Raymond T. Spiegel
B: January 25, 1889, Pittsford, NY
D: November 3, 1931, Canandaigua, NY
HS: No
College: No
Ht: 5'9" Wt: 157
Seasons: 1911, '13–14

Stewart—E, B
Wt: 160
Seasons: 1919

John Stigelmeier—T, B
John C. Stigelmeier
B: March 1, 1889, Buffalo, NY
D: February 11, 1980, Buffalo, NY
HS: Depew (NY)
College: No
Ht: 5'11" Wt: 185
Seasons: 1917

Joe Still—T, E, G
Joseph W. Still
B: June 29, 1889, Rochester, NY
D: December 24, 1971, Broward County, FL
HS: No
College: No
Ht: 5'8" Wt: 158
Seasons: 1909, '13

Storrier—G
Wt: 176
Seasons: 1919

Sullivan—C
Seasons: 1918

Sweeney—G
Seasons: 1910

Chase Tarbox—T
George M. Tarbox
B: November 15, 1894, Rochester, NY
D: March 5, 1966, Staten Island, NY
HS: East High (Rochester)
College: Mechanics Institute (Rochester)

Ht: 6'2" Wt: 205
Seasons: 1917–18

V.P. Thomas—B
Vivian Paul Thomas
B: February 1, 1897, Maquoketa, IA
D: December 10, 1927, Rock Island, IL
HS: Rock Island High (IL)
College: No
HT: 5'11" Wt: 155
Seasons: 1916–17

Hi Tiffany—T, G
Hiram D. Tiffany
B: March 17, 1886, Rochester, NY
D: May 3, 1935, Batavia, NY
HS: No
College: No
Ht: 5'9" Wt: 177
Seasons: 1908, '11

Toole—T, E
Wt: 168
Seasons: 1918

Vacheron—C
Seasons: 1916

Vaughn—E
Seasons: 1912, '15

Billy Warren—E
Seasons: 1915

Art Webb—G, B
Arthur S. Webb
B: June 19, 1888, Rochester, NY
D: December 31, 1954, Rochester, NY
HS: East Rochester High (East Rochester, NY)
College: Genesee Wesleyan Seminary
Ht: 5'10" Wt: 210
Seasons: 1912, '14–17, '19

Jim Weldon—E, B
James W. Weldon
B: September 26, 1888,

D: June 15, 1983
HS: East High (Rochester)
College: No
Ht: 5'10" Wt: 155
Seasons: 1908–9

Wilcox—B
Seasons: 1911

Wilson—G
Seasons: 1917

Bob Witter—E, B
Robert Ellsworth Witter
B: August 16, 1897, Perry, NY
D: March 6, 1976, East Aurora, NY
HS: Warsaw (NY)
College: Alfred (NY)
Ht: 5'10" Wt: 158
Seasons: 1917–18

Ray Witter—E, B
Ray Charles Witter
B: February 19, 1896, Perry, NY
D: August 4, 1983, Batavia, NY
HS: Warsaw (NY)
College: Syracuse, Alfred (NY)
Ht: 5'10" Wt: 183
Seasons: 1917–19

Jimmy Woods—T, G
James John Woods
B: May 5, 1894, Jamestown, NY
D: December 1966, Salamanca, NY
HS: Jamestown (NY)
College: No
Ht: 5'9" Wt: 196
Seasons: 1917, '19

Ben Ziegler—B, E
J. Benjamin Ziegler
B: May 29, 1889, Rochester, NY
D: May 1, 1947
HS: West High (Rochester)
College: No
Ht: 5'7" Wt: 160
Seasons: 1908–10, '12

2. Rochester Jeffersons APFA/NFL Era

In compiling the demographic information for the players who appeared in at least one league-recognized game for the Rochester Jeffersons between 1920 and 1925, the authors used *Total Football II: The Official Encyclopedia of the National Football League* as the starting point. An exhaustive search for any missing or questionable pieces ensued. Every conceivable potential source was explored, including census reports, military records, college records, newspapers, game programs, and sometimes Leo Lyons' personal journal. While acknowledging a few holes still remain, the authors believe this to be the most accurate and comprehensive listing of each player's vital statistics possible. Players whose names are preceded by an asterisk [*] appeared in nonleague games only.

Joe Alexander—C
Joseph A. Alexander
 (Doc)
B: April 1, 1897, Silver Creek, NY
D: September 12, 1975, New York, NY
HS: Syracuse Central (NY)
College: Syracuse
Ht: 5'11" Wt: 220
Seasons: 1921–22, '24

Eddie Anderson—E
Edward Nicholas Anderson
B: November 13, 1900, Oskaloosa, IA
D: April 26, 1974, Belleair, FL
HS: Mason City (IA)
College: Notre Dame
Ht: 5'10" Wt: 176
Seasons: 1922

Will Anderson—B
Willard August Anderson
B: May 5, 1897, Muskegon, MI
D: April 24, 1982, Hinsdale, IL
HS: Muskegon (MI)
College: Syracuse
Ht: 5'10" Wt: 173
Seasons: 1923–24

Bob Argus—B
Robert Anthony Argus
B: January 21, 1894, Hammondsport, NY
D: December 8, 1945, Rochester, NY
HS: Corning Free Academy (NY), West
 High (Rochester)
College: No
Ht: 5'10" Wt: 193
Seasons: 1920–25

Joe Bachmaier—C, G, T, E
Joseph William Bachmaier
B: March 11, 1895, Rochester, NY
D: January 14, 1974, Rochester, NY
HS: West High (Rochester)
College: No
Ht: 5'9" Wt: 175
Seasons: 1920–24

Hugh Bancroft—E
Hugh Norman Bancroft
B: August 4, 1894, Wethersfield Springs,
 NY
D: October 31, 1974, Dunedin, FL
HS: Warsaw (NY)
College: No
Ht: 5'10" Wt: 165
Seasons: 1923

Jim Barron—T
James Martin Barron
B: November 10, 1888, Boston, MA
D: February 6, 1936, Boston, MA
HS: Boston College (MA)
College: Georgetown
Ht: 6' Wt: 195
Seasons: 1921

John Barsha—B
John F. Barsha

B: December 25, 1898, Russia
D: February 18, 1976, New York, NY
HS: Boys (Brooklyn, NY)
College: Syracuse
Ht: 5'11" Wt: 180
Seasons: 1920

Reaves Baysinger—E
Reaves Henry Baysinger
B: February 22, 1902, Doylestown, OH
D: December 4, 1994, Hilton, NY
HS: Central (Akron, OH)
College: Syracuse
Ht: 6' Wt: 180
Seasons: 1924

Gene Bedford—E
William Eugene Bedford
B: December 2, 1896, Dallas, TX
D: October 6, 1977, San Antonio, TX
College: Centre, SMU
Ht: 5'9" Wt: 165
Seasons: 1925

Howard Berry—B
Joseph Howard Berry, Jr.
B: December 31, 1893, Philadelphia, PA
D: April 29, 1976, Philadelphia, PA
HS: Northeast (PA)
College: Muhlenberg (PA)
Ht: 5'11" Wt: 165
Seasons: 1921

Benny Boynton—B
Ben Lee Boynton
(The Purple Streak)
B: December 6, 1898, Waco, TX
D: January 23, 1963, Dallas, TX
HS: Waco (TX)
College: Williams
Ht: 5'9" Wt: 170
Seasons: 1921–22, '24

Denny (Dinny) Cahill—G
William Dennis Cahill
B: May 6, 1889, Rochester, NY
D: January 12, 1953, Rochester, NY

HS: East High (Rochester)
College: No
Ht: 6' Wt: 225
Seasons: 1920

Bart Carroll—T
Bart J. Carroll
B: December 29, 1893, Louisville, NY
D: March 27, 1967, Schenectady, NY
HS: Massena (NY)
College: Colgate
Ht: 5'11" Wt: 180
Seasons: 1920

Babe Clark—B, C, T
Harold K. Clark
B: January 14, 1891, Avon, NY
D: April 18, 1951, Rochester, NY
HS: East High (Rochester)
College: Cornell
Ht: 5'8" Wt: 170
Seasons: 1920

Butch Clark—E, B
Harold R. Clark
B: June 11, 1896, Rochester, NY
D: June 29, 1980, Rochester, NY
HS: Cathedral (Rochester)
College: Fordham
Ht: 5'10" Wt: 195
Seasons: 1920, '22–25

Fred Clarke—E
Frederick S. Clarke
B: May 25, 1900, Rochester, NY
D: August 7, 1964, Rochester, NY
HS: West High (Rochester)
College: No
Ht: 5'9" Wt: 160
Seasons: 1920

Ben Clime—G, E, B
Benjamin Sidney Clime
B: October 14, 1891, Philadelphia, PA
D: January 13, 1973, Fort Lauderdale, FL
HS: Philadelphia Central (PA)
College: Swarthmore

Ht: 5'11" Wt: 190
Seasons: 1920–21

John Coaker—T, G
John F. Coaker
B: September 17, 1902, Rochester, NY
D: July 5, 1966, Jamaica, NY
HS: West High (Rochester)
College: No
Ht: 5'9" Wt: 170
Seasons: 1924

Bill Connell—B
William Joseph Connell
B: October 19, 1893, Rochester, NY
D: March 1, 1976, Canandaigua, NY
HS: West High (Rochester)
College: No
Ht: 6' Wt: 181
Seasons: 1920

Ham Connors—E
Hamilton C. Connors
B: February 22, 1898, Pittsburgh, PA
D: February 27, 1967, East Rochester, NY
HS: East High (Rochester)
College: No
Ht: 5'10" Wt: 190
Seasons: 1925

Frank Culver—C
Franklin Zham Culver
B: April 24, 1897, Toledo, OH
D: January 13, 1969, Yonkers, NY
HS: V.W. Scott (Toledo, OH)
College: Syracuse
Ht: 5'11" Wt: 175
Seasons: 1924

John Dooley—T, G
John M. Dooley
B: September 29, 1897, Camillus, NY
D: October 31, 1991, Syracuse, NY
HS: Camillus (NY)
College: Syracuse, Bucknell
Ht: 6'2" Wt: 224
Seasons: 1922, '24–25

Jim Dufft—G, T
James Henry Dufft
B: June 25, 1896, New York, NY
D: May 28, 1960
HS: Kelvin School (Mount Vernon, NY)
College: Rutgers, Fordham
Ht: 6'6" Wt: 250
Seasons: 1921

Joe DuMoe—E
Joseph Thomas DuMoe
B: July 30, 1895, Nickerson, MN
D: February 23, 1959, Los Angeles County, CA
HS: Central (Duluth, MN)
College: Syracuse, Fordham, Lafayette
Ht: 5'9" Wt: 178
Seasons: 1920–21

Red Emslie—G
Percy Gordon Emslie
B: April 29, 1895, Buffalo, NY
D: August 3, 1964, Buffalo, NY
College: No
Ht: 5'9" Wt: 185
Seasons: 1923

Bill Erwig—T
William E. Erwig
B: October 4, 1894, Berlin, Germany
D: January 5, 1952, Freeport, NY
HS: Morris High (NY)
College: Fordham, Syracuse
Ht: 5'9" Wt: 160
Seasons: 1920

Earl Ettenhaus—G
(see Bill Kellogg)
Seasons: 1921

Guil Falcon—B
Guilford W. Falcon
(Hawk)
B: December 15, 1892, Evanston, IL
D: July 28, 1982, Hollywood, FL
HS: Evanston (IL)
College: No

Ht: 5'10" Wt: 220
Seasons: 1925

Ben Forsyth—C
Charles Benjamin Forsyth
B: June 4, 1890, Webster, NY
D: November 11, 1968, Webster, NY
HS: West High (Rochester)
College: Rochester, Syracuse
Ht: 5'11" Wt: 190
Seasons: 1920

Fred Foster—B
Frederick Frank Foster
B: April 25, 1898, Niagara Falls, NY
D: December 19, 1968, Tallahassee, FL
HS: Niagara Falls (NY)
College: Syracuse
Ht: 5'11" Wt: 185
Seasons: 1923–24

***Walter French**—B
Walter Edward French
B: July 12, 1899, Moorestown, NJ
D: May 13, 1984, Mountain Home, AR
HS: Moorestown (NJ), Pennington Prep (NJ)
College: Rutgers, Army
Ht: 5'7" Wt: 155
Seasons: 1922

Walt Frickey—E
Walter Henry Frickey
B: August 8, 1895, Rochester, NY
D: March 12, 1972, Rochester, NY
HS: West High (Rochester)
College: No
Ht: 5'11" Wt: 220
Seasons: 1920

Mike Gavagan—B
Maurice Thomas Gavagan
Born: April 10, 1900, Warsaw, NY
Died: January 9, 1957, Warsaw, NY
HS: Warsaw (NY)
College: St. Bonaventure

Ht: 5'10" Wt: 176
Seasons: 1923

Cecil Grigg—B
Cecil Burkett Grigg
(Tex)
B: February 15, 1891, Nashville, TN
D: September 5, 1968, Houston TX
HS: Sherman (TX)
College: Austin, Texas
Ht: 5'11" Wt: 191
Seasons: 1924–25

John Hasbrouck—B, E
Robert Lyncdon Hasbrouck
B: November 21, 1893, Grundy Center, IA
D: February 9, 1976, Garland, TX
HS: Peekskill (NY)
College: Rutgers
Ht: 6' Wt: 190
Seasons: 1921

Pete Heinlein—G, T
Edward August Heinlein
B: June 22, 1890, Rochester, NY
D: March 30, 1957, Rochester, NY
HS: No
College: No
Ht: 5'11" Wt: 230
Seasons: 1920

Ralph Henricus—B
Ralph Charles Henricus
B: June 2, 1896, Rochester, NY
D: August 27, 1949, Alameda County, CA
HS: Cathedral (Rochester)
College: Cornell
Ht: 6' Wt: 175
Seasons: 1922

Jake Hoffman—B
Jacob Harry Hoffman
B: July 21, 1895, Syracuse, NY
D: February 11, 1977, Jordan, NY
HS: East Syracuse (NY)
College: No

Ht: 5'8" Wt: 170
Seasons: 1925

*M. Hummel—T
Seasons: 1922

Dutch Irwin—B, E
Harry Stanton Irwin
B: August 11, 1899, Rochester, NY
D: June 6, 1967, Fairport, NY
HS: East High (Rochester)
College: Mercer
Ht: 5'7" Wt: 170
Seasons: 1920

Jim Kane—G
James Harold Kane
B: November 28, 1896, Rochester, NY
D: April 10, 1976, Rochester, NY
HS: East High (Rochester)
College: No
Ht: 5'11" Wt: 200
Seasons: 1920

Cy Kasper—B
Thomas Cyril Kasper
B: May 27, 1895, Faribault, MN
D: December 28, 1991, Bismarck, ND
HS: Faribault (MN), Shattuck Military Academy (MN)
College: Notre Dame
Ht: 5'10" Wt: 170
Seasons: 1923

*Stan Keck—T, G
James Stanton Keck
B: September 11, 1897, Greensburg, PA
D: January 20, 1951, Pittsburgh, PA
HS: Kiski (Saltsburg, PA), Bellefonte Academy (PA)
College: Princeton
Ht: 5'11" Wt: 205
Seasons: 1923

Bill Kellogg—B
William J. Kellogg
(also played as Earl Ettenhaus, 1921)
B: March 3, 1897, Pittsburgh, PA
D: November 28, 1969, Syracuse, NY
HS: Allegany (NY)
College: Indiana (PA), Syracuse
Ht: 5'10" Wt: 178
Seasons: 1925

Tex Kelly—G
Clarence Ashley Kelly
B: October 29, 1898, Duncan, OK
D: February 4, 1978, Shawnee, OK
College: No
Ht: 6'3" Wt: 220
Seasons: 1925

Jim Kendrick—B
James Marcellus Kendrick
B: August 22, 1893, Hillside, TX
D: November 17, 1941, Waco, TX
HS: Douglas-Shuler Academy (TX)
College: Texas A&M
Ht: 6' Wt: 195
Seasons: 1925

Dick King—B
Richard Stewart Cutter King
B: February 9, 1895, Boston, MA
D: October 16, 1930, Bogotá, Colombia
HS: Boston Latin (MA)
College: Harvard
Ht: 5'8" Wt: 175
Seasons: 1922

John Kwist—T
Eric John Kwist
B: February 6, 1899, Sweden
D: May 16, 1954, Rochester, NY
College: No
Seasons: 1920

Jim Laird—B
James Tyler Laird
B: September 10, 1897, Montpelier, VT
D: August 16, 1970, Windham, CT
HS: Holderness School (NH)
College: Colgate

Ht: 6' Wt: 194
Seasons: 1920–21

Chris Lehrer—B
John Christian Lehrer
D: November 26, 1947
College: No
Wt: 185
Seasons: 1922

Jim Leonard—T
James Michael Leonard
B: January 2, 1899, Geneseo, NY
D: February 2, 1979, Naples, FL
HS: Geneseo (NY)
College: Geneseo State, Colgate
Ht: 6' Wt: 205
Seasons: 1923

Darby Lowery—G, E, T
Chester Lowery
B: January 30, 1894, Greenwich, OH
D: August 1982, Geneva, NY
HS: Greenwich High (OH)
College: Oberlin
Ht: 6' Wt: 213
Seasons: 1920–25

Ed Lynch—E
Edward James Lynch
B: October 4, 1896, Northampton, MA
D: August 24, 1967, Dearborn, MI
HS: St. Michael's (MA)
College: Catholic University of America
Ht: 6' Wt: 191
Seasons: 1925

Roy Mackert—T
Charles LeRoy Mackert
B: February 2, 1894, Sunbury, PA
D: February 12, 1942, Washington, DC
HS: Conway Hall (PA)
College: Lebanon Valley (MD)
Ht: 6'2" Wt: 200
Seasons: 1925

Roy Martineau—G
Daniel Roy Martineau
B: August 20, 1900, Syracuse, NY
D: October 25, 1961, Syracuse, NY
HS: Solvay (NY)
College: Buffalo, Syracuse
Ht: 6' Wt: 210
Seasons: 1924–25

Frank Matteo—T, G
Francis Pasquale Matteo
B: April 2, 1896, Syracuse, NY
D: December 19, 1983, Oneida, NY
HS: North (Syracuse, NY)
College: Syracuse
Ht: 5'11" Wt: 195
Seasons: 1922–25

Joe McShea—G
John Maurice McShea
B: December 13, 1899, Rochester, NY
D: December 21, 1985, Rochester, NY
HS: Charlotte (NY)
College: Rochester
Ht: 5'8" Wt: 185
Seasons: 1923

Dutch Mellody—B, G
Walter John Mellody
Born: February 17, 1893, Rochester, NY
Died: May 27, 1943, New York, NY
HS: No
College: No
Ht: 5'8" Wt: 188
Seasons: 1920

Paul Meyers—E
Paul Duncan Meyers
B: November 19, 1895, Chicago, IL
D: July 2, 1966, Millville, NJ
HS: East Division (WI)
College: Wisconsin–Milwaukee, Wisconsin
Ht: 5'11" Wt: 170
Seasons: 1922

Frank Morrissey—G
Francis Joseph Morrissey
B: March 11, 1899, Boston, MA
D: November 19, 1968, Wynnewood, PA
HS: Medford (MA)
College: Boston College
Ht: 6'1" Wt: 203
Seasons: 1921

Pop Morrison—T, E
Stewart E. Morrison
B: March 2, 1892, Penn Yan, NY
D: April 28, 1980, Rochester, NY
HS: West High (Rochester)
College: No
Ht: 6'3" Wt: 205
Seasons: 1920

*****Dan Mulvey**—E
Daniel P. Mulvey
B: April 20, 1900, Lockport, NY
D: April 28, 1966, Lockport, NY
HS: Lockport (NY)
College: No
1921

Bob Nash–T
Robert Arthur Nash
(Nasty)
B: December 16, 1892, Ireland
D: February 1, 1977, Winsted, CT
HS: Bernards (NJ)
College: Cornell, Rutgers
Ht: 6'1" Wt: 205
Seasons: 1924

Nielson—B
Seasons: 1924

Jerry Noonan—B
Gerard Michael Noonan
B: July 31, 1897, Bayonne, NJ
D: August 24, 1971, Los Angeles, CA
College: Notre Dame, Fordham, Santa Clara, New York University
Ht: 6'1" Wt: 189
Seasons: 1921, '22–24

*****Tom Noonan**—B
Thomas F. Noonan
B: December 21, 1894, Bayonne, NJ
D: November 9, 1946, San Diego, CA
Seasons: 1921

Clem Nugent—B
Clement Earl Nugent
B: November 9, 1899, Algona, IA
D: December 20, 1950, Los Angeles, CA
HS: Algona (IA)
College: Iowa
Ht: 5'9" Wt: 155
Seasons: 1924

Elmer Oliphant—B
Elmer Quillen Oliphant
(Ollie)
B: July 9, 1892, Bloomfield, IN
D: July 3, 1975, New Canaan, CT
HS: Washington (IN), Linton (IN)
College: Purdue, Army
Ht: 5'7" Wt: 175
Seasons: 1920

Red Pearlman—T, G
Irving Ralph Pearlman
B: July 31, 1898, Pittsburgh, PA
D: November 28, 1985, Hollywood, FL
HS: Fifth Avenue (PA)
College: Pittsburgh
Ht: 6' Wt: 195
Seasons: 1924

Pepper–G
Seasons: 1920

Leo Peyton–B
B: November 4, 1899, Canton, NY
D: April 9, 1989, Carthage, NY
HS: Canton (NY)
College: No
Ht: 5'11" Wt: 190
Seasons: 1923–24

*****Chief Poodry**—E, B, C
Aaron Hawthorn Poodry

B: December 12, 1891, Tonawanda
    Reservation, NY
D: February 7, 1945, Rochester, NY
HS: Carlisle Indian (PA)
College: No
Ht: 6'
Seasons: 1921

Mike Purdy—B
Clair Joseph Purdy, Jr.
B: January 24, 1895, Auburn, NY
D: January 10, 1950, Auburn, NY
HS: Dean Academy (MA)
College: Brown
Ht: 5'10" Wt: 179
Seasons: 1920

Red Quigley—B
Gerald Quigley
B: December 18, 1895, Rochester, NY
D: September 21, 1966, Rochester, NY
HS: Cathedral (Rochester)
College: No
Ht: 5'9" Wt: 155
Seasons: 1920

Billy Rafter—B
William John Rafter
B: October 7, 1895, Troy, NY
D: June 28, 1966, Syracuse, NY
HS: Lansingburg (NY)
College: Syracuse
Ht: 5'6" Wt: 155
Seasons: 1921, '24

Harry Robertson—T
Harold John Robertson
B: March 4, 1896, Chambly, Quebec
D: January 7, 1962, Coral Gables, FL
HS: Somerville (MA), Worcester (MA)
College: Syracuse
Ht: 5'10" Wt: 185
Seasons: 1922

Spin Roy–E
Elmer T. Roy
B: October 23, 1896, Alexander, NY

D: April 28, 1947, North Tonawanda, NY
HS: North Tonawanda (NY)
College: No
Ht: 6' Wt: 175
Seasons: 1921–25

Bill Ryan—T
William Ryan
B: March 15, 1905
HS: Englewood (IL)
College: Fordham
Ht: 5'11" Wt: 190
Seasons: 1924

Herm Sawyer–B
Herman Sawyer Schlossberg
Born: October 18, 1898, Missoula, MT
D: September 25, 1968, New York, NY
HS: Missoula (MT)
College: Syracuse
Ht: 5'8" Wt: 170
Seasons: 1922

Shag Sheard—B
Alfred Scotchard Sheard
B: November 17, 1898, Canton, NY
D: November 11, 1980, Canton, NY
HS: Canton (NY)
College: St. Lawrence
Ht: 5'11" Wt: 177
Seasons: 1923–25

Hank Smith—C, G, T
Henry A. Smith
(The Watertank)
B: July 23, 1893, Lancaster, NY
D: February 3, 1985, Buffalo, NY
HS: Lancaster High (NY)
College: No
Ht: 6'1" Wt: 189
Seasons: 1920–25

Lou Smyth–B
Louie Lehman Smyth
B: March 19, 1898, Cleburne, TX
D: September 11, 1964, Long Beach, CA
HS: Sherman (TX)

College: Texas, Centre
Ht: 6'1" Wt: 200
Seasons: 1924–25

Cliff Steele–B
Clifford Francis Steele
B: October 8, 1896, Duluth, MN
D: September 3, 1974, Palm Beach, FL
HS: Mechanic Arts (MN)
College: Syracuse, Fordham
Ht: 5'8" Wt: 150
Seasons: 1921–22

Charlie Stewart—G
Charles Edward Stewart
B: July 8, 1890, Pittsfield, MA
D: December 18, 1965, North Grafton, MA
HS: Williston Northampton School (MA)
College: Cornell, Colgate
Ht: 5'9" Wt: 160
Seasons: 1920

George Tandy—C, E
George Wendell Tandy
B: November 27, 1893, Franklin, IL
D: May 11, 1969, Springfield, IL
College: North Carolina
Ht: 6'1" Wt: 210
Seasons: 1920

Carl Thomas—T, E
Carl Herbert Thomas
B: March 2, 1897, Philadelphia, PA
D: October 30, 1961, Philadelphia, PA
HS: Frankford (PA), Central (PA)
College: Pennsylvania
Ht: 5'10" Wt: 195
Seasons: 1920–21

V.P. Thomas—B
Vivian Paul Thomas
B: February 1, 1897, Maquoketa, IA
D: December 10, 1927, Rock Island, IL
HS: Rock Island High (IL)
College: No
HT: 5'11" Wt: 155
Seasons: 1920

Tiny Thompson—G
George Bryan Thompson
B: December 24, 1897, New York, NY
D: October 26, 1961, Fulton, NY
HS: Luzerne (PA)
College: Syracuse
Ht: 5'10' Wt: 233
Seasons: 1922

Lou Usher—T, G
Louis Childs Usher
B: June 27, 1897, Lincoln, NE
D: January 1, 1927, Hammond, IN
HS: Hyde Park Academy (IL)
College: Detroit Mercy, Syracuse
Ht: 6'2" Wt: 240
Seasons: 1920–21

Elmer Volgenau—G
Elmer Porter Volgenau
B: August 2, 1900, New Haven, CT
D: December 6, 1965, Clarence, NY
HS: Masten Park (NY)
College: Colgate
Ht: 6'2" Wt: 190
Seasons: 1924

Gordon Wallace—B, C
Gordon Lewis Wallace
B: August 6, 1899, Rochester, NY
D: July 9, 1931, Rochester, NY
HS: East High (Rochester)
College: Rochester
Ht: 5'10" Wt: 170
Seasons: 1923–24

Art Webb—G
Arthur S. Webb
B: June 19, 1888, Rochester, NY
D: December 31, 1954, Rochester, NY
HS: East Rochester High (East Rochester, NY)
College: Genesee Wesleyan Seminary
Ht: 5'10" Wt: 210
Seasons: 1920

Jim Welsh–G
James Edward Welsh
B: September 17, 1902, Malden, MA
D: February 12, 1958, Lake County, FL
HS: Malden (MA)
College: Colgate
Ht: 5'11" Wt: 250
Seasons: 1923

Larry Weltman—B
Lawrence Abraham Weltman
B: January 26, 1899, Pittsfield, MA
D: September 12, 1959, Troy, NY
HS: Pittsfield (MA)
College: Syracuse
Ht: 5'10" Wt: 175
Seasons: 1922

Frank Whitcomb—G, T, C
Frank E. Whitcomb
B: December 7, 1896, Granby, NY
D: July 31, 1977, Fulton, NY
HS: Mercersburg Academy (PA)
College: Syracuse
Ht: 6'3" Wt: 217
Seasons: 1920–21

Mike Wilson—E, B
Samuel Marshall Wilson
B: December 2, 1896, Edge Hill, PA
D: May 16, 1978, Boynton Beach, FL
HS: Northeast (PA)
College: Lehigh
Ht: 5'10" Wt: 167
Seasons: 1922

Ray Witter—E, B, G
Ray Charles Witter
B: February 19, 1896, Perry, NY
D: August 4, 1983, Batavia, NY
HS: Warsaw (NY)
College: Syracuse, Alfred
Ht: 5'10" Wt: 183
Seasons: 1920–23

Jimmy Woods—C, T, G
James John Woods
B: May 5, 1894, Jamestown, NY
D: December 3, 1966, Salamanca, NY
HS: Jamestown High (NY)
College: No
Ht: 5'9" Wt: 196
Seasons: 1920–24

Chet Wynne—B
Chester Allen Wynne
B: November 23, 1898, Long Island, KS
D: July 17, 1967, Chicago, IL
High School: Norton (KS)
College: Notre Dame
Ht: 6' Wt: 180
Seasons: 1922

*Swede Youngstrom—G
Adolf Frederick Youngstrom
B: May 24, 1897, Waltham, MA.
D: August 5, 1968, Boston, MA.
High School: Waltham (MA)
College: Dartmouth
Ht: 6'1" Wt: 187
Seasons: 1925

Dave Ziff—E
David Samuel Ziff
B: January 18, 1902, Northampton, MA
D: October 17, 1977, New York, NY
HS: Northampton (MA)
College: Syracuse, St. John's
Ht: 6' Wt: 195
Seasons: 1925

Chapter Notes

Leo Lyons was an inveterate notetaker. Although unquestionably disorganized, Lyons memorialized nearly every important football-related event he experienced onto whatever material was within his grasp at the moment. He jotted notes in a day planner, on scraps of paper, on the covers and pages of magazines, the backs of placards, or any other surface on which he could commit his impressions for posterity. In our effort to write as complete and comprehensive a biography as possible, we felt it essential to use Lyons' own words whenever we could. To do this, it was often necessary to cull quotes from pieces of paper that had no dates. Sometimes the tiniest undated scraps held the most vital information about a game, meeting, or other important event. As a result of the disorganization of the material, the authors have chosen to use a generalized citation when quoting from or referring to Lyons' notes, unless the note includes a specific identifiable date.

Chapter 1

1. *Rochester Democrat & Chronicle*, April 28, 2019, pp. 1D, 6D.
2. Rochester's population in 1900, according to the website www.waterworkshistory.us, was 162,608.
3. *Rochester Democrat & Chronicle*, October 3, 1892, p. 10.
4. *Rochester Democrat & Chronicle*, July 29, 1893, p. 10.
5. *Rochester Democrat & Chronicle*, September 16, 1897, p. 11.
6. Residential and employment history pieced together using Rochester city directories and New York State Census reports.
7. Lyons' personal notes, June 8, 1929.
8. Leo Lyons Oral History from Pro Football Hall of Fame, date not known.
9. Leo Lyons interview with Kevin C. Bosner, August 1969.
10. Leo Lyons interview with Robert Wheeler, July 1, 1967. Voice recording transcript. Used by permission.
11. Bob Carroll, "The Town That Hated Pro Football," *The Coffin Corner*, Volume III, 1981.
12. *Rochester Democrat & Chronicle*, October 1, 1925, p. 28.
13. Sabina Bosner Steffenhagen interview with John Steffenhagen, June 2002.
14. Leo Lyons interview with Robert Wheeler, July 1, 1967. Voice recording transcript. Used by permission.
15. Leo Lyons interview with Kevin C. Bosner, August 1969.
16. Lyons' personal notes, June 8, 1929.
17. *Rochester Democrat & Chronicle*, November 9, 1908, p. 13.
18. Elbert Angevine, *Parade of the Grid Ghosts: The Story of Football in Rochester*, p. 37.
19. *Rochester Democrat & Chronicle*, November 17, 1908, p. 17.
20. *Rochester Democrat & Chronicle*, November 23, 1908, p. 13.
21. Lyons' personal notes, June 8, 1929.
22. Sabina Bosner Steffenhagen interview with John Steffenhagen, June 2002.
23. *Ibid.*
24. *Ibid.*
25. Bob Carroll, "The Town That Hated Pro Football," *The Coffin Corner*, Volume III, 1981.
26. Elbert Angevine, *Parade of the Grid Ghosts: The Story of Football in Rochester*, pp. 40–41.
27. *Ibid.*
28. *Ibid.*
29. *Ibid.*
30. Letter from Will Caulfield to Leo and Catharine Lyons, March 7, 1936.
31. Sabina Bosner Steffenhagen interview with John Steffenhagen, June 2002.
32. *Ibid.*
33. *Ibid.*
34. *Ibid.*
35. *Ibid.*
36. *Ibid.*
37. Lyons' personal notes, January 6, 1976.
38. Elbert Angevine, *Parade of the Grid Ghosts: The Story of Football in Rochester*, p. 47.
39. *Rochester Democrat & Chronicle*, October 31, 1912, p. 21.
40. Leo Lyons Oral History from Pro Football Hall of Fame, date not known. Used by permission.
41. *Rochester Democrat & Chronicle*, October 31, 1912, p. 21.

42. Sabina Bosner Steffenhagen interview with John Steffenhagen, June 2002.
43. *Rochester Democrat & Chronicle*, December 16, 1912, p. 17.
44. Sabina Bosner Steffenhagen interview with John Steffenhagen, June 2002.
45. *Rochester Democrat & Chronicle*, December 1, 1913, p. 17.

Chapter 2

1. The account of Leo and Catherine's wedding as told by their daughter Sabina Lyons Bosner and transcribed by John and Kevin Bosner, Leo's grandchildren, November 6, 1997.
2. *Rochester Democrat & Chronicle*, August 16, 1914, p. 28.
3. *Rochester Democrat & Chronicle*, October 7, 1914, p. 19.
4. Leo Lyons interview with Kevin C. Bosner, August 1965. Written transcript. Used by permission.
5. *Rochester Democrat & Chronicle*, November 18, 1914, p. 18.
6. *Rochester Democrat & Chronicle*, February 7, 1915, p. 31.
7. *Rochester Democrat & Chronicle*, February 20, 1915, p. 18.
8. *Rochester Democrat & Chronicle*, February 22, 1915, p. 15.
9. Sabina Bosner Steffenhagen (Leo Lyons' granddaughter) interview with John Steffenhagen (coauthor), February 23, 2023.
10. Leo V. Lyons, "How Pro Football Was Born," *TV Guide,* 1964 (exact date not known).
11. *Rochester Democrat & Chronicle*, December 26, 1963, p. 6D.
12. Leo Lyons interview with Kevin C. Bosner, August 1965. Written transcript. Used by permission.
13. Lyons' personal notes, January 6, 1976.
14. Leo Lyons Interview with Kevin C. Bosner, August 1965. Written transcript. Used by permission.
15. *Rochester Democrat & Chronicle*, October 18, 1915, p. 17.
16. *Buffalo Times*, October 24, 1915, p. 51.
17. *Rochester Democrat & Chronicle*, October 25, 1915, p. 19.
18. *Rochester Democrat & Chronicle*, November 1, 1915, p. 19.
19. *Rochester Democrat & Chronicle*, November 26, 1915, p. 27.
20. Sabina Bosner Steffenhagen (Leo Lyons' granddaughter) interview with John Steffenhagen (coauthor), February 23, 2023.
21. *Rochester Democrat & Chronicle*, January 23, 1916, p. 30.
22. *Rochester Democrat & Chronicle*, January 29, 1916, p. 20.
23. Lyons personal notes, July 13, 1916
24. Lyons personal notes, March 3, 1924.
25. *Rochester Democrat & Chronicle*, November 13, 1916, p. 17.
26. Elbert Angevine, *Parade of the Grid Ghosts: The Story of Football in Rochester*, pp. 57–58.
27. *Buffalo Courier*, December 4, 1916, p. 8.
28. *Rochester Democrat & Chronicle*, December 4, 1916, p. 17.
29. Readmikenow, "Walter Camp: The Father of American Football," *How They Play* (https://howtheyplay.com/team-sports/Walter-Camp-The-Father-of-American-Football), May 17, 2022.
30. Letter from Walter Camp, New Haven, CT, to Leo V. Lyons, Rochester, NY, December 8, 1916.
31. *Rochester Democrat & Chronicle*, December 20, 1916.

Chapter 3

1. *Rochester Democrat & Chronicle*, October 7, 1917, p. 34.
2. Leo Lyons interview with Robert Wheeler, July 1, 1967, voice recording transcript. Used by permission.
3. Leo V. Lyons, "How Pro Football Was Born," *TV Guide,* date unknown.
4. Leo Lyons interview with Robert Wheeler, July 1, 1967. Voice recording transcript. Used by permission.
5. *Canton Daily News*, October 28 and 29, 1917, p. 19.
6. Leo Lyons interview with Robert Wheeler, July 1, 1967. Voice recording transcript. Used by permission.
7. Robert W. Peterson, *Pigskin: The Early Years of Pro Football*, p. 174.
8. Keith McClellan, *The Sunday Game: At the Dawn of Professional Football*, p. 408.
9. Robert W. Wheeler, *Jim Thorpe: World's Greatest Athlete*, p. 206.
10. Leo Lyons interview with Robert Wheeler, July 1, 1967. Voice recording transcript. Used by permission.
11. *Rochester Democrat & Chronicle*, November 5, 1917, p. 17.
12. Lyons' personal notes, December 2, 1917.
13. Ibid.
14. *Rochester Democrat & Chronicle*, December 3, 1917, p. 17.
15. *Rochester Democrat & Chronicle*, October 6, 1918, p. 35.
16. Lyons' personal notes, no date provided.
17. *Rochester Democrat & Chronicle*, December 1, 1918, p. 39.
18. *Rochester Democrat & Chronicle*, January 11, 1939, p. 20.
19. *Rochester Democrat & Chronicle*, October 6, 1919, p. 23.
20. *Buffalo Courier*, December 1, 1919, p. 8.
21. *Rochester Democrat & Chronicle*, December 1, 1919, p. 27.

Chapter 4

1. *Canton Daily News*, August 21, 1920.
2. Letter from Ralph E. Hay, general manager

of Canton Bulldogs football team, to L.V. Lyons of Rochester, NY, September 9, 1920.
3. *Rochester Democrat & Chronicle*, September 14, 1920.
4. Lyons' personal notes, September 13, 1920.
5. George S. Halas, with Gwen Morgan and Athur Veysey, *Halas: An Autobiography*, p. 60.
6. Lyons' personal notes, no date provided.
7. Jeffrey J. Miller, *Buffalo's Forgotten Champions: The Story of Buffalo's First Professional Football Team and the Lost 1921 Title*, pp. 13–14.
8. *New York Times*, September 19, 1920.
9. Lyons' personal notes, exact date unavailable.
10. Chris Willis, *Joe Carr: The Man Who Built the National Football League*, p. 127.
11. Lyons' personal notes, January 6, 1976.
12. Lyons' personal notes, no date provided.
13. Lyons' personal notes, September 27, 1920.
14. Lyons' personal notes, July 1923.
15. https://www.jnj.com/our-heritage.
16. Robert Peterson, *Pigskin: The Early Years of Pro Football*, p. 62.
17. Lyons' personal notes, no date provided.
18. Lyons' personal notes, no date provided.
19. *Rochester Democrat & Chronicle*, November 25, 1920.
20. Lyons' personal notes, no date provided.
21. *Rock Island Argus*, November 19, 1920, p. 32.
22. *Rochester Democrat & Chronicle*, December 6, 1920, p. 21.

Chapter 5

1. George S. Halas, with Gwen Morgan and Athur Veysey, *Halas: An Autobiography*, p. 91.
2. *Canton Daily News*, May 2, 1921.
3. Lyons' personal notes, April 30, 1921.
4. *Mansfield* [OH] *News*, June 19, 1921.
5. Letter from Geo. Eastman, Eastman Kodak Company, Rochester, NY, to Leo V. Lyons of Rochester, NY, January 13, 1921.
6. Letter from Irl E. LaGrange, Pulver Company, Inc., Rochester, NY, to Leo V. Lyons of Rochester, NY, June 8, 1920.
7. Lyons' personal notes, no date provided.
8. Lyons' personal notes, August 27, 1921.
9. *Wisconsin State Journal*, August 28, 1921.
10. *Rochester Democrat & Chronicle*, September 29, 1921, p. 24.
11. Leo Lyons Oral History from Pro Football Hall of Fame, date not known.
12. *Rochester Democrat & Chronicle*, February 4, 1934, p. 30; also Lyons' personal notes, no date provided.
13. Lyons' personal notes, no date provided.
14. Lyons' personal notes, January 18 and February 19, 1921.
15. Lyons' personal notes, October 16, 1921.
16. Letter from Arch Turner, Thomas E. Wilson & Co., to Leo V. Lyons, January 3, 1922.
17. George S. Halas, with Gwen Morgan and Athur Veysey, *Halas: An Autobiography*, p. 74.
18. Lyons' personal notes, October 19, 1921.
19. John Maxymuk, *NFL Head Coaches: A Biographical Dictionary, 1920–2011*, p. 353.
20. Lyons' personal notes, March 3, 1931.
21. Sara Morrison, "The NFL Team That Only Survived Long Enough to Lose One Game," *Pacific Standard*, June 14, 2017.
22. Joe Alexander—unidentified article.
23. Lyons' personal notes, November 12, 1921.
24. *Rochester Democrat & Chronicle*, November 16, 1921, p. 24.
25. Lyons' personal notes from day planner, November 19, 1921.
26. "Jordan Calls Off Pro Grid Battle," *Washington Herald*, December 5, 1921; Lyons' personal notes, December 5, 1921.
27. The $3,270.37 Lyons lost in 1921 is equivalent to $57,279.44 in 2024 (U.S./CPI Inflation Calculator).
28. Chris Willis, *Joe Carr: The Man Who Built the National Football League*, p. 146.
29. George S. Halas, with Gwen Morgan and Athur Veysey, *Halas: An Autobiography*, pp. 75–76.
30. Jeffrey J. Miller, *Buffalo's Forgotten Champions: The Story of Buffalo First Professional Football Team and the Lost 1921 Title*, pp. 55–56.
31. Bob Braunwart and Bob Carroll, "The Taylorville Scandal," *The Coffin Corner*, Volume 2, No. 6 (1980), p. 3.
32. Lyons' personal notes, January 28, 1922.
33. *Canton Daily News*, January 29, 1922.
34. George S. Halas, with Gwen Morgan and Arthur Veysey, *Halas: An Autobiography*, p. 92.
35. [Rushville, IN] *Daily Republican*, December 28, 1921, p. 5.
36. Bob Braunwart and Bob Carroll, "The Taylorville Scandal," *The Coffin Corner*, Volume 2, No. 6 (1980), pp. 2–4.
37. *Lima* [OH] *News*, January 30, 1922, p. 6.
38. *Fort Wayne* [IN] *Sentinel*, January 29, 1922, p. 15.
39. *Akron Beacon-Journal*, February 1, 1922, p. 14.
40. *Yonkers* [NY] *Herald*, February 10, 1922, p. 11.

Chapter 6

1. David Zimmerman, *Lambeau: The Man Behind the Mystique*, pp. 62–63.
2. Lyons' personal notes, no date provided.
3. George S. Halas, with Gwen Morgan and Athur Veysey, *Halas: An Autobiography*, p. 91.
4. *The* [Sandusky, OH] *Review*, June 25, 1922.
5. Lyons' personal notes, no date provided.
6. *Rochester Democrat & Chronicle*, September 27, 1922, p. 25.
7. Lyons' personal notes, October 9, 1922.
8. *Akron Beacon*, October 7, 1922.
9. Lyons' personal notes, October 9, 1922.
10. Lyons' personal notes, October 12, 1922.
11. *Rock Island Argus*, October 23, 1922, p. 10.

12. *Rock Island Argus*, October 18, 1922.
13. Lyons' personal notes, October 22, 1922.
14. Lyons' personal notes, October 29, 1922.
15. *Rochester Democrat & Chronicle*, October 31, 1922, p. 25.
16. Lyons' personal notes, November 30, 1922.
17. In 1922, two of the most highly respected coaches in the game, Guy Chamberlin of Canton and George Halas of Chicago, posted All-Pro teams. Both chose Alexander as the center on the First Team. Halas picked Boynton as one of four backs on his Second Team. Bob Carroll, Michel Gershman, David Neft, and John Thorn, *Total Football II: The Official Encyclopedia of the National Football League*, pp. 392–393.
18. *Rochester Democrat & Chronicle*, September 16, 1923, p. 42.
19. *Rochester Democrat & Chronicle*, September 23, 1923, p. 42.
20. This was the average attendance for the two homes games the Jeffersons played in 1922 (600 and 2,200).
21. Lyons' personal notes, November 30, 1922.
22. Lyons' personal notes, June 2, 1952.
23. John Eisenberg, *The League: How Five Rivals Created the NFL and Launched a Sports Empire*, p. 89.
24. Jeff Davis, *Papa Bear: The Life and Legacy of George Halas*, p. 59.
25. Lyons' personal notes, February 24, 1936.
26. National Football League Owners Meeting Minutes, January 20, 1923. Carl Storck, recording secretary.
27. Lyons' personal notes, October 7, 1923.
28. *Rochester Democrat & Chronicle*, November 24, 1923, p. 25.
29. *Rochester Democrat & Chronicle*, November 27, 1923, p. 29.
30. National Football League Owners Meeting Minutes, January 26–27, 1924. Carl Storck, recording secretary.
31. *Racine Journal-News*, January 28, 1924, p. 12.

Chapter 7

1. *Rochester Evening Journal and the Post Express*, July 22, 1924.
2. Secretary Carl Storck placed the wrong dates of this meeting at the top of the minutes submitted to the league. Storck mistakenly entered the dates of the meeting as "July 25th & 26th, 1924." The actual dates were Saturday, July 26, and Sunday, July 27.
3. *Rochester Herald*, July 26, 1924, p. 14.
4. National Football League Owners Meeting Minutes, July 26–27, 1924. Carl Storck, recording secretary.
5. Letter from Carl Storck, Dayton, OH, to Leo V. Lyons, Rochester, NY, March 21, 1924.
6. Lyons' personal notes, March 3, 1924.
7. *Rochester Democrat & Chronicle*, September 27, 1924, p. 24.
8. F. B. Field, "Pro Grid Players Kicking Over Traces," *Collyer's Eye*, October 18, 1924, p. 5.
9. *Buffalo Morning Express*, October 3, 1924, p. 14.
10. Lyons' personal notes, September 28, 1924.
11. *Rochester Democrat & Chronicle*, October 12, 1924, p. 45.
12. *Rochester Democrat & Chronicle*, October 17, 1924, p. 37.
13. Lyons' personal notes, August 1924.
14. *Buffalo Evening News*, October 15, 1924, p. 26.
15. *Buffalo Enquirer*, October 16, 1924, p. 8.
16. Lyons' personal notes, October 19, 1924.
17. *Rochester Evening Journal and the Post Express*, November 6, 1924, p. 11.
18. *Rochester Democrat & Chronicle*, November 19, 1924, p. 33.
19. Although the NFL recognizes Johnny Murphy as the Jeffersons' head coach for the final four games of the 1924 season, there is no evidence to indicate he in fact coached the team at any time. Given his previous statement regarding having seen the Jeffs play only once since taking over as club manager, his presence at future games is also questionable.
20. *Rochester Democrat & Chronicle*, November 21, 1924.
21. The Maroons, being an independent team, could not have been competing for a league championship.
22. Bob Matthews, "This Could Have Been Another Green Bay," *Upstate*, January 19, 1975, pp. 12–15.
23. Bob Matthews, "This Could Have Been Another Green Bay," *Upstate*, January 19, 1975, pp. 12–15.
24. National Football League Owners Meeting Minutes, January 24–25, 1925. Carl Storck, recording secretary.
25. Lyons' personal notes, August 1924.
26. John Eisenberg, *The League: How Five Rivals Created the NFL and Launched a Sports Empire*, pp. 33–34.
27. *Harrisburg Telegraph*, September 16, 1925, p. 16.
28. Lyons' personal notes, September 28, 1925.
29. [Zanesville, OH] *Times Recorder*, August 29, 1925, p. 10; [Massillon, OH] *Evening Independent*, September 1, 1925, p. 9.
30. Jeffrey J. Miller, *Buffalo's Forgotten Champions: The Story of Buffalo's First Professional Football Team and the Lost 1921 Title*, p. 100.
31. Lyons' personal notes, October 4, 1925.
32. Lyons' personal notes, October 18, 1925
33. Lyons' personal notes, October 25, 1925.
34. *Hartford Courant*, November 9, 1925, pp. 8–9.
35. Lyons' personal notes, November 11, 1925.
36. [Pottsville] *Republican and Herald*, November 12, 1925, p. 7.
37. "Alfio Boscarino Dies; Ex-'Bootlegger King,'" *Rochester Democrat & Chronicle*, March 10, 1961, p. 18.

38. Postcard sent from Leo V. Lyons to Ed Schlegel, postmarked August 2, 1925.
39. Chris Willis, "Red Grange Had Three Managers for Famous Barnstorming Tour," *Pro Football Journal* (online magazine), March 12, 2020.
40. "Pro Football Wheezed 1st in Canton, Ohio." *Hollywood Sun-Tattler*, March 30, 1961, p. 13.
41. Robert W. Wheeler, *Jim Thorpe: World's Greatest Athlete*, p. 264.
42. Lars Anderson, *The First Star: Red Grange and the Barnstorming Tour That Launched the NFL*, p. 141.
43. George S. Halas, with Gwen Morgan and Arthur Veysey, *Halas: An Autobiography*, p. 107.
44. Lyons' personal notes, November 1925.
45. Lyons' personal notes, November 22, 1925.
46. [Atlantic City] *Daily Press*, December 3, 1925, p. 18.
47. [Atlantic City] *Daily Press*, December 3, 1925, p. 18.
48. www.mapquest.com
49. Bob Carroll, Michel Gershman, David Neft, and John Thorn, *Total Football II: The Official Encyclopedia of the National Football League*, p. 394.

Chapter 8

1. Chris Willis, *Joe Carr: The Man Who Built the National Football League*, p. 209.
2. *Albuquerque Morning Journal*, February 8, 1926, p. 2.
3. Willis, *Joe Carr*, p. 214.
4. National Football League Owners Meeting Minutes, February 6-7, 1926. Carl Storck, recording secretary.
5. Lyons' typed copy of proposal to Rueckheim Bros. & Eckstein, 1926.
6. Beckett Collectibles, LLC (https://www.beckett.com/football/1935/national-chicle).
7. National Football League Owners Meeting Minutes, July 10-11, 1926. Carl Storck, recording secretary.
8. National Football League Owners Meeting Minutes, February 5-6, 1927. Carl Storck, recording secretary.
9. National Football League Owners Meeting Minutes, April 23, 1927. Carl Storck, recording secretary.
10. National Football League Owners Meeting Minutes, July 16-17, 1927. Carl Storck, recording secretary.
11. Lyons' personal notes, June 8, 1929.
12. Bob Carroll, "The Town That Hated Pro Football," *The Coffin Corner*, Volume III, 1981.

Chapter 9

1. Lyons' personal notes, February 24, 1936.
2. Lyons' personal notes, no date provided.
3. Letter from Leland H. Joannes, Green Bay, WI, to Leo V. Lyons, Rochester, NY, March 19, 1931.
4. Letter from Joe F. Carr, Columbus, OH, to Leo V. Lyons, Rochester, NY, September 4, 1936.
5. [Dubuque, IA] *Telegraph-Herald*, April 15, 1940, p. 8.
6. First-known list of memorabilia collected by Leo V. Lyons, personally typed and handwritten, dated March 4, 1940.
7. Letter from Carl Storck, Dayton, OH, to Leo V. Lyons, Rochester, NY, August 1, 1940.
8. Letter from Bert Bell, Philadelphia, PA, to Leo Lyons, Rochester, NY, November 7, 1953.
9. National Football League Owners Meeting Minutes, March 11-13, 1960.
10. Harry March, *Pro Football: It's "Ups" and "Downs,"* pp. 3-7.
11. *Lima* [OH] *News*, April 28, 1961, p. 15.
12. Letter from Pete Rozelle to Leo Lyons reprinted in the *Greater Greece Press*, February 15, 1962, p. 5.
13. Chris Willis, "The Pro Football Hall of Fame—The Beginning," *The Coffin Corner*, Volume 16, No. 5 (1994).
14. Letter from Leo V. Lyons, Rochester, NY, to Pete Rozelle, New York, NY, February 11, 1963.
15. [Columbus, NE] *Daily Telegram*, November 9, 1962, p. 8.
16. Multiple letters between Leo V. Lyons, Rochester, NY, and Pete Rozelle, New York, NY (February 11, 1963, March 14, 1966, September 24, 1966, April 16, 1969).
17. *Rochester Democrat & Chronicle*, May 19, 1976, p. 50.
18. *Rochester Democrat & Chronicle*, October 19, 1954, p. 21.
19. George Halas' Pro Football Hall of Fame enshrinement speech (https://www.profootballhof.com/players/george-halas).
20. [Monessen, PA] *Valley Independent*, January 25, 1964, p. 7.
21. [Syracuse] *Port-Standard*, September 6, 1964, p. 25.
22. Letter from Pete Rozelle, New York, NY, to Leo Lyons, Rochester, NY, March 5, 1965.
23. Clay Moorhead, "Revenue Sharing and the Salary Cap in the NFL: Perfecting the Balance Between NFL Socialism and Unrestrained Free-Trade," *Vanderbilt Journal of Entertainment & Technology Law*, Volume 8, Issue 3 (Summer 2006).
24. David Mosse, "What if the NFL Didn't Employ Revenue Sharing?" *ESPN.com* (https://www.espn.com/nfl/news/story?id=2781759), February 1, 2007.
25. Craig R. Coenen, *From Sandlots to the Super Bowl: The National Football League, 1920-1967*, pp. 201-220.
26. Leo V. Lyons, "How Pro Football Was Born," *TV Guide*, 1964 (exact date unknown), pp. 15-17.
27. Robert Wheeler interview with Jeffrey J. Miller (coauthor), January 11, 2024.
28. *Rochester Democrat & Chronicle*, July 22, 1957, p. 5.
29. Bob Carroll, "The Town That Hated Football," *The Coffin Corner*, Volume III, 1981.

30. *Rochester Democrat & Chronicle,* November 11, 1936, p. 24; October 30, 1937, p. 18.
31. Robert W. Wheeler, *Jim Thorpe: World's Greatest Athlete,* p. 265.
32. *Rochester Democrat & Chronicle,* November 27, 1940, p. 25.
33. *Rochester Democrat & Chronicle,* August 27, 1953, p. 32; September 2, 1954, p. 30.
34. Joe Bock interview with Jeffrey J. Miller (coauthor), December 28, 2023.
35. Text from plaque presented to Leo V. Lyons to commemorate enshrinement in the Rochester–Monroe County High School Athlete's Hall of Fame, 1974. Also *Rochester Courier-Journal,* November 20, 1974, p. 16.
36. *Rochester Democrat & Chronicle,* May 19, 1976, pp. 50–51.
37. *Rochester Democrat & Chronicle,* July 5, 1977, p. 14; April 9, 2003, p. 3.
38. Letter from Jim Campbell, Pro Football Hall of Fame, Canton, OH, to Catharine Lyons, Rochester, NY, August 25, 1976.
39. Jim Campbell interview with Jeffrey J. Miller (coauthor), January 17, 2024.

Chapter 10

1. Robert W. Peterson, *Pigskin: The Early Years of Pro Football,* p. 174.
2. www.ebbets.com/collections/rochester-jeffersons
3. Bob Carroll, "The Town That Hated Football," *The Coffin Corner,* Volume III, 1981.

Bibliography

Books

Anderson, Lars. *The First Star: Red Grange and the Barnstorming Tour That Launched the NFL*. New York: Random House, 2009.

Angevine, Elbert. *Parade of the Grid Ghosts: The Story of Football in Rochester*. Rochester, NY: Harold P. Bittner, 1949.

Benter, Michael D. *The Badgers: Milwaukee's NFL Entry of 1922-1926*. Haworth, NJ: St. Johann Press, 2013.

Bowles, Mark. *The First NFL Season: 1920*. Cuyahoga Falls, OH: Belle History, 2019.

Carroll, Bob, Michael Gershman, David Neft, and John Thorn. *Total Football II: The Official Encyclopedia of the National Football League*. New York: HarperCollins, 1997.

Carroll, John M. *Fritz Pollard: Pioneer in Racial Advancement*. Urbana: University of Illinois Press, 1992.

Coenen, Craig R. *From Sandlots to the Super Bowl: The National Football League, 1920-1967*. Knoxville: University of Tennessee Press, 2005.

Davis, Jeff. *Papa Bear: The Life and Legacy of George Halas*. New York: McGraw-Hill, 2005.

Eisenberg, John. *The League: How Five Rivals Created the NFL and Launched a Sports Empire*. New York: Basic Books, 2018.

Fleming, David. *Breaker Boys: The NFL's Greatest Team and the Stolen 1925 Championship*. New York: ESPN Books, 2007.

Frederick, Chuck. *Leatherheads of the North: The True Story of Ernie Nevers & the Duluth Eskimos*. Duluth, MN: X-Communication, 2007.

Halas, George, with Gwen Morgan and Arthur Veysey. *Halas: An Autobiography*. Chicago: Bonus Books, 1986.

March, Harry A. *Pro Football: Its "Ups" and "Downs."* Albany: J.B. Lyon, 1934.

Maxymuk, John. *NFL Head Coaches: A Biographical Dictionary, 1920-2011*. Jefferson, NC: McFarland, 2012.

McClellan, Keith. *The Sunday Game: At the Dawn of Professional Football*. Akron: University of Akron Press, 1998.

Miller, Jeffrey J. *Buffalo's Forgotten Champions: The Story of Buffalo's First Professional Football Team and the Lost 1921 Title*. Philadelphia: Xlibris, 2004.

Miller, Jeffrey J. *Pop Warner: A Life on the Gridiron*. Jefferson, NC: McFarland, 2015.

Peterson, Robert W. *Pigskin: The Early Years of Pro Football*. New York: Oxford University Press, 1997.

Professional Football Researchers Association. *The Early History of Professional Football*. Guilford, NY: PFRA Publications, 2011.

Rozendaal, Neal. *Duke Slater: Pioneering Black NFL Player and Judge*. Jefferson, NC: McFarland, 2012.

Smith, Robert. *Pro Football: The History of the Game and the Great Players*. Garden City, NY: Doubleday, 1963.

Wheeler, Robert W. *Pathway to Glory: Jim Thorpe*. New York: Carlton Press, 1975. (Republished in 1979 as *Jim Thorpe: World's Greatest Athlete*)

Willis, Chris. *The Columbus Panhandles: A Complete History of Pro Football's Toughest Team, 1900-1922*. Lanham, MD: Scarecrow, 2007.

Willis, Chris. *Joe F. Carr: The Man Who Built the National Football League*. Lanham, MD: Scarecrow, 2010.

Ziemba, Joe. *Bears vs. Cardinals: The NFL's Oldest Rivalry*. Jefferson, NC: McFarland, 2012.

Zimmerman, David. *Lambeau: The Man Behind the Mystique*. Eagle Books, 2003.

Magazines/Periodicals

Braumwart, Bob, and Bob Carroll. "The Taylorville Scandal." *The Coffin Corner*, Vol. 2, No. 6 (1980), p. 3.

Carroll, Bob. "The Town That Hated Pro Football." *The Coffin Corner*, Vol. 3, No. 11 (1981).

Field, F.B. "Pro Grid Players Kicking over Traces." *Collyer's Eye*, October 18, 1924, p. 5.

Lyons, Leo V. "How Pro Football Was Born." *TV Guide*, 1964 (exact date unknown).

Matthews, Bob. "This Could Have Been Another Green Bay." *Upstate*, January 19, 1975, pp. 12-15.

Moorhead, Clay. "Revenue Sharing and the Salary Cap in the NFL: Perfecting the Balance Between NFL Socialism and Unrestrained Free-Trade." *Vanderbilt Journal of Entertainment & Technology Law*, Vol. 8, No. 3 (2006).

Willis, Chris. "The Pro Football Hall of Fame—The Beginning." *The Coffin Corner*, Vol. 16, No. 5 (1994).

Bibliography

Letters (Chronological Order)

Walter Camp, New Haven, CT, to Leo V. Lyons, December 8, 1916.
Erl E. LaGrange, Pulver Company, Inc., Rochester, NY, to Leo V. Lyons, June 8, 1920.
Ralph E. Hay, general manager of Canton Bulldogs football team, to L.V. Lyons, September 9, 1920.
Geo. Eastman, Eastman Kodak Company, Rochester, NY, to Leo V. Lyons, New York, January 13, 1921.
Arch Turner, Thomas E. Wilson & Co., to Leo V. Lyons, January 3, 1922.
Carl Storck, Dayton, OH, to Leo Lyons, January 16, 1924.
Carl Storck to Leo V. Lyons, March 21, 1924.
Postcard sent from Leo V. Lyons to Ed Schlegel, postmarked August 2, 1925.
Leland H. Joannes, Green Bay, WI, Columbus, OH, to Leo Lyons, March 19, 1931.
George S. Halas, Chicago, to Leo Lyons, November 19, 1934.
Joe F. Carr, Columbus, OH, to Leo V. Lyons, March 11, 1936.
Joe F. Carr to Leo V. Lyons, September 4, 1936.
Will Caulfield to Leo and Catharine Lyons, March 7, 1936.
Carl Storck to Leo V. Lyons, August 1, 1940.
Elmer Layden, Chicago, to Leo Lyons, September 25, 1942.
Bert Bell, Philadelphia, to Leo Lyons, November 7, 1950.
George S. Halas to Leo Lyons, February 7, 1957.
Telegram from Pete Rozelle, New York, to Leo Lyons, January 4, 1962.
Pete Rozelle, New York, to Leo Lyons, February 15, 1962.
Pete Rozelle to Leo V. Lyons, June 27, 1962.
Pete Rozelle to Leo V. Lyons, August 9, 1962.
Pete Rozelle to Leo V. Lyons, February 8, 1963.
Leo V. Lyons to Pete Rozelle, February 11, 1963.
Pete Rozelle to Leo V. Lyons, June 18, 1963.
Pete Rozelle to Leo V. Lyons, September 24, 1964.
Pete Rozelle to Leo Lyons, March 5, 1965.
Leo V. Lyons to Pete Rozelle, March 14, 1966.
Pete Rozelle to Leo Lyons, August 26, 1966.
Leo V. Lyons to Pete Rozelle, September 24, 1966.
Leo Lyons to Pete Rozelle, Jim Kensil, and Thelma C. Elkjer, New York, April 26, 1969.
Pete Rozelle to Leo Lyons, July 13, 1972.
Jim Campbell, Pro Football Hall of Fame, Canton, OH, to Catharine Lyons, Rochester, NY, August 25, 1976.

NFL Meeting Minutes (Chronological Order)

September 17, 1920
April 30, 1921
June 18, 1921
August 27, 1921
January 28, 1922
June 24–25, 1922
August 20, 1922
January 20, 1923
July 28–29, 1923
January 26, 1924
July 26–27, 1924 (misdated as July 25–26)
January 24–25, 1925
August 1–2, 1925
February 6–7, 1926
July 10–11, 1926
February 5–6, 1927
April 23, 1927
July 16–17, 1927
July 7, 1928

Interviews (Chronological Order)

Hugh E. Irwin (son of Harry "Dutch" Irwin) interviewed by John D. Steffenhagen, July 19, 2010.
Gary S. Maybee (grandson of Art Webb) interviewed by John D. Steffenhagen, June 17, 2019.
Sabina Bosner Steffenhagen interviewed by John D. Steffenhagen, June 2002 and February 20, 2023.
Joe Bock interviewed by Jeffrey J. Miller, December 28, 2023.
Robert Wheeler interviewed by Jeffrey J. Miller, January 11, 2024.
Jim Campbell interviewed by Jeffrey J. Miller, January 17, 2024.

Oral Histories (Chronological Order)

Leo V. Lyons interviewed by Robert W. Wheeler, July 1, 1967.
Leo V. Lyons interviewed by Kevin C. Bosner, August 1969.
Sabina Lyons Bosner interviewed by Kevn C. Bosner, November 6, 1997.

Web Articles

Mosse, David. "What if the NFL Didn't Employ Revenue Sharing?" *ESPN.com*. (https://www.espn.com/nfl/news/story?id=2781759), February 1, 2007.
Readmikenow. "Walter Camp: The Father of American Football." *How They Play* (https://howtheyplay.com/team-sports/Walter-Camp-The-Father-of-American-Football), May 17, 2022.
Willis, Chris. "Red Grange Had Three Managers for Famous Barnstorming Tour." *Pro Football Journal*, March 12, 2020.

Helpful Websites

Beckett Collectibles (https://www.beckett.com/football/1935/national-chicle)
Newspaper Archive/World Archives Holdings (https://newspaperarchive.com)

Pro Football Hall of Fame (https://www.profootballhof.com/players/george-halas)
Pro Football Journal (https://nflfootballjournal.blogspot.com)
Pro Football Reference (https://www.pro-football-reference.com)
Professional Football Researchers Association (https://profootballresearchers.com)
Rochester Jeffersons (https://www.rochesterjeffersons.org)

Newspapers

Akron Beacon-Journal
Albuquerque Morning Journal
Buffalo Courier
Buffalo Enquirer
Buffalo Evening News
Buffalo Morning Express
Buffalo Times
Canton Daily News
Chicago Tribune
[Atlantic City] *Daily Press*
[Rushville, Indiana] *Daily Republican*
[Columbus, Nebraska] *Daily Telegram*
[New Philadelphia, Ohio] *Daily Times*
Davenport [Iowa] *Democrat and Leader*
[Massillon, Ohio] *Evening Independent*
Fort Wayne [Indiana] *Sentinel*
Greater Greece [New York] *Press*
Harrisburg [Pennsylvania] *Telegraph*
Hartford Courant
Hollywood Sun-Tattler
Lima [Ohio] *News*
Mansfield [Ohio] *News*
[Allentown, Pennsylvania] *Morning Call*
New York Times
Philadelphia Inquirer
Pittsburgh Post-Gazette
The [Syracuse, New York] *Post-Standard*
Racine [Wisconsin] *Journal-News*
[Pottsville, Pennsylvania] *Republican and Herald*
The [Sandusky, Ohio] *Review*
Rochester Democrat and Chronicle
Rochester Evening Journal and the Post Express
Rochester Herald
Rock Island Argus
The [Zanesville, Ohio] *Signal*
[Dubuque, Iowa] *Telegraph-Herald*
[Zanesville, Ohio] *Times Recorder*
[Monessen, Pennsylvania] *Valley Independent*
Washington [D.C.] *Herald*
Wisconsin State Journal

Index

Acme Packing 71, 83, 85
Akron Numatics 57, 87
Akron Pros 5, 57–59, 61–62, 65, 68–69, 76, 83, 86, 88–89, 93, 101–102, 105, 130–131, 145, 152, 165–166
Alexander, Joe (Doc) 75–80, 87, 90, 93–95, 98–99, 105–106, 110, 119, 131, 134, 143, 179
All-Buffalo 35, 38, 41–42, 45, 49–50, 53, 62, 72
All-Rochester 20, 29, 38, 52
All-Syracuse 20, 50, 53, 87, 162, 164–165
All-Tonawanda Lumberjacks 45, 49–50, 53, 64, 71, 77, 87
Alling, Joseph T. 10
American Chicle Company 39, 70, 135
American Football Coaches Association 83
American Professional Football Association (APFA) 59–66, 69, 71–72, 76–80, 82–85, 92, 112, 135, 153, 157, 165, 179
Angevine, Elbert 12, 18, 50, 169, 189–190, 195
Angevine, Oliver 19, 32, 40, 169
Aquinas Stadium 144–145
Argus, Bob 29, 32, 36, 40, 50–53, 65, 72, 87–90, 93, 105, 113–114, 169, 179, 192
Ashton, Chuck 19–20, 22, 169
Atlantic City Blue Tornadoes 124–125, 167
Atlantic City Roses 110, 167

Bachmaier, Joseph 40, 50, 52, 62, 72, 87, 105, 169, 179
Barsha, Johnny 61–62, 64, 66–67, 75, 179
Baseball Park (Bay Street) 27, 29, 31, 36, 49, 52–53, 57, 62–64, 79, 87, 98, 162–166
Bauer, Billy 23, 28, 36, 47, 170
Bausch and Lomb Senecas 27, 51, 53
Bell, Bert 6, 136–137, 139, 144, 193, 196

Bender's Tavern 82
Benz, Eddie 11, 13, 22, 32, 40, 170
Benzoni, Herbert (Rip) 41–42, 49, 62
Berry, Joe Howard, Jr. 73–75, 78–79, 87, 98, 121, 131, 134, 156, 159, 180
Bethlehem Steel 76
Bock, Joe 145–146, 194, 196
bootlegging 96–97
Boscarino, Alfio 122–123
Bosner, John, Jr. (J.A.) 144, 148–149
Bosner, John, Sr. 143, 147
Bosner, Kevin 14, 16, 144, 148–149, 189–190, 196
Bosner, Leo (Vin) 144, 148–149
Bosner, Maureen (Katie) 144
Bosner, Sabina Ellen Lyons 2, 30, 36–37, 132, 143, 147–148
Boynton, Ben 73, 76–80, 87–92, 94–95, 98, 105, 108, 110, 121, 131, 180, 192
Brewer, Untz 89
Brown, Chubby (Alexander) 49–51, 170
Buffalo All-Americans 57–58, 61, 63–65, 68–69, 72, 75–78, 80–81, 92–95, 99, 101, 104, 108, 110, 134
Buffalo Bills 1, 5, 145–146
Buffalo Bisons 105, 108–109, 113, 115, 132, 166–167
Buffalo Prospects 53–55, 63, 92–93, 164

Cahill, Denny 22, 26, 32, 40, 50, 170, 180
Camp, Walter 42–43, 61, 63, 75, 83, 115
Campbell, Jim 148, 194, 196
Canandaigua Academy 16
Cansdale, Dave 27, 32, 40
Canton Bulldogs 2, 44, 46–48, 57–59, 61–62, 65, 77–78, 89, 95, 97, 101, 109, 112–115, 131, 140, 152–153, 157, 164, 166–167
Carr, Joe 5, 68–69, 71, 77–79, 81–83, 85, 92, 97, 102, 104–108, 111–112, 124–125, 127–128, 130–131, 133–134, 136, 139, 152
Carroll, Bob 9, 14, 131, 153–154, 189, 191–195
Caske, Shorty (William) 10, 13, 15, 32, 40, 171
Caufield, Bill 10, 13, 15, 171
Chicago Bears 1–3, 52, 74, 81, 89–91, 100, 102, 111, 121–125, 128, 130, 133, 136, 139–140
Chicago Cardinals 59, 61, 68, 73, 97, 99–102, 124–125, 127, 130, 136, 166, 195
Chicago Staleys 72, 74, 79, 81, 134, 149–151, 156, 165
Chicago Tigers 61, 66, 131
Clark, Babe (Harold K.) 22, 26, 28–30, 32, 35–36, 50–53, 62
Clark, Butch (Harold R.) 52, 62, 105, 113–114, 124, 171, 180
Cleveland Bulldogs 108, 112, 131, 166
Cleveland Indians (football) 59, 108, 112
Cleveland Tigers 45, 61, 131
Cofall, Stan 57–59, 68
Columbus Panhandles 5, 61–62, 66, 68–69, 78–79, 86, 95, 97, 102, 107, 130–131, 134, 139, 154, 157, 165
Columbus Tigers 106, 109, 166
Connell, William 40, 50, 171, 181
Connors, Hamilton 32, 40, 113, 171, 181
Conshohocken Ironworkers 92–93, 166
Conzelman, Jim 52, 91, 112, 124, 136
Coolley, Doc (Marion) 122
Cooperstown (Baseball HOF) 3, 133, 136–137
Country Club of Rochester 13
Court Plymouths 18
Courtland Hotel 46, 81
Cracker Jack Candy 15, 38–39, 70, 104, 128–129, 135
Crippen, Ken 2, 149

199

Index

Cubs Park 3, 72–73, 89, 91, 149–151, 156, 165
Cusack, Jack 46, 57

Dayton Triangles 44, 57–59, 61–62, 68–69, 86, 95, 102, 130, 152, 157
Decatur Staleys 2, 52, 58, 62, 64
Delmont Hotel 58
Detroit Heralds 44–45, 51, 53–54, 61, 66, 69, 164
Detroit Panthers 112–113, 123–124, 130–131, 167
Doane, Cameron 15, 171
Doane, William 11, 171
Dooley, John 87–88, 106, 113–114, 171, 181
Dow, Dutch (Walter) 26, 50, 172
Driscoll, Harry 19, 172
Driscoll, Paddy (John) 52, 99
Dumoe, Joseph 61, 72, 74, 181
Dunning, Frank 13–14
Durnherr, Percy 100, 103, 107, 111–112

East High Orientals 9, 16, 22–24
East Syracuse 40–41, 163
Eastman, George 7, 13, 21, 39, 63, 69–70, 96, 134, 149, 155
Edgerton Park 105–107, 125
Empire Fence Company 19
Ettenhaus, Earl 79, 113; see also Kellogg, Bill
Exposition Park 72

Fairport, New York 1, 7, 20, 148, 162
Falcon, Guil 181
Fawcett Stadium 137, 141
Fleming, Ward 47, 172
Flint Independents 53
Forsyth, Benjamin 182
Forsyth, Jack 10, 13, 52–53, 61–62, 72, 80
Fort Porter 63, 165
Frankford Yellow Jackets 93–94, 99, 104–105, 111, 121, 125, 127, 130–131, 166
Frickey, Walter 27, 32, 34, 40, 50, 172, 182

Genesee Valley Park 18, 23, 161–162
Geneva Glenwoods 35–36, 163
Geneva Hogarths 14, 161
Geneva Rogan and Johnson 41, 163
Glavin, William 11–12
Grange, Lyle 122
Grange, Red (Harold) 121–126, 128, 134, 136, 139, 141, 149, 151, 193, 195–196

Gray, Don 19, 22, 26, 32, 40, 172
Green Bay Packers 3, 71, 81–85, 92, 100, 115–118, 133, 136, 149, 167
Grigg, Cecil (Tex) 109, 113–118, 120, 124, 140, 182
Groot, Adrian 13, 15, 17, 19, 22, 173
Guyon, Joe 65

Hagen, Walter 9, 13–14, 18, 25, 31
Halas, George 1–2, 5, 52, 58–60, 64, 68, 72–74, 79, 81–83, 85, 89–90, 97, 104, 113, 121–122, 124–126, 128–130, 132–134, 136–137, 139–143, 147–148, 152–154, 191–193, 195–197
Hammond Pros 5, 52, 57, 59, 61, 68–69, 91, 102, 127
Hartford Blues 118, 130, 167
Hasbrouck, John 182
Hay, Ralph 5, 57–61, 68, 77, 108, 139, 152–153, 190, 196
Heinlein, Pete 22, 26, 32, 40, 45, 50, 52, 62, 173, 182
Henricus, Ralph 87, 182
Hockaday Paint Co. 97, 122, 132
Hoffman, Jake 114, 182
Holy Sepulchre Cemetery 147
Hornell Football Team 98, 166
Horning, Steamer (Clarence) 49, 53–54, 173
Horrigan, Joe 1, 148
Horth, Al 15, 22, 173
Horween, Arnold 73–74, 89, 99, 113
Houdini, Harry 12
Hughitt, Tommy 63, 81, 104

Immaculate Conception Church 25
Immaculate Conception School 8–9, 12, 15, 17
Irwin, Dutch (Harry) 22–23, 26–27, 32, 34–36, 40–43, 45–46, 50–52, 62, 173, 183, 196
Irwin, Hugh E. 33, 196

Jardine, John W. 100, 103, 107
Jefferson Club 10, 61
Joannes, L.H. 133
Jordan, Tim 79, 81, 85, 92
Joris, Kim 6

Kane, Jim 173, 183
Keck, Stan 99, 183
Kellogg, Bill 79, 113, 117–118, 183; see also Ettenhaus, Earl
Kelly, Tex (Clarence) 113–114, 183
Kendle, John
King, Dick 91, 93, 110, 183
Klehr, Herman 22, 173

Klehr, Joe 26, 28, 174
Knights of Columbus 100, 144
Kretchmer, Bill 13, 174

Laird, Jim 62–64, 67, 72, 74–75, 77–79, 183
Lambeau, Curly (Earl) 3, 6, 71, 85, 116–117, 133–134, 139, 149, 158
Lancaster football team 20, 22–24, 31, 35, 38, 40, 53, 162–164
Langslow, Acton 24, 28–29, 40, 174
Lehrer, Chris 90, 184
Lengeman, Nels 26, 32, 40, 50, 52, 174
Leo V. Lyons Paint Co. 132–133, 136, 138, 144, 148
Long, Dr. Graydon 72, 174
Loughlin, John 15, 174
Lowery, Darby (Chester) 72, 87–88, 105, 111, 113–114, 116, 174, 184
Lynch, Edward 113–115, 120–121, 125, 184
Lyons, Catharine 1, 8, 12–13, 15–17, 25–26, 30, 36–38, 132–133, 138, 143, 146–148, 194, 196
Lyons, Catherine Zelda 30–31, 37, 132, 143
Lyons, Donald (Bucket) 8
Lyons, Edward, Jr. 7
Lyons, Edward, Sr. 6–9, 25, 132
Lyons, Frank 8
Lyons, Irene 7, 15
Lyons, John 8
Lyons, Mary 7
Lyons, William 7, 22, 24, 26, 32, 174

MacLellan, Charlie 19, 22, 32, 40, 175
Major League Football 21, 85
Man-Afraid-of-His-Wife 31, 175; see also Lyons, Leo V.)
Mara, Jack 140–141
Mara, Timothy 6, 97, 112, 119, 124, 128, 137, 139
Marino, Dan 1
Marshall, George Preston 69, 139
Martineau, Roy 106, 114, 184
Massillon Tigers 44, 57–59
Matteo, Frank 87–88, 105, 113–114, 184
Maybee, Gary Sherman 34, 53, 196
McCann, Dick 138, 143
McCarty, William 13, 16–17, 19–20, 22, 175
McCrohan, John 41, 50, 175
McDonald, Henry 16–20, 22–23, 31–32, 35–36, 40–41,

Index

47–50, 52–53, 75, 146, 149, 152, 155, 175
McNeil, Chester 92–93
McNeil, Frank 58, 68, 72, 77, 81, 104, 139
McShea, Joe 184
Mechanics Institute 21, 80
Mellody, Dutch (Walter) 8, 13, 17, 19–20, 22, 25–26, 28, 30, 32, 34, 36, 45–46, 50, 52, 62, 72, 175, 184
Merchants Despatch Transportation (M.D.T.) 8–9
Miller, Heine 63, 88
Morrison, Charles 13, 19, 175
Morrison, Pop (Stewart) 13, 15, 19–20, 22, 26, 28, 32–33, 40, 50, 52, 175, 185
Morrison Hotel 122, 124
Morrissey, Frank 78, 101, 185
Muncie Flyers 5, 59, 61–62, 66, 69, 131
Murphy, Johnny 107–109, 192

Nash, Bob 105, 121, 185
National Chicle Gum Company 129, 135, 153
National Football League (NFL) 1–6, 58–59, 61, 69, 71, 77, 79–80, 85–86, 90–93, 97–98, 101, 103–104, 105, 107, 110–115, 118, 121, 125, 128–131, 133–134, 137, 139–142, 144–150, 153–154, 158
Nazareth College 132, 143
Neale, Greasy (Earl) 48
Nesser brothers 78, 89, 106, 139
New York Giants 3, 112, 114, 118–120, 124, 128, 130, 134, 136, 140, 159, 167
New York State Armory 29–31, 38, 163
Nied, Frank 57–59, 61, 68, 76, 88–89, 104, 152
Noonan, Jerry 72, 78–79, 105, 107, 109, 185
Noonan, Tom 185

O'Brien, Chris 58–59, 68, 99, 127
O'Brien, Joe 32, 176
O'Brien, Morgan 58–59, 68, 82
O'Brien, Punk (William) 15, 176
Odd Fellows building 58
O'Donnell, Jimmy 57, 59, 85
Ohio League 57, 114
Oliphant, Elmer 63–64, 66–67, 75–76, 87, 98, 131, 185
Oneida Northside A.C. 48–50
O'Neil, Rev. Augustine 25
Onondaga Indians 41, 50

Pennsylvania Railroad 68, 78, 150, 157

Pfaudler, Mike 13, 15, 19, 22, 176
Philadelphia Quakers 77–78, 165
Pitcairn Quakers 44, 50, 62
Pittsburgh Pirates (football) 97, 135–136, 150, 159
Pittsburgh Steelers 1, 139–141, 144–145, 150
Polo Grounds 3, 119–120, 167, 185
Poodry, Chief (Aaron) 176
Portage Hotel 68
Pottsville Maroons 110–113, 120–121, 124–125, 127, 130, 167
Powers, John 72, 100, 103, 107
Premier Park 16, 161–162
Pro Football Hall of Fame 1–2, 62, 137–141, 143, 147–149, 151, 153–154, 189, 191, 193–197
Providence Steam Roller 109, 112, 118, 131, 136, 154, 166–167
Pulver Gum Company 39, 70
Purdy, Mike 63–64, 66–67, 186
Pyle, C.C. (Charles) 122, 124, 128

Quigley, Red (Gerald) 53, 62, 176, 186

Racine Legion 81, 83, 85, 91–92, 102, 115, 130, 166
Rafter, Bill 186
Ranney, Art 57–59, 61, 68–69, 83–84
Reid's Field 11, 14, 20, 23, 27–28, 31, 161–162
Rice, Ray 15, 19, 176
Rochester Atlantics 27
Rochester Belmonts 9, 11
Rochester Chamber of Commerce 72, 100, 107, 144
Rochester Columbias 9, 11–12
Rochester Crimsons 38
Rochester Democrat and Chronicle 11–12, 18–20, 23, 27–28, 30–31, 33, 35–36, 38, 42, 45, 48–51, 53, 55, 58, 64, 66, 72, 78, 92, 94–95, 100, 105, 107, 111, 145, 147–148
Rochester Free Academy 9
Rochester Hustlers 27
Rochester Oxfords 9, 14–18, 20, 22, 125, 152
Rochester Pullmans 23, 28–29, 38, 162
Rochester Rotary 143–144
Rochester Scalpers 10–12, 15–18, 20–21, 23–24, 27–31, 35–36, 38, 41, 47, 49–50, 53, 64–65, 77, 161–165
Rochester Telephone 12, 17, 26
Rochester X-Rays 9, 11–12, 161
Rock Island Independents 5,

44, 57, 59, 61–62, 65, 68–69, 72, 86, 93, 95, 99, 102, 128, 166
Rockefeller, Gov. Nelson 146, 149, 158
Rooney, Art 1, 6, 97, 140–141, 144, 147–148, 150, 159
Roy, Spin (Elmer) 87–89, 105, 113, 186
Rozelle, Pete 2, 137–139, 141–142, 146, 149, 158, 193, 196
Rueckheim Brothers 39, 70, 128
Ruhling, F.E. 70

Scanlon, Joseph 100, 103, 107
Schiebel, Walter 40, 176
Schiller, George 50, 52, 177
Schlegel, Ed 107, 114, 122, 127, 129, 193, 196
Sheard, Shag (Alfred) 98, 100–101, 105–106, 109, 113–114, 118, 120–121, 125, 186
Sheehan's Field 11, 18–20, 27, 31–32, 35, 40–41, 46, 48, 51, 161–164
Slattery, Jack 10, 19, 177
Smith, Hank 55, 62, 72, 87–88, 91, 93, 105, 113–114, 131, 177, 186
Smyth, Lou 109–110, 113–118, 120–121, 124, 186
Spalding 73, 89–90, 113, 134
Spiegel, Ray 10, 13, 22, 26, 32, 177
Steele, Cliff 87–89, 91, 187
Steffenhagen, Eddie 1
Steffenhagen, Joann 1, 148
Steffenhagen, Julie 2
Steffenhagen, Sabina Bosner 1, 11–12, 16, 30, 37, 144, 147–148, 189–190, 196
Still, Joe 19, 177
Stinchcomb, Pete 90
Storck, Carl 57, 59, 68–69, 71, 82, 97, 102, 104, 127–129, 131, 134, 136, 152
Striegel, Doc (Dr. John) 110, 121, 127
Stuhldreher, Harry 115, 118, 140
Sweeney, Richard 15, 177
Syracuse 47th U.S. Army Infantry 46–47
Syracuse Pros 79, 165
Syracuse Stars 63, 165
Syracuse University 31, 41, 46, 55, 61–63, 67, 75, 77, 79, 87, 100, 106, 113, 142, 163
Syracuse Westcotts 32, 35, 38, 163

Tehan, Ellen 7
Thompson, Tiny (George) 87, 187

Thorpe, Jim 2, 5, 38, 47–49, 57–61, 64–65, 68, 73, 85–87, 114, 119, 134, 136, 139, 143–144, 149, 152–153
Toledo Maroons 109–101, 104, 113, 166
Tonawanda Kardex 71, 77, 165

United States School of Air Photography 51
University of Illinois 52, 83, 121–122
University of Pennsylvania 73, 75
University of Rochester 10, 24, 28, 40, 51–52, 94, 107, 144, 174, 177
Usher, Lou 61, 64, 66–67, 95, 187

Utica Knights of Columbus (Team) 100, 144

Van Zandt, Mayor Clarence 93
Volgenau, Elmer 106, 187

Washington Pros 79, 81–82, 85, 92, 105, 165
Waterbury Blues 115, 167
Webb, Art 27, 32, 34, 40, 47, 50, 52–53, 62, 178, 187, 196
Weldon, Jim 10, 178
Welsh, Jim 188
Weltman, Larry 87–88, 188
West End Park 13–14, 18, 161
West High Occidentals 9, 15, 24, 27–28, 52, 161
Wheeler, Robert 142–144, 189–190, 193–196

Wilkes-Barre Panthers 99, 166
Willis, Chris 128, 138, 191, 193, 195–196
Wilson Sporting Goods 73–74, 89–90, 113, 134, 151, 153
Witter, Bob 50, 178
Witter, Ray 48–49, 52, 87, 178, 188
Woods, Jimmy 50, 62, 72, 143, 178
Wrigley Field see Cubs Park
Wrigley Gum 39, 104, 129

Youngstrom, "Swede" 63, 188

Ziegler, Ben 19, 178
Ziff, Dave 113, 188

www.ingramcontent.com/pod-product-compliance
Lightning Source LLC
Chambersburg PA
CBHW060343010526
44117CB00017B/2948